The Harold Samuel Collection

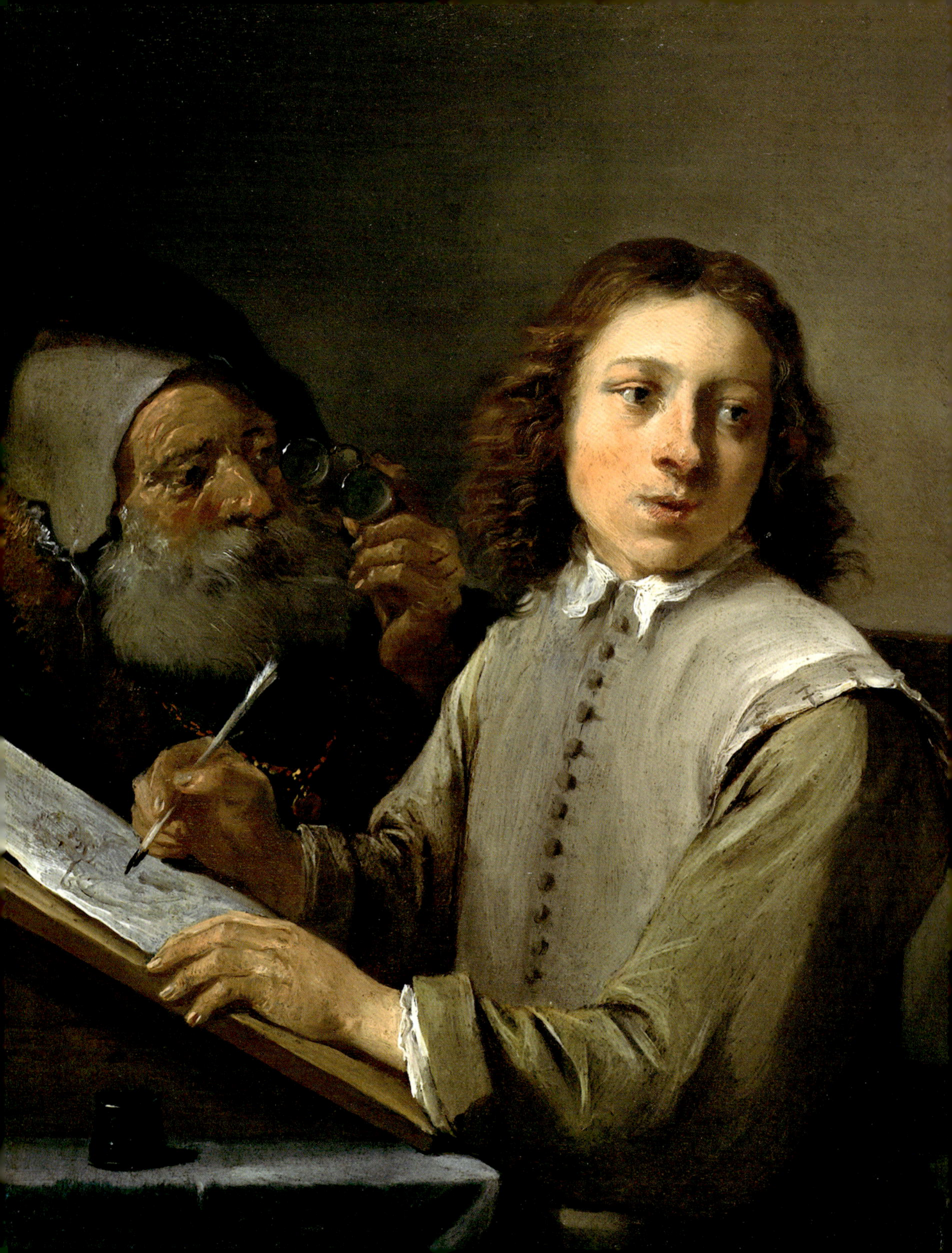

THE HAROLD SAMUEL COLLECTION

A GUIDE TO THE DUTCH AND FLEMISH
PICTURES AT MANSION HOUSE

Michael Hall

with an introduction
by Clare Gifford

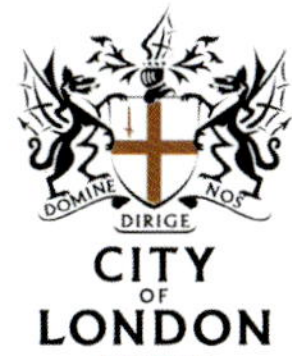

Paul Holberton publishing

ISBN 978 1 907372 41 4

British Library Cataloguing in Publication Data
A catalogue record for this book is available from the British Library

Produced by Paul Holberton publishing,
89 Borough High Street, London SE1 1NL
www.paul-holberton.net

Designed by Laura Parker

Map by Martin Lubikowski, ML Design

Origination and printing by E-graphic, Verona, Italy

FRONT COVER Wallerant Vaillant, *A you man copying a painting* (no. 60)
BACK COVER Palamedes Palamesesz, *A cavalry battle on a bridge* (no. 59)
FRONTISPIECE David Teniers the Younger, *The Five Senses: Sight* (no. 13), detail

USING THE GUIDE

This guide to the 84 Dutch and Flemish pictures in the Samuel collection that hang at Mansion
House is geographical, in that it follows the collection from the first pictures the visitor
encounters on the ground floor, up the Red Staircase turning right into the Long Parlour, into
the Salon, across to the North and South Drawing Rooms and back into the Salon Vestibule
leading from the Salon.

The entries give the guide number; the name of the artist, as commonly recognized; the
artist's places and dates of birth and death; the title of the work; the medium – usually panel
(without identifying the wood type), copper or canvas; the size in centimetres, height before
width. Signatures are noted but without describing how or where, as are dates but only if found
on the work or if known from documentary evidence. This is followed by the number in Peter
Sutton, Dutch and Flemish Seventeenth-Century Paintings: The Harold Samuel Collection (London
1992), which gives biographies of the artists and provenance, exhibitions, literature, condition,
comparisons and sources of the paintings.

CONTENTS

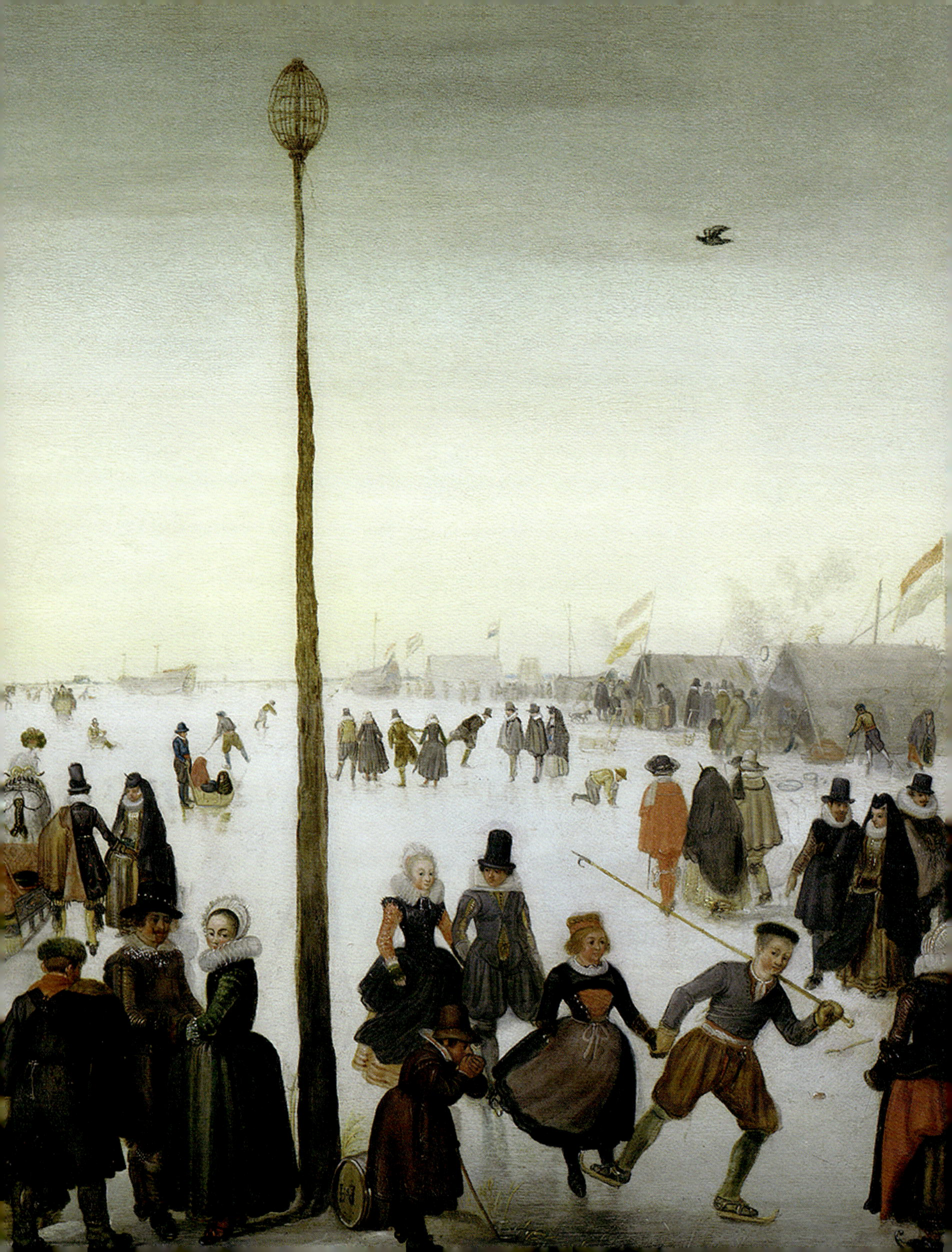

Foreword

Lord Samuel of Wych Cross died in 1987 aged seventy-five, leaving his priceless collection of seventeenth-century Dutch and Flemish paintings to the Corporation of London in a remarkable act of philanthropy, expressly to be hung together in Mansion House. Although his widow was left the pictures to enjoy for her lifetime, Lady Samuel decided instead that she wished to see the pictures in their new home at Mansion House. The collection was formally handed over to the City of London at the end of November 1987. Sir Robert Bellinger, the Lord Mayor at the time and a lifelong friend of Samuel's, received the bequest, describing it as "the greatest gift of art ever conveyed to the Corporation of the City of London in all the centuries of its existence".

These paintings had not been exhibited in the UK in the twentieth century, and were not known to the general public nor to many art historians at the time of the bequest. Before the pictures were hung at Mansion House they were exhibited at the Barbican Art Gallery for eight weeks in the autumn of 1988. In 1991–92 Mansion House was refurbished, and the opportunity was taken for some of the paintings to tour before a wider public. In 1992 another Barbican exhibition, *The Celebrated City*, had part of the collection as its centrepiece, a selection of paintings were shown at several galleries in the USA, and a comprehensive catalogue of the collection was produced by Peter Sutton.

This new guidebook to the paintings as they hang today in Mansion House is published on the occasion of the 25th anniversary of Harold Samuel's bequest. The anniversary has also provided the stimulus to enhance accessibility, with increased opportunities for members of the public and those with a particular interest in Dutch and Flemish painting to see the pictures.

My wife Clare, who has created this book, and I very much hope you will enjoy viewing this amazing collection, of which the City of London is the proud and privileged custodian.

Roger Gifford
Lord Mayor 2012–13

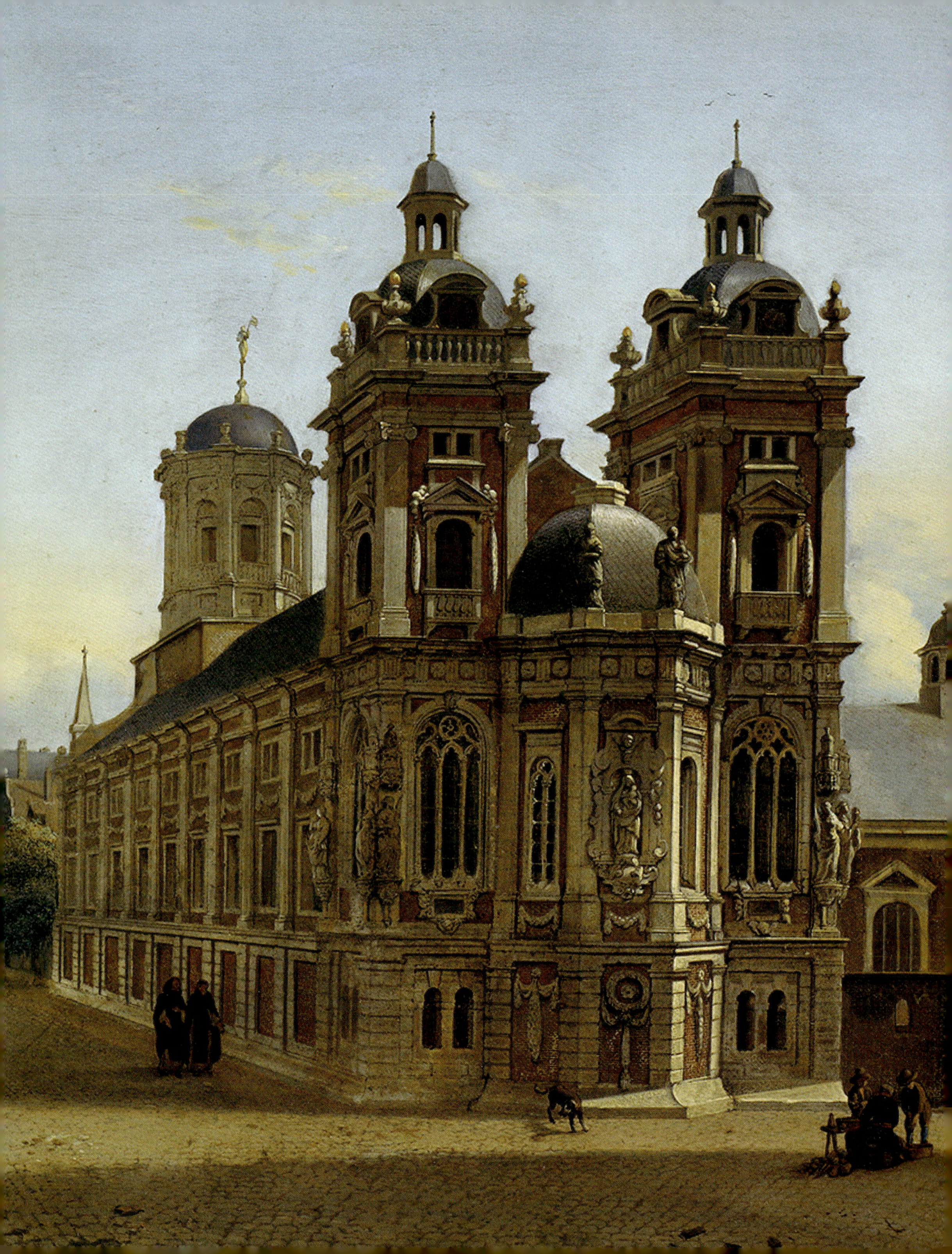

Harold Samuel
The Collection and the Collector

THE HAROLD SAMUEL COLLECTION was the finest private collection of seventeeth-century Dutch paintings assembled in the UK in the twentieth century.

The pictures, collected by Lord Samuel over a period of thirty-five years, were chosen very much in accordance with his personal taste, as well as that of his wife and daughters. He rarely acquired a painting without Lady Samuel either seeing the original or at least a photograph of it. Samuel's motivation in collecting was not fashion, nor social advancement or kudos. He bought works which appealed to his meticulous, even fastidious, personality.

The paintings were entirely for his own personal enjoyment, though he took pride in showing the collection to anyone whom he felt would appreciate it. All the pictures were hung in the family home, Wych Cross Place, which was bought in 1954 from Geoffrey and Dorothy Hart, a couple who may also have been responsible for kindling his interest in Dutch Old Masters. Wych Cross, designed by the architect Edmund Fisher, was built in 1902, set in rolling Sussex countryside and with extensive gardens landscaped by Thomas Manson. Harold Samuel took immense delight in his home and garden, also becoming known for his horticultural skill and the enormous and magnificent flowers he grew.

This may go some way to explain the singular lack of floral still-life paintings in his collection, a significant omission as these were popular and frequent subjects in the 'Golden Age' of Dutch painting. In fact, the collection was in no way intended to be a comprehensive representation of Dutch seventeenth-century painting, and other specific absences are portraiture and historic and religious subjects. Samuel's pictures were mainly, though not all, cabinet-sized and designed to be displayed in a domestic setting, as they were at Wych Cross. The paintings hung throughout the house, very much at home among the fine English furniture that Samuel also loved.

Harold Samuel was an intensely private man. He enjoyed spending hours in his gardens, looking at his pictures or among the books in his extensive library.

He amassed a major collection of art books, which was eventually bequeathed to the Israel Museum, Jerusalem.

Harold Samuel founded his company in 1944, when he bought Land Securities Investment Trust Ltd, which owned three houses in Kensington and some government stock, for under £20,000. He then built up the company through prudent acquisition of London property and shrewd domestic takeovers. He bought West End properties in the late 1940s and acquired Devonshire House in 1949. One of the most visionary developers of his age, Samuel was responsible for much post-war re-development, providing financial backing to secure bombsites in London, Plymouth, Exeter, Hull, Coventry and Bristol. With an encyclopaedic knowledge of the industry, he was set to become the first post-war millionaire by the 1950s, and by the 1980s Land Securities was the leading property company in the world, valued at over £3 billion. Samuel was a hero and mentor to the generation following him in property, and is credited with being the first to observe three things that matter most when it comes to property: location, location, location.

Samuel was a great philanthropist, although his very generous gifts were quietly bestowed out of the public eye and without flamboyance. He gave many millions of pounds to institutions such as the Royal College of Surgeons, the University of Cambridge, University College London and the British Heart Foundation. He also founded and was president of the Central London Housing Trust for the Aged, as well as acting as a trustee for his old school, Mill Hill.

Knighted in June 1963, Harold Samuel was the first in the property profession to receive this honour for public and charitable services, and he was created Baron Samuel of Wych Cross in the County of Sussex in June 1972.

Lord Samuel – founder, Chairman, and "architect of the greatness" of Land Securities – died in 1987 and was felt to be irreplaceable. There was some anxiety about the future of the company without his all-pervasive personality at the helm, but it has continued to grow from strength to strength. A landmark development by Land Securities in the heart of the City of London opened in 2010 – One New Change, designed by Jean Nouvel – home to retailers, offices, restaurants and cafes.

Samuel was the most successful and trusted property developer of his era. He was an extremely focused individual, and the only other thing that came close to his interest in property was his interest in seventeeth-century Dutch paintings. Samuel was a man of habit. When in London he lived at a handsome house in Avenue Road, near Regent's Park. Always immaculately dressed, he lunched each day at the Ritz or the Savoy. He was a shy, kind man, always keen to avoid publicity, and who disliked public speaking. Those who knew him well found him a man of unusual humour beneath the formal exterior, a friend of unparallelled

loyalty and a man of uncompromising integrity. He chose his colleagues and
advisors with considerable care, preferring to select colleagues rather than appoint
through a competitive applications process. He was unusual in having acquired
almost all of his collection through one dealer, Edward Speelman, an old friend.
In Speelman Harold Samuel had chosen an art dealer at the top of his profession,
the best of his generation, and a man of trustworthiness and integrity in his own
field equal to Samuel's in his. By buying in this way Samuel was able to preserve
his anonymity and also have access to the best possible expert opinion beyond that
of the auction house and the condition reports with the sales.

Samuel did not buy from other dealers, nor directly from auction houses. Just
thirteen of the pictures were purchased at auction by Speelman acting for Samuel,
and only three pictures were bought without Speelman's direct help, though not
without his consultation. Speelman did not keep much stock himself but would
identify items for sale which might interest a client, such as Samuel, and he would
then acquire them on their behalf. Speelman had an unwavering eye and, despite
the commission involved in this method of acquisition, he had a very satisfied
clientele. Sometimes Speelman would buy a picture that he thought Samuel
would be interested in and would telephone from his gallery in nearby Piccadilly
to Samuel at his office in Berkeley Street. Samuel would then go round to look at
it and if he liked it he would arrange for it to be taken down to Wych Cross for the
weekend with detailed instructions, including a diagram, about where to hang
it. Over the weekend he would consult with his wife and daughters, and on the
Monday he would call Speelman to accept (or more rarely reject) the deal. He never
tried to negotiate the asking price and paid in full by return. In fact he was never
heard to talk about a picture in money terms, though of course he would often
refer to the cost or value of a building. He sought works in excellent condition
and with well-documented provenance and expected the same precision and
perfection in the painting that he delivered in his own work.

When Samuel first started to buy paintings he began with still-life pictures
by Spaendonck, which he later sold, and then a mother-and-child scene by the
French painter Boilly. He also bought some Italian *vedute* – by Canaletto, Marieschi
and Guardi, amongst others – which he parted with as his interest in Dutch
paintings escalated. He acquired some flower paintings early on, including some by
Bartholomeus van der Ast, Rachel Ruysch and Jan van Huysum, but sold them.

The acquisition of Dutch paintings from the seventeenth century was to
some extent following the fashion among a long line of wealthy Londoners and
merchants like the Walters, as well as the Rothschilds, great nineteenth-century
French collectors, and millionaires such as Beit. This particular collection of

paintings, however, very much represents Harold Samuel's own taste, and in many ways his personality too. It consists entirely of works painted in the Netherlands in the first three quarters of the seventeenth century, a period of extraordinary artistic productivity often referred to as the 'Golden Age' of Dutch painting. This generation of Dutch artists enlarged and developed traditions from earlier Flemish painters, made accessible because some of them had settled in Amsterdam. The great wealth of the Netherlands, its rapid growth and development, world trading and international power was the backdrop to this enormous activity in the arts.

The Northern provinces were at war with Spain, gaining independence in 1648. Artists were among the many Protestant settlers from the Southern provinces who travelled to Amsterdam. The Dutch had valuable colonies, controlled by the Dutch East India Company (founded in 1602) and the Dutch West India Company (1621). Trade with their possessions made 'Holland' and the Dutch provinces the commercial centre of Europe, with Amsterdam at its heart. Its citizens prospered, having the highest per-capita income at any time in the seventeenth century in Europe. The very large middle class found themselves able to afford luxuries such as oil paintings, and many quite ordinary households would have genre scenes, cabinet-sized, on their walls.

In this bourgeois society more than 60% of Netherlanders were city dwellers and they enjoyed owning naturalistic landscapes of their native land, as well as familiar townscapes. Some pictures had a moral or didactic content, their allusive signs and symbols often rather obscured by the passing of time. Those that remain easy to identify include the constant reminders of mortality, seen in the distant gallows in the winter scenes of Averkamp and 'Cabel', the grave and skull in De Witte's church interior, or a clock or watch appearing in still-life paintings such as those of Claesz. The extraordinarily lifelike still-life compositions, representing everyday objects with what now looks like almost photographic execution, were very popular, and these clearly appealed to Harold Samuel, with his very exacting and focused character.

Painting was perceived at the time as a craft rather than a creative process. Subjects were treated in a true-to-life manner, although the compositions were frequently idealized and arranged in the studio rather than being taken directly from life. Demand was high, prices reasonable and artists worked fast and mostly on a small scale in order to keep up the supply for clients. Many artists specialized, for instance in landscapes, ice or snow scenes, still-life or genre paintings.

A large number of seventeenth-century Dutch paintings survive, partly as a result of the large number that were produced and probably also because of the high quality of the materials used and craftsmanship involved. Painters learned as paying apprentices in studios of established artists, beginning by helping to prepare paints and surfaces, and moving on to copying, as depicted in the painting by Vaillant on the cover of this book.

The most refined and detailed handling of paint was possible only on a very smooth, firm surface. Copper panels provided the best surface – also the most expensive and therefore usually small – followed by oak panels, which could be larger, such as the Hals *Merry Lute Player*. Canvas was the most difficult surface to paint on in fine detail, but allowed for a larger size, such as the landscapes of Ruysdael and Koninck. In the collection there are fifteen paintings on copper, 52 on oak panel and only seventeen on canvas, again reflecting Harold Samuel's fascination with the exactitude of the artists' skills.

Samuel bought the first pictures that remained in his collection in 1956, having bought a few in the years preceding which were later sold. Many of the paintings came from renowned collections in Europe, or further afield, some having changed hands several times – the Hobbema, for instance, which had been in private collections in Britain, the USA and Paris, or the five Teniers, in England, Montreal, Paris and Florence. Samuel acquired through Speelman two groups of paintings from single sources, together making up a quarter of his final collection, and all bought in or around 1959. This was a somewhat unusual approach at the time though had been a more acceptable, even admired, method of collecting in the nineteenth century. It seems now to be contrary to the notion of developing a personal taste, something which Samuel undoubtedly did as his collection grew. However, it was relatively early in the creation of his collection and Samuel would have been reassured by the proven quality, taste and authenticity bestowed by the association with an already established and respected collector. There are seven paintings which came from the Beit collection, including Wouwermans's lively *Landscape with kermis*, and fourteen pictures from Etienne Nicolas, the wine producer, including *Cattle by a river* by Cuyp, with its exquisite light, and Jan Steen's perfect *Sleeping Couple*. After these major group purchases Samuel continued to add steadily to the collection, buying 55 pictures between 1959 and 1970. After that he bought more slowly, with the last being purchased in 1980.

The biggest single group is that of the thirteen winter landscapes, an archetypal sub-group of Dutch landscape painting, with their intriguing detailed activities on the frozen waterways. Another theme prominent in Samuel's collection is the landscape panorama, which includes some of the largest works in the collection, such as those by Ruysdael and Koninck as well as smaller works such as those by Cuyp. There are also two very fine Brazilian landscapes by Frans Post, who accompanied Count Johan-Maurits of Nassau-Seigen to Brazil. The National Gallery in London does not possess an example by him but has one on longterm loan from the Rijksmuseum, Amsterdam.

There are a number of indoor domestic and genre scenes, including works by Steen, de Hooch and Maes, a series of tavern scenes by Ostade, and the Five Senses by Teniers the Younger. The Harold Samuel collection also has a number of marvellous cityscapes, a sub-genre of landscape painting that began to flourish after about 1650, with six paintings by van der Heyden and two extraordinarily photographic works by Berckheyde. These are likely to have been especially attractive to Samuel as a man of property.

Trading by sea was incredibly active in the seventeenth century in the Netherlands and as many as one in ten men and boys were at sea at any one time. Life at sea, harbours, boats at anchor or sailing with billowing sails under huge skies were all popular subjects, and Samuel bought a number of evocative examples by a master of this genre, Willem van de Velde the Younger.

For many people still-life arrangements remain the most immediately recognizable and typical pictures from the Golden Age of Dutch painting. Avoiding floral subjects, Samuel collected a number of ravishing paintings of everyday objects, food and drink, simple in composition, yet utterly masterful in execution. It is with awe and astonishment that we look at the glass *roemer* in the Claesz, the silver pilgrim flask by Kalf, or the cheese and biscuits of van Schooten.

Perhaps the best known of all the artists in the collection is Frans Hals. There are two paintings by him, one until recently attributed to a follower. *The Merry Lute Player* is the most famous picture in the collection, and one of the finest by Hals in existence. Its purchase in 1963 from New York was notorious at the time not only because of the record sale price for the artist, but because it was achieved via transatlantic bidding on the telephone (by Edward Speelman). Although Samuel had flown over to view the picture, he managed, typically for him, to remain anonymous throughout the process.

Notable paintings were also sold by Samuel during this period, which looking back now is somewhat puzzling. These include a Saenredam, *Interior of Saint Bavo* (sold back to Speelman in 1985, now in the J. Paul Getty Museum, Los Angeles), which would have been an ideal addition to his group of architectural paintings. He also bought and resold a Rembrandt whose authenticity was felt to be dubious because of anomalies in the signature. This is now also in the Getty, and has been cleaned and finally and definitely attributed to Rembrandt from his Leiden period (hence the different signature). He owned at various stages as many as six paintings by Cuyp, one of which is now in the Getty and another which was bought for Lady Samuel and ultimately bequeathed to the Israel Museum. Samuel also sold a painting by Metsu in 1985.

Samuel had completed his collection by about 1980. Because it is so deliberately not a comprehensive review of the period, it is clear that the pictures in Mansion House are the ones he loved and felt a real connection with, and as such they allow us an intimate glimpse of the man he was.

The transplanting of such a group of paintings from the domestic interior of Wych Cross, the sort of environment in which the artists intended them to be hung, to the grandeur of Mansion House, was no easy task. The curator of the Guildhall Art Gallery at the time, Vivien Knight, had the Victorian paintings and portraits of past Lord Mayors removed back to the Art Gallery to make way for the collection. Challenging, large, ornate spaces now had to be home to intimate cabinet pictures, and Vivien approached the problem with great imagination and intelligence. Framed in the eighteenth-century ornate gilded frames favoured by Speelman, the paintings look more at home in Mansion House that they might have done had they remained in their original plain black ebony frames.

The pictures are mainly grouped by theme, displaying artists together who were related by style, working practice, school or town. Winter landscapes and other tonal landscape pictures are on the Red Staircase, with the major Frans Hals picture making a bold statement halfway up and introducing the genre paintings at the top of the stairs and in the Long Parlour. This room is not ideal for hanging pictures, with only narrow spaces between the windows, but the detailed genre scenes and small landscapes, for instance the four Brueghels, can be studied at close quarters, with only those above the two fireplaces being more difficult to appreciate fully. Larger pictures are displayed to great effect in the Salon, including large interior scenes by Steen and de Hooch and still lifes very suitable for a dining area. The hang in the drawing rooms has been brilliantly conceived, very like an eighteenth-century collector's display of cabinet pictures, by taking one or two large works and placing the smaller works around and beneath them. Once more, artists related to each other and similar subjects are grouped together, producing a highly attractive and dramatic overall effect.

Here the depiction by Vaillant of a studio apprentice copying a painting is hung below the actual painting by Palamedesz that the young boy is copying. The locating and acquisition of the Palamedesz must have been the most thrilling coup for Samuel and is any collector's dream, but it must especially have satisfied his very meticulous nature and desire for thoroughness and completion.

CLARE GIFFORD

This book was produced with the support and collaboration of the staff of
the Guildhall Art Gallery, Mansion House and London Metropolitan Archive,
City of London.

Author's Acknowledgements

The author wishes to thank Roger Gifford and his wife Clare for the opportunity
to write this guide. John Morton Morris and Jan Six have been generous and
supportive to a fault. Thanks are due also to the following: Douglas Bartram-
Weight, Christopher Breyne, Martin van den Broeke, John Davies, Anne Deils,
Jay Gam, Ross Garcia, Geoffrey and Carole Lawson, Fiona Lings, Seamus McKenna,
Guy and Marion Naggar, Otto Naumann, Laura Parker, David Pearson, Geoffrey
Pick, Kathy Reichenbach, Scott Schaefer, Sabine Schlosser, Daniel Simpson, Sonia
Solicari, Anthony Speelman, Schlomit Steinberg, Peter Sutton, Julia Armstrong
Totten, Amy Walsh, Laurence Ward and Anne Woolett.

Cat. 33, detail

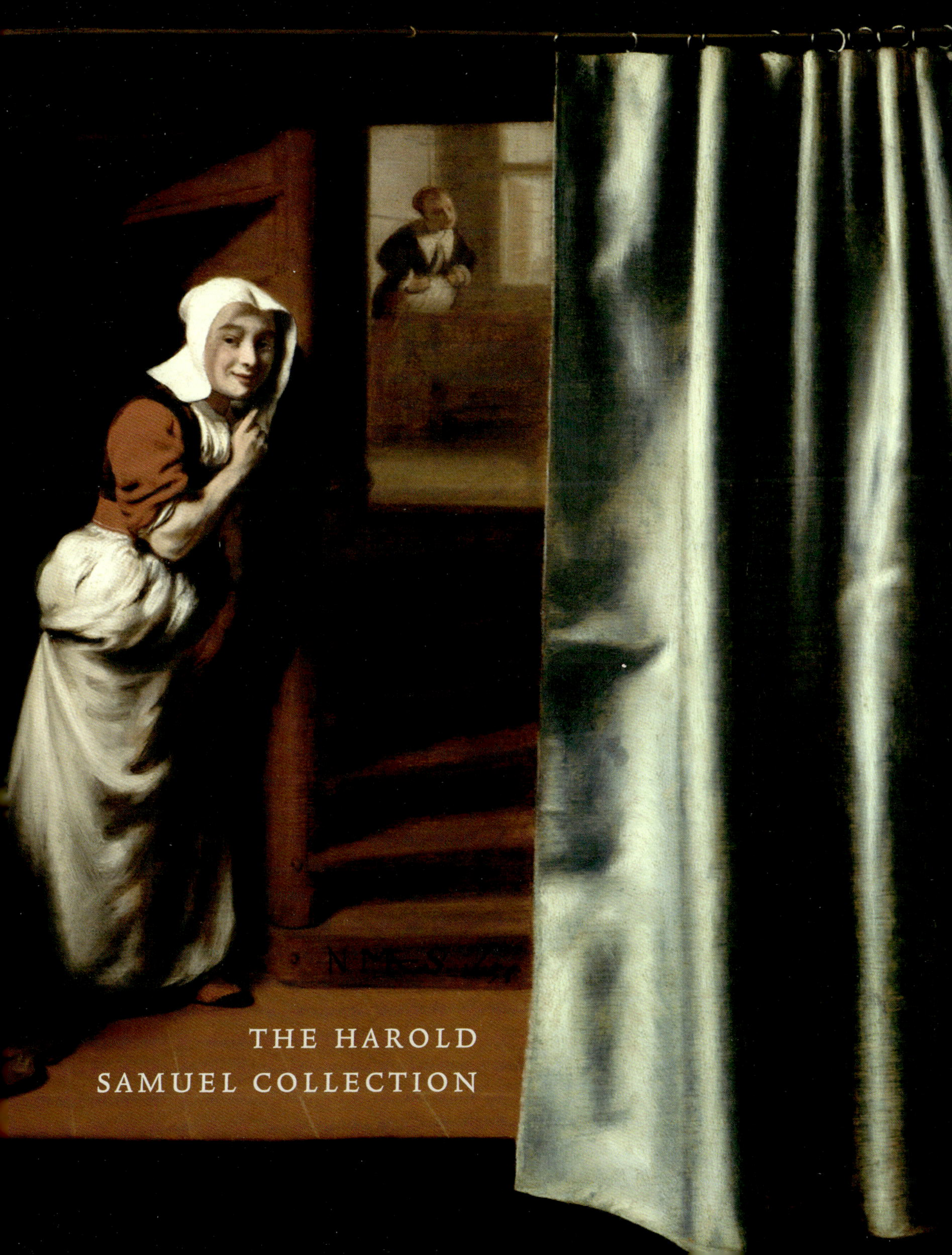

THE HAROLD
SAMUEL COLLECTION

THE RED STAIRCASE

The collection begins on the ground floor of the Red Staircase

The main entrance to Mansion House is through the Walbrook Door into the
Walbrook Hall on the ground floor. The hall occupies an area originally designed
as domestic offices and stables by the architect, George Dance the Elder. The
house stands on the long, narrow site of a small church, destroyed in the Great
Fire of 1666 and subsequently an open-air market. Work began in 1739 and when
the house was first occupied, in 1752, entry was via a double flight of external
stairs facing the Bank of England and the Royal Exchange, under the portico and
through the Vestibule, now offices. The centre of the first floor was an open court,
covered over by George Dance the Younger in 1795, when the Grand Stair in the
north-east corner was also removed and Walbrook Hall created as the main visitor
entrance. Though it was adapted in 1861 by James Bunstone Bunning and again in
1991–93, the principal layout of 1795 remains.

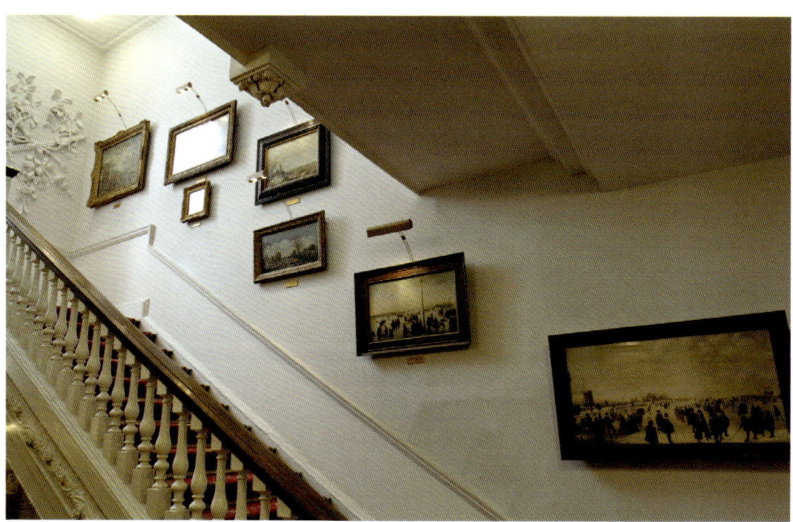

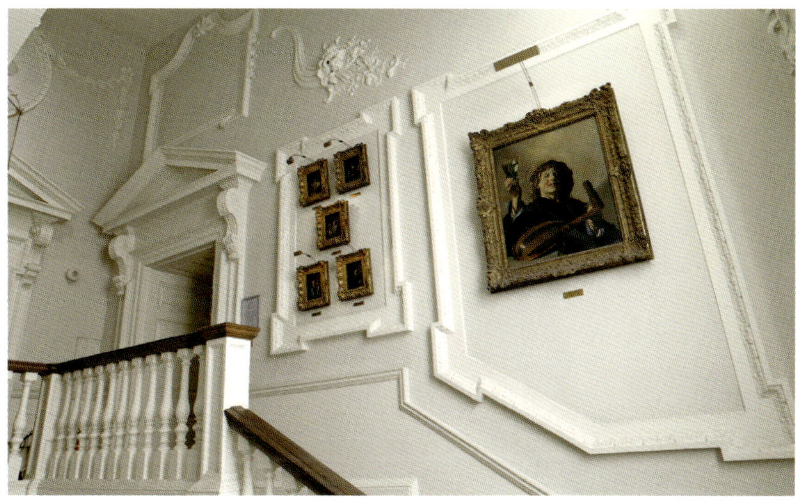

Originally a service stair but now the main route of access to the first floor, the Red Staircase is mainly hung with winter landscapes, one of the strongest areas of the Samuel collection. A plaque to the left of the door from the Hall commemorates the gift by Lord Samuel in 1987. On either side of the door and at the bottom of the stairs hang the earliest of these landscapes, by Cabel and by Hendrick Averkamp, starting the tour. Lord Samuel's love of landscape and winter landscapes in particular is well represented here, and the theme continues with early works by Jan van Goyen and Aelbert Cuyp. Samuel also acquired a significant group of genre pictures, which include a set of Five Senses by David Teniers and the collection's famous work by Frans Hals, hanging on the upper stair, which make a striking and fitting prelude to the rest of the collection. The blind-panel decoration of Kentian frames with outset corners and egg-and-dart moulding are well suited to the display, though those on the lower stairs were removed in 1991–93 to allow more paintings to be hung.

At the top of the stairs turn right into the Long Parlour

1

ARENT ARENTSZ, CALLED CABEL
Amsterdam 1585/86–1631

Winter landscape with figures on a bridge, a hunter and skaters

Oil on panel, 35.6 × 63.1 cm, signed
Sutton no. 1

One of the great strengths of the Samuel collection is the depth and breadth of the Dutch landscapes, of which winter scenes are such an integral part. Intended when they were painted for a purely local market, these scenes are redolent with familiar associations – the physical geography of the Low Countries, the pleasure of outdoor pursuits – which they combine with a delightful social realism.

The flat, watery and frozen countryside is carefully managed by the artist, who finds a place for the figures on the right, up on the wooden bridge for dramatic effect. The snowy return in the bottom right-hand corner – which breaks the monotony of water, snow and the flat horizon – is mirrored by the reed beds tapering down to the boats frozen in the water. The mast of the little boat on the left, mirrored on the far right by the tall pole that acts as a navigation marker, adds verticality to an otherwise strongly horizontal scene. The layers of colour that make the sky are particularly evocative of a bitterly cold day. The range of colours and tone, though limited, is skilfully employed to create contrasts, particularly in the instance of the darkly clad kneeling hunter set against the warm browns of the reeds. Two observers stand out against the horizon, completing the quintessentially Dutch scene. While the contemporary audience would have enjoyed the subject of duck hunting and the incidental winter pleasure of the skaters and a pair of *kolf* players, it would also certainly have noticed the man hanging from the gibbet on the left horizon.

Working in Amsterdam in the early seventeenth century, Cabel got his nickname from the cable-maker's house in which he lived. Though skilled and highly regarded as a landscape artist, he relied on others for direct inspiration, notably Hendrick Averkamp, also well represented at Mansion House (see nos. 3 and 4).

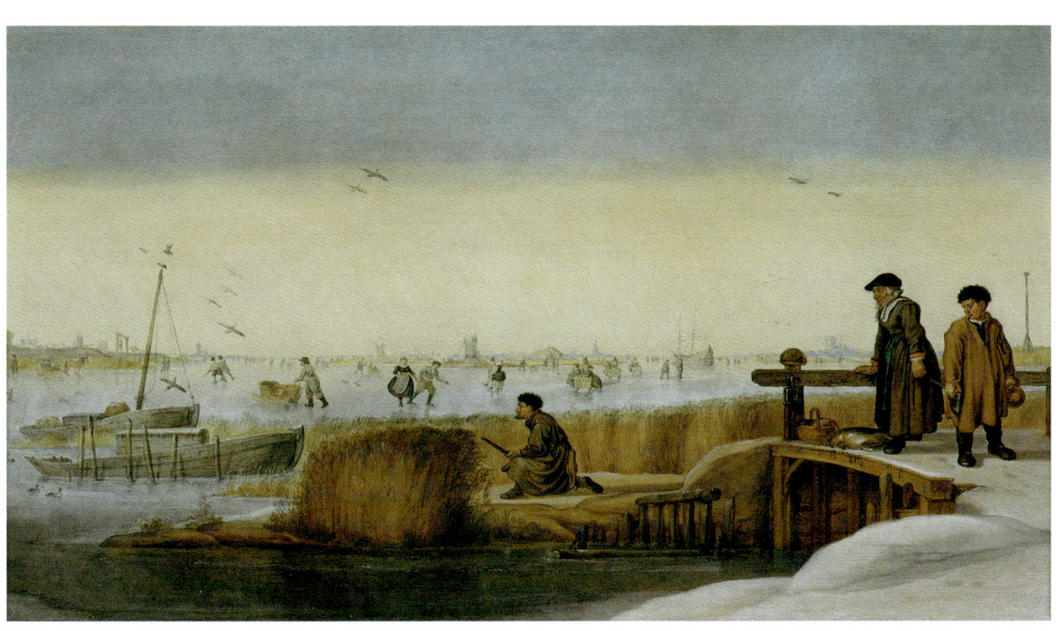

2

ARENT ARENTSZ, CALLED CABEL
Amsterdam 1585/86–1631

Winter landscape with a duck hunter

Oil on panel, 32 × 58 cm, signed
Sutton no. 2

Like so many of Cabel's works, this painting is based on another by Hendrick Averkamp. Here the artist has used a navigation pole (*seinpalen* in Dutch) effectively to cut the picture in two, though not in halves nor completely vertically. By placing another *seinpalen* on the far side of the frozen river, Cabel sets up the pictorial space, which would have been hard to visualize, since it otherwise consists of little more than sky, a faint horizon to the frozen river and two spits of land on the right. In representing the flat polders and canals that comprise so much of Holland, some form of verticality – buildings, figures, ships – was needed to establish distance, a technical feat made even more difficult when the sky and water were represented in subtle winter colours.

This work is not in the best condition. The paint has been much worn and over-painted and layers of yellowing varnish have dulled the distinction between the sky and the ice. This wear is often worst where the layers of paint are thinnest. Conversely, where the paint is thickest, usually on the figures, the condition is far better, increasing the contrast yet further.

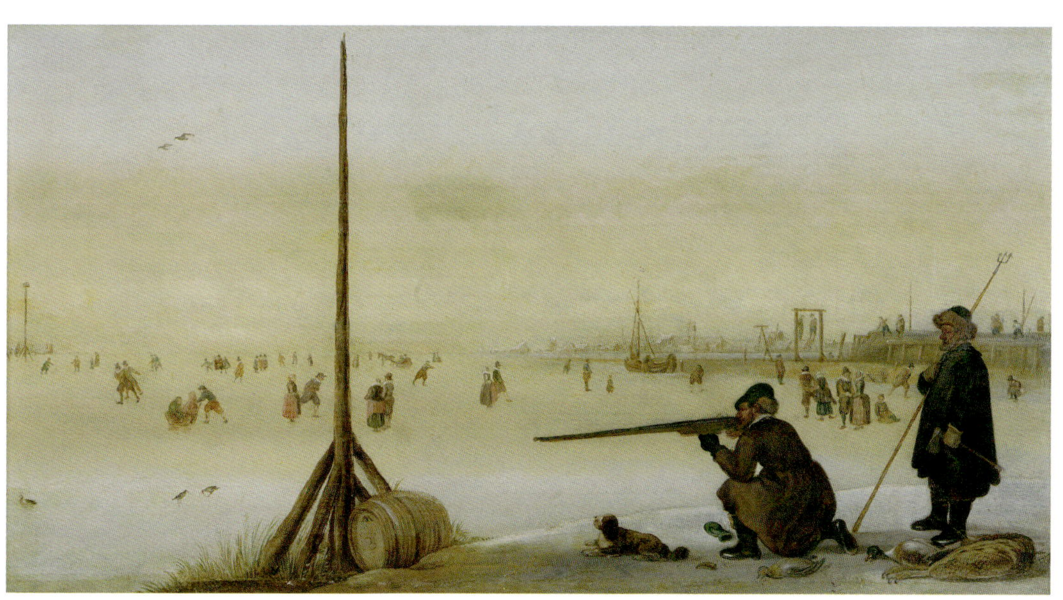

3

Winter landscape on the River IJsel near Kampen

Oil on panel, 53 × 96.6 cm, signed
Sutton no. 3

Averkamp was a mute. He came from a well-educated and prosperous family,
who settled in the town of Kampen that lies on the River IJsel, a tributary of the
Scheldt, in the southern Netherlands. His mother, concerned that he might not
be able to support himself, left him an annuity of 100 guilders from the family
inheritance. He was sent north to study in Amsterdam, but his earliest works
show strong influences from Flemish artists such as Pieter Brueghel I. Despite his
disability, on returning home he was to become the first and best known of all the
winter-landscape painters.

Averkamp's works are populated with great numbers of people of every variety,
in a multitude of pursuits, that fully answer our expectations of incident and
accident in Dutch art. Typical of his work from about 1615, the Samuel collection
painting has a low horizon and a viewpoint from the centre of the River IJsel,
with the two banks converging on the horizon and with Kampen itself on the
far left. Averkamp produced many figure studies, which he used repeatedly for
his compositions and which reflected the wide variety of orders in Dutch society.
On the left, two wealthy ladies occupy a fine horse-drawn sleigh. In the centre,
an elegant couple, the lady heavily veiled against the cold, walk arm in arm,
while in the right foreground spectators gather to watch a game of *kolf*, played
using wooden-shafted, metal-headed clubs and leather balls filled with cow
hair. Further off, skaters ignore the gruesome gibbet on the right bank. Though
sometimes presented with a moral theme – the ice and the danger of slipping on it
hinting at the uncertainties of life, and the hanged men at transience and futility
– such works were more often merely pleasant reminders of what were everyday
scenes, anecdotal and delightful in their detail and familiarity.

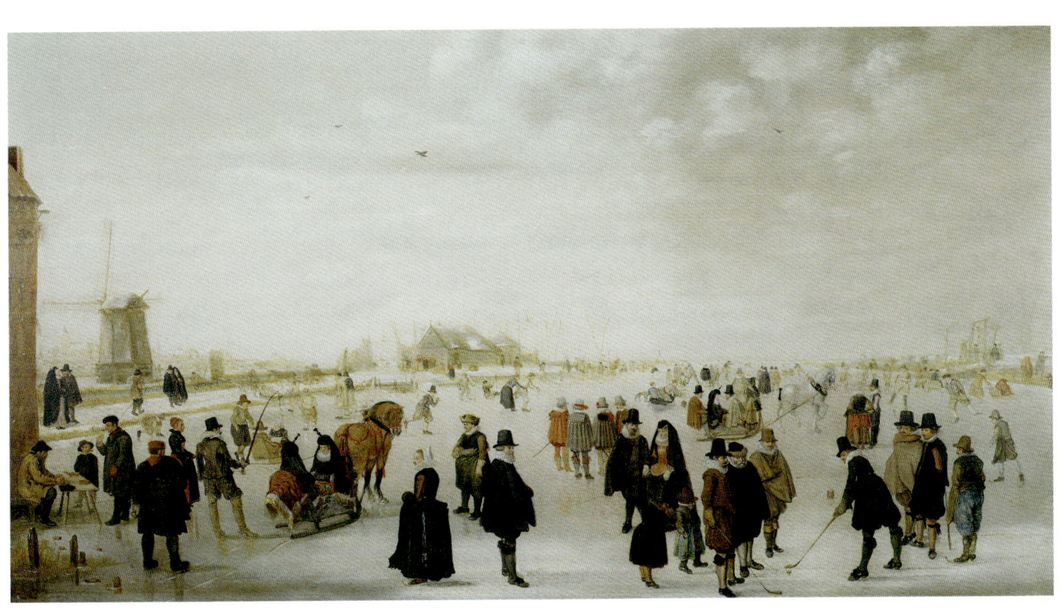

4

HENDRICK AVERKAMP
Amsterdam 1585–1635 Kampen

Winter landscape with a frozen river and figures

Oil on copper, 40.5 × 64.5 cm, signed
Sutton no. 4

This picture is painted on copper, which provides a smoother surface and is less prone to damage than either panel or canvas, often resulting in far better preserved layers of paint. Averkamp has again set his scene on a frozen river, the receding banks – with flag-bedecked booths on the right and a dyke on the left – leading the eye towards a distant town and a sizable ship, frozen in the ice.

Like the work by Cabel – who copied Averkamp's work extensively, often with few changes – the scene is bisected by a navigation post, crowned with an upturned eel-trap to make it more visible from a distance for boatmen. The post has two functions. In design terms it offers some relief from the inevitably strong horizontals and, read in relation to the flagpoles on the right-hand bank and the mast of the distant ship, allows depth to be created – as the gradual diminution of the figures and the changes in the tones of the ice and sky also do. In terms of symbolism, we know from Dutch emblematic literature that the beacon post, or *seinpalen* – useful only to a helmsman with an understanding of navigation – signified the importance of specialized knowledge. The distant gallows on the left bank offered another moral lesson, facing as they do on the other bank the cheerful, worldly booths for refreshments and entertainment – one with a leafing branch hanging in front, a well-known sign for a tavern.

Averkamp's studio practice was such that he often re-used figure groups in his pictures, making extensive use of preparatory drawings. Some of the more completed and coloured drawings he may also have produced for sale. For example, the young couple to the immediate right of the post, arm in arm, occur in a drawing in the Royal Collection at Windsor, in which the girl has tentatively been identified as Averkamp's sister Femmetje.

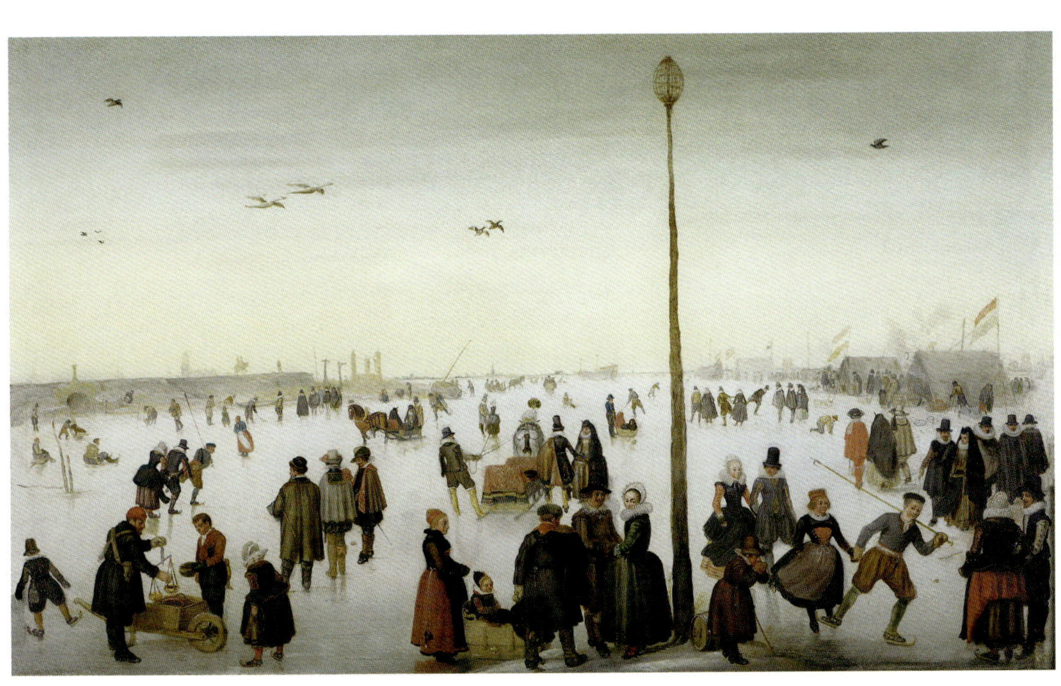

5

Panoramic landscape with shepherds, sheep and a town in the distance

Oil on panel, 38 × 54.7 cm, signed
Sutton no. 16

There are two works at Mansion House by Aelbert Cuyp, one of the most
important of all the seventeenth-century Dutch landscape artists. His images
of cows beside gently flowing rivers and of lush pastures in the golden light of
either morning or evening epitomize the agrarian wealth and well-being of the
time. Though the second of the Samuel pictures is more typical of Cuyp's style,
this early work of about 1640 sheds light on both his origins and aspirations.
Influenced by the tonal works of a slightly older generation of landscapists led
by Jan van Goyen, Cuyp uses a very limited range of colours, dominated by what
might best be described as a faded straw yellow. With this he delineates figures,
foliage and livestock, blending them off into the middle distance to the tower of a
village church. Only by using an imaginary hill can he create a vantage point from
which to show the full extent of the flat terrain. The interest of the work, sparse in
composition and limited in tone, lies in the silhouetted shepherds and the range
of textures achieved within these constraints. In the faintly blue sky some colour
relieves the severity.

Son of the most distinguished artist in his home town of Dordrecht, Cuyp
was greatly influenced by his father in his compositions, particularly those that
are rhythmic and balanced. Though he quickly developed away from the limited
tonal range we see here, he always maintained an understanding, learned from
van Goyen, of how colours relate in a harmonic way. From those Dutch artists
who had been to Italy, particularly Jan Both, he was to learn about light. While
Harold Samuel never bought works by this group of Italian-influenced artists
that included Adam Pynacker and Nicolaes Berchem, in the second Cuyp (no. 52)
and other pictures at Mansion House (nos. 10 and 19, for example) we can see the
immense impact they had on Dutch painting.

Cuyp, who only ever travelled along the Rhine and on the rivers Maas and Waal,
has become synonymous with Dutch landscape. This work is a valuable indicator
of his early influences and ability.

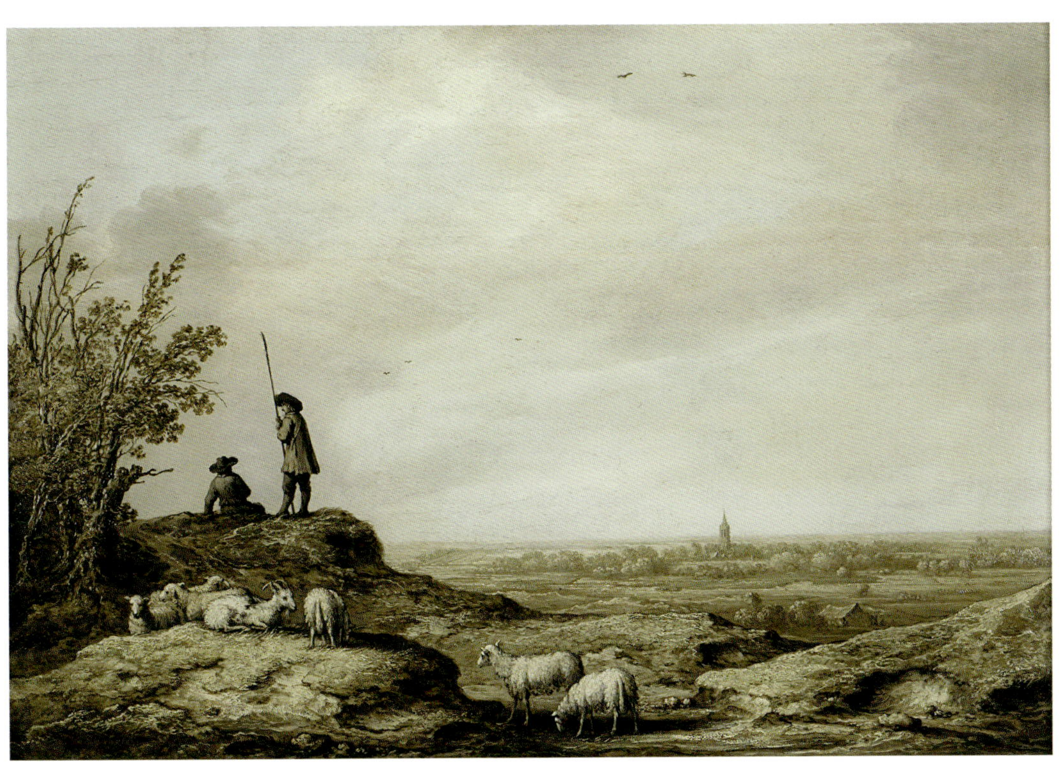

6

JAN VAN GOYEN
Leiden 1596–1656 The Hague

Winter landscape with a walled castle

Oil on panel, 32.1 × 59.3 cm, signed and dated *1626*
Sutton no. 19

This is an early example of van Goyen's work, more conventional than his later, tonal works which were to have such an influence on Aelbert Cuyp. Apprenticed at the age of ten to a local artist in his native Leiden, van Goyen travelled for a year through France in 1615–16 and spent another formative year in the Haarlem studio of Esaias van den Velde, whose style he followed into his late twenties. In this early work we detect his future style in the way he uses subdued and subtle tones, particularly in the walls and roofs of the castle and the building on the right.

The wide frozen river acts as a moat for the turreted castle. Drifts of smoke from the castle and the house on the right bank, along with the skein of birds in flight, add emphasis to the depiction of a bitterly cold day. The elongated format of the painting well suits the narrative of the scene. Filled with figures in a variety of activities, the wide composition is carefully framed by the buildings and by the inward-arching, darkly bare trees. The horizon is set below the middle of the picture and the low clouds act as a foil for the elegant browns and greys of the buildings and the frost-covered trees. Occasional touches of red are used to lead the eye to the activity on the ice. They are judiciously spaced to the left, right, in the foreground and in the distance, in different sizes and shades, to seem natural but to add points of focus in an otherwise uniform tonality. This aspect of Dutch seventeenth-century painting was avidly picked up by English landscape artists in the late eighteenth and nineteenth centuries, by Gainsborough, Turner and Constable amongst others.

This early work gives depth to the group of five pictures by van Goyen in the Samuel collection as it shows his style before it changed considerably after his move to the more cosmopolitan centre of The Hague in 1632.

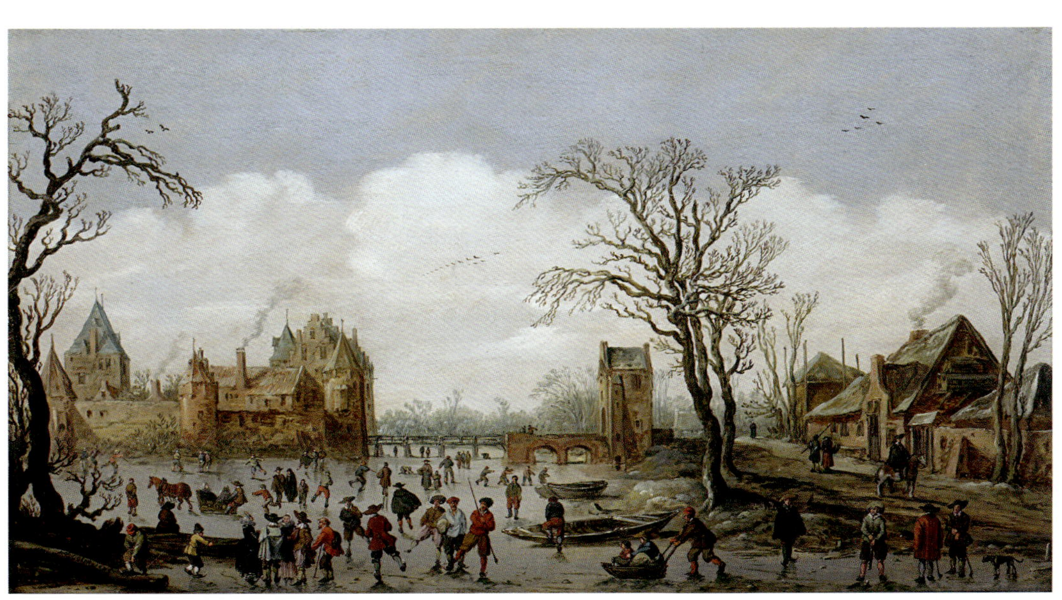

7

JAN VAN GOYEN
Leiden 1596–1656 The Hague

Winter landscape with skaters before 's-Hertogenbosch

Oil on panel, 45.6 × 76.6 cm, signed and dated 1646
Sutton no. 21

Here Jan van Goyen has moved to the more mature style of his later years, dispensing with the framing devices of trees and buildings, called *coulisses*, that we saw in the previous work, and lowering the horizon to create a vast sky, with the land taking up barely a quarter of the picture. The range of colours is reduced to a minimum, bar the odd touch of red, notably on the jacket of the man who has fallen on the ice in the left foreground and, slightly duller, the red of the jacket of the woman seated in the sleigh to the left. Otherwise, the greys and browns of the bare landscape, with patches of pale blue in the cloudy sky, admirably evoke the Dutch winter. The faint spits of land on either side direct the eye across the frozen scene towards the cathedral of 's-Hertogenbosch on the horizon.

A great advantage in the study of works by van Goyen is that he almost always signed and often dated them. Dendrochronological evidence coupled with this useful habit of dating works shows that he preferred to use wood panels from freshly felled trees. The use of under-seasoned wood in this instance has led to problems of conservation: the panel has been reduced in thickness and a supporting cradle has been fitted to the back to prevent splitting, which had begun in the top left-hand corner. As large areas of paint are thinly applied – particularly in the ice and in the sky, where little work was needed to achieve the desired effect – some wear has occurred and re-touching was required.

This picture was previously owned by two distinguished collectors – in the mid nineteenth century by the Russian Prince Paul Demidoff, who lived in self-imposed exile in Florence, and then, after 1890, by the Princes of Liechtenstein, who sold it in 1948. Harold Samuel almost always bought his pictures through the London dealer Edward Speelman, if not directly, then acting for him at auction. Samuel bought all his works by van Goyen from Speelman in the 1960s when supply, and therefore choice, was far greater than today. Taking Speelman's advice on quality and suitability, Samuel formed a group of well-related works that show the range of van Goyen's style and the scale on which he worked. This picture is one of the larger and more sophisticated of the group.

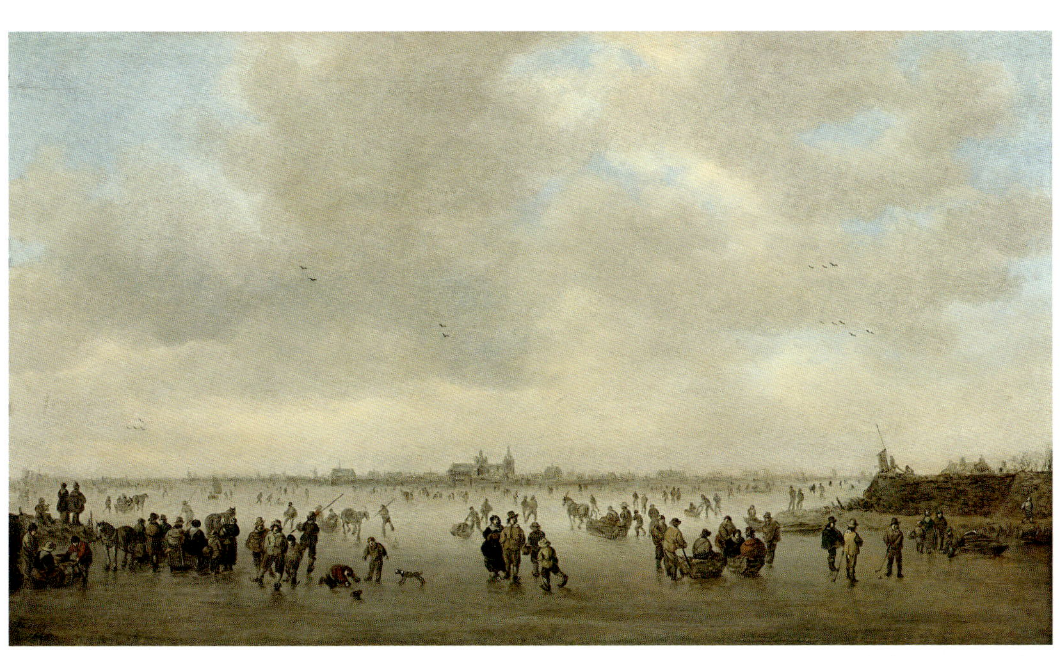

8

Winter landscape with skaters

Oil on panel, 21.7 × 21.1 cm, signed
Sutton no. 73

Adriaen van de Velde, the son and brother of the distinguished marine painters
Willem van de Velde, Elder and Younger, is best known for his small-scale bucolic
landscapes with exceptionally well-studied animals and figures. He was devoted
to making outdoor sketches and at least once a week, his biographer tells us, he
carried his drawing equipment into the countryside. These farm-animal and
landscape studies from nature were worked up into preliminary compositional
sketches and finished drawings before he began a picture. Solid, well-observed
and realistically posed figures and animals, in carefully constructed groups, often
dominate his work. Such was his skill that other Amsterdam artists, including
Ruisdael, Hobbema and van der Heyden, had Adriaen provide the 'staffage' of their
own landscapes.

The very low horizon, the diminutive scale of the figures and the choice of
a small, upright panel make this an unusual work for van de Velde. The use of
perspective in which the vanishing points are way outside the picture plane
creates an excellent view of ice-bound pedestrian traffic on a diagonal to the right.
The church buildings and the child on the sled draw the eye diagonally to the left.
This clever composition is coupled with a subtle use of colour; three quarters of
the picture are taken up by the sky, which only at the very highest point becomes
the rich, pale blue of winter.

The surface of the panel has suffered noticeable losses where the rises in the
grain, which runs vertically, are thinly painted and have become worn. On such
a small scale these losses are noticeable.

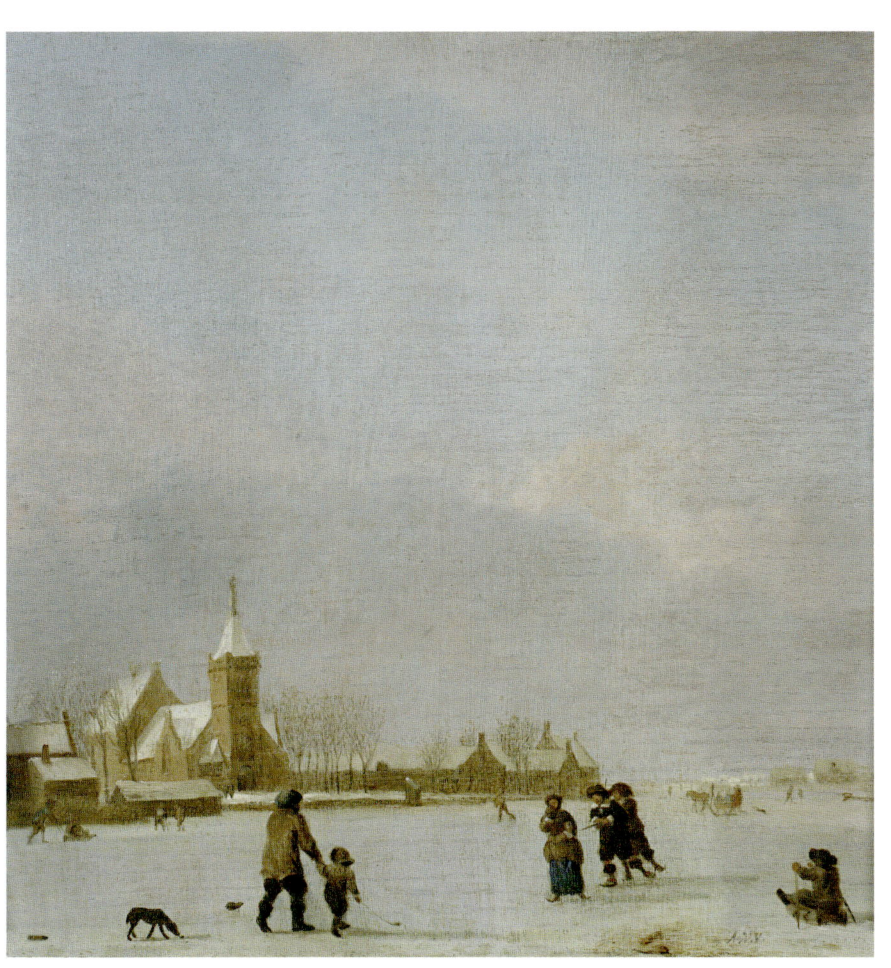

9

AERT VAN DER NEER
Amsterdam 1603/04–1677

Winter landscape with skaters

Oil on canvas, 59.4 × 74.6 cm, signed
Sutton no. 43

Born in Amsterdam, Aert van der Neer worked for some years as the steward of
the estates of the Lords of Arkel that lay to the east of Dordrecht. He came late to
painting and it was not until his early thirties, probably under the influence of
his artist friends the brothers Rafael and Jochem Camphuyzen, that he began to
paint. Though he is now a well-known name amongst Dutch seventeenth-century
landscapists, in his own lifetime he was less than successful in his new career,
moving to Amsterdam and turning his hand to tavern-keeping to make ends
meet. He died in poverty, his paintings hardly valued.

Van der Neer's style is easily recognized and, despite the fact that he varied the
times of day and year at which his scenes were set, rather formulaic. He usually
painted from a higher viewpoint than either Averkamp or van Goyen, the two
slightly older artists who clearly influenced him, and preferred a central standpoint
above water. Coupled with strong features of houses or tall trees on one side only
and an open plain to face them, a path or riverbank often runs across the foreground in his paintings. Van der Neer paid great attention to climatic conditions,
ably depicting cloud formations and the changes in colours they produced, as here,
where the ice reflects the lowering clouds in a rich golden haze of expectant snow.
Landscape artists had rarely attempted to define the time of day, but Aert van der
Neer became adept at sunrises and sunsets, winter scenes and, his most distinctive
contribution to the genre of Dutch landscape, the moonlit river landscape.

The usual cast of characters make up the action down the frozen river, with *kolf*
players, passengers in a horse-drawn sleigh and idle strollers on the ice. Several
figures, wrapped up against the coming snow, shelter in the lee of the houses
on the left. Some washing is optimistically hung to dry on a cottage fence.

As so little appears to change within van der Neer's restricted subject matter
or develop in the treatment of his subjects, his works are notoriously hard to date
stylistically. Sutton has dated this work to the 1650s, however, given the size of the
figures, which are slightly larger than normal, and their costumes, which are of
that date.

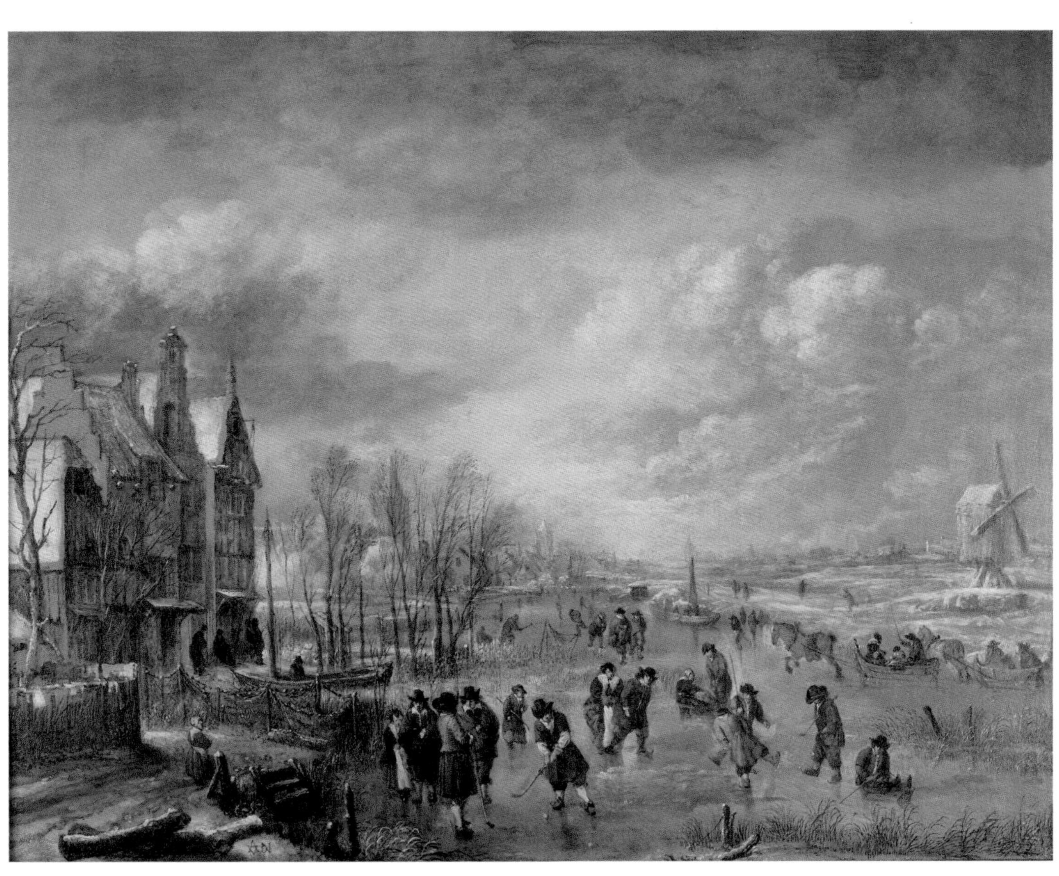

10

FRANS HALS
Antwerp *c.* 1582/83–1666 Haarlem

The Merry Lute Player

Oil on panel, 90.4 × 75 cm, signed

Sutton no. 24

Undoubtedly the most important and recognized picture in the Samuel collection, *The Merry Lute Player* marks a break from the fine succession of landscapes seen so far. Frans Hals is best known as a portraitist, but this picture of a young man in slightly theatrical costume, resting his lute and raising a glass, in fact comes under the category of genre. The young model, who is depicted in several other works by Hals, strikes a pose derived from contemporary Italian paintings, in which half-length figures are accompanied by the attributes of music and drink. Brought over the Alps by a group of Dutch Caravaggists that included Hendrick ter Bruggen and Gerard van Honthorst, these works influenced a whole generation of Dutch artists. Hals never followed the Caravaggist experimentation with strong lighting effects or their more polished technique, preferring instead to use more fluid and rapid brushstrokes. He did, however, draw from their lively poses, heads tilted, arms raised in gestures that often entailed dramatic foreshortening, as seen here in the young man's left hand. The player holds the neck of the lute and points directly at the viewer with only the thumb and little finger lit, the rest in shadow, brilliantly suggesting the lightness of the instrument. Hals's painterly technique is seen here in the wisps of hair and, in particular, in the flashes of blue that line the sleeves of the jacket. With a minimum of brushstrokes the effect of rich fabric is effortlessly achieved. A stroke of blue on the table, half hidden beneath the lute, represents reflected light from the blue lining. A change in design (called a *pentimento* or *repentir*) can be seen at the upper rim of the wineglass, which Hals reduced in size, and now is revealed by changes in the paint over time.

Another Italianate aspect of Hals's style is his use of very simple settings, backgrounds devoid of detail. He often used an umber ground colour, achieved with lead white, yellow ochre and black, and this can be seen in the passage in which the young man's hair and collar meet. To achieve fluidity Hals painted 'alla prima', that is, wet paint on to wet paint. The looseness in his brushwork that gives a somewhat frayed appearance, though greatly admired in Haarlem, where he spent the best part of his long life, was also seen as symbolic of his loose

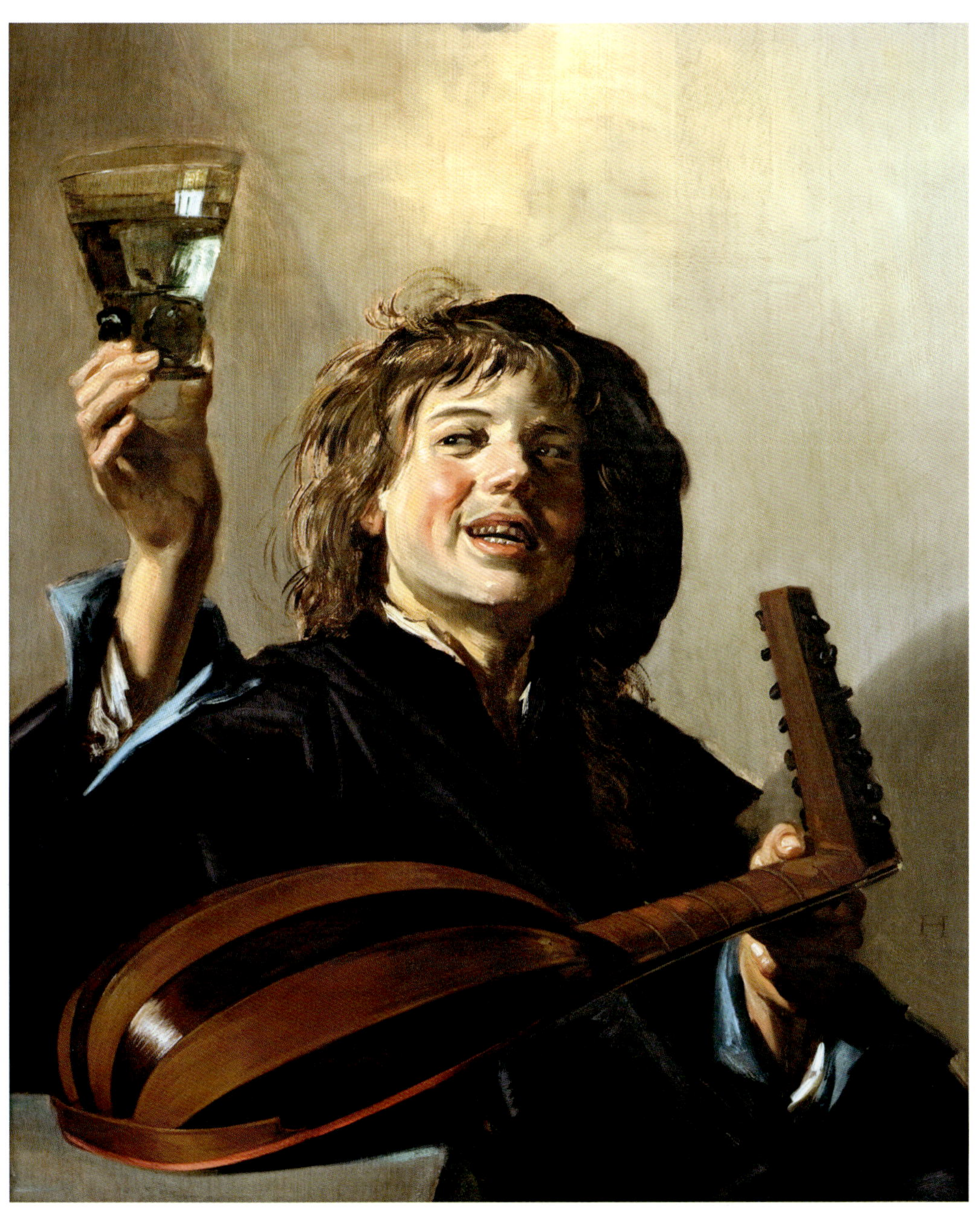

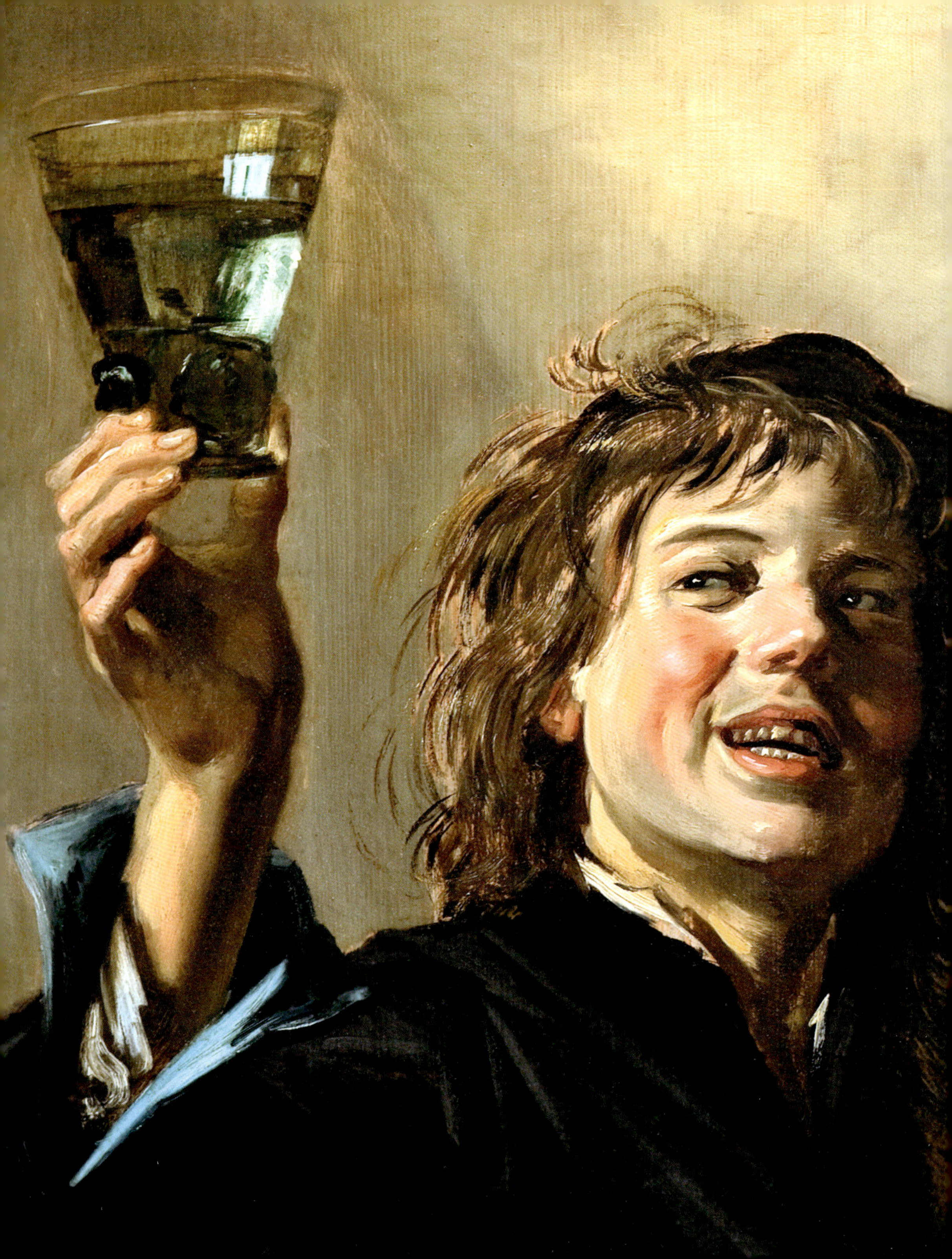

morals. Constantly beset with financial worries and accused of loving drink too much, Hals died in comparative poverty, the recipient of a pension from the town council. In his lifetime his fame was fairly localized. After his death his reputation entered a long period of quiet as his style did not appeal to eighteenth-century taste. He was rescued in the 1860s almost single-handedly by the French art critic Théophile Thoré, who regarded Hals's life and art as exemplifying spontaneity, being full of joy and individuality, the qualities most admired of the new Dutch Republic of the seventeenth century.

11

DAVID TENIERS THE YOUNGER
Antwerp 1610–1690 Brussels

The Five Senses: Taste

Oil on copper, 21.8 × 16.5 cm, signed
Sutton no. 70

This work is as much a portrait of a glass as it is an allegory on the sense of taste. Raised high by the young but well-proportioned man, the great bowl of glass, nearly filled to the brim with wine, gleams invitingly in careful hands. With his mouth wide open after tasting the contents, the subject is probably the landlord of a tavern known to the artist in his native Antwerp. A boy behind him carries a large earthenware pitcher, ready to refill the glass when needed. Teniers's use of muted earth colours in the fabrics and background is enlivened by splashes of stronger colours, notably in the blue hat with gold braid and the elegant, jaunty feather.

The glass is of *roemer* form, a type common in northern Europe, made of sand, wood ash and lime. The need for large quantities of ash limited the areas of production to wooded areas of Germany, the eastern Netherlands and Flanders, and the high iron content of northern sands produced characteristic green tones, giving it the name of 'waldglas' or 'forest glass'. The thick stem is decorated with prunts or rosettes of glass, which have the double function of decoration and forming a grip for greasy hands unused to knives and forks. Depictions of *roemers* can be found in other Samuel collection pictures (see nos. 34 and 40, for example).

Teniers often included carefully arranged still lifes in his genre scenes. Guardrooms are shown with piles of gleaming arms and armour, kitchens with overturned copper pots and pans stacked high and luscious vegetables – excellent excuses for the artist to show off his technical prowess and the skilful use of tones and depiction of light that caused him to be greatly admired and copied.

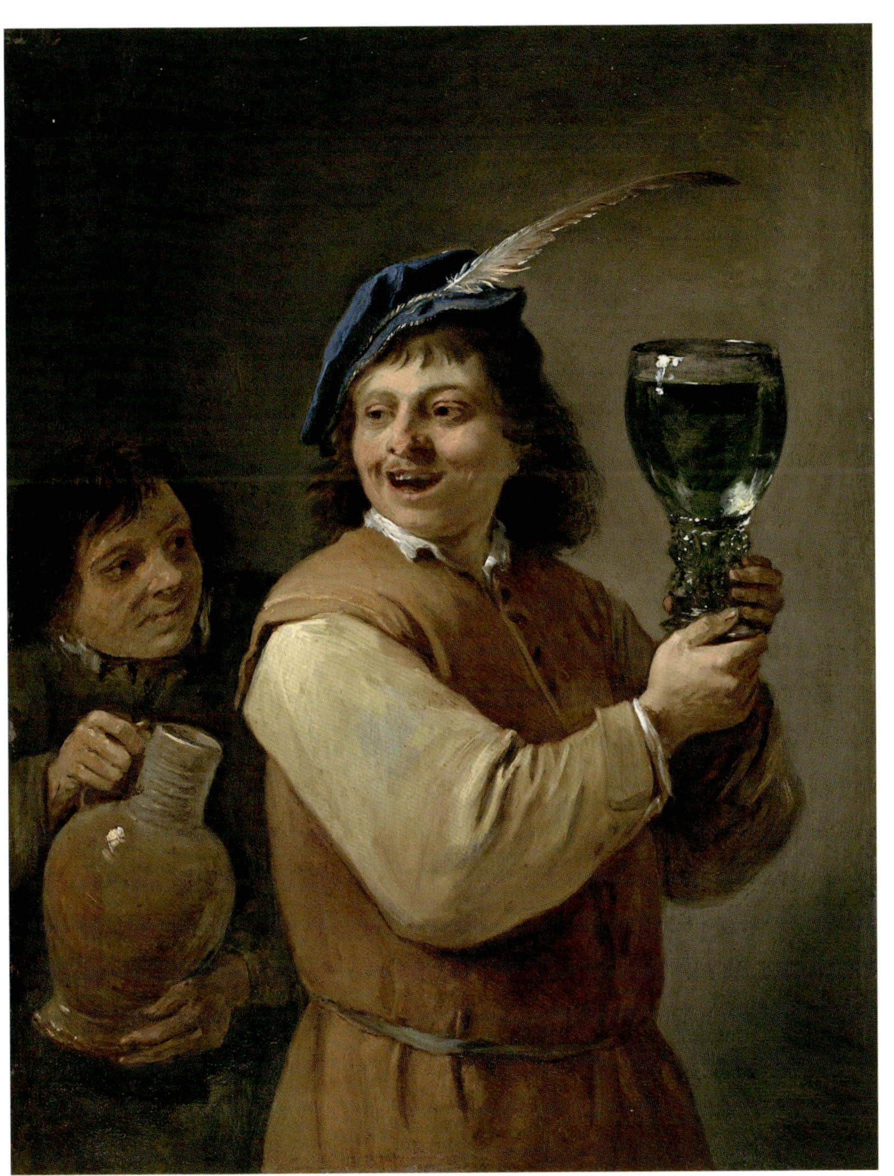

12

DAVID TENIERS THE YOUNGER
Antwerp 1610–1690 Brussels

The Five Senses: Feeling

Oil on copper, 21.8 × 16.5 cm, signed
Sutton no. 71

Aristotle defined the five senses as human perceptions that have no tangible expression. Using everyday figures in everyday settings, Teniers has overcome the problem of representing the senses visually, and, even for a modern audience, he manages to capture these abstract perceptions with remarkable accuracy. Who hasn't felt the twinge of painful pleasure at removing a plaster? Here a young man, seated beside a woman who can probably be classified as a 'kopster', or village quack, gingerly removes a dressing from his wrist, the feeling of pain captured on his face. The nurse, evidently delighted at the result, prepares a new dressing over a brazier of hot charcoal. High up on the wall a shelf, well out of reach of curious small hands or rodents, carries a range of pots and packets, the *kopster's* stock in trade. Teniers's skill at depicting detail and his subtle colouring shines out, notably on the top of the chair-back and in the brilliant white of the man's headgear.

The senses had a strong tradition in Flemish art, as represented by the five works of an artist from Antwerp of an earlier generation, Marten de Vos (1532–1603), which were engraved by Adriaen Collaert before 1618 and would undoubtedly have been known by Teniers. Even more likely as a source of inspiration are the set of engravings by Jan Saenredam after paintings by Hendrick Goltzius (1558–1617), which, though far more elaborate and baroque than Teniers's works, with their simple, peasant-like figures, share the three-quarter-length format and two-figure composition. Teniers's success was his popular appeal, which resonated with so many branches of society and guaranteed him prosperity.

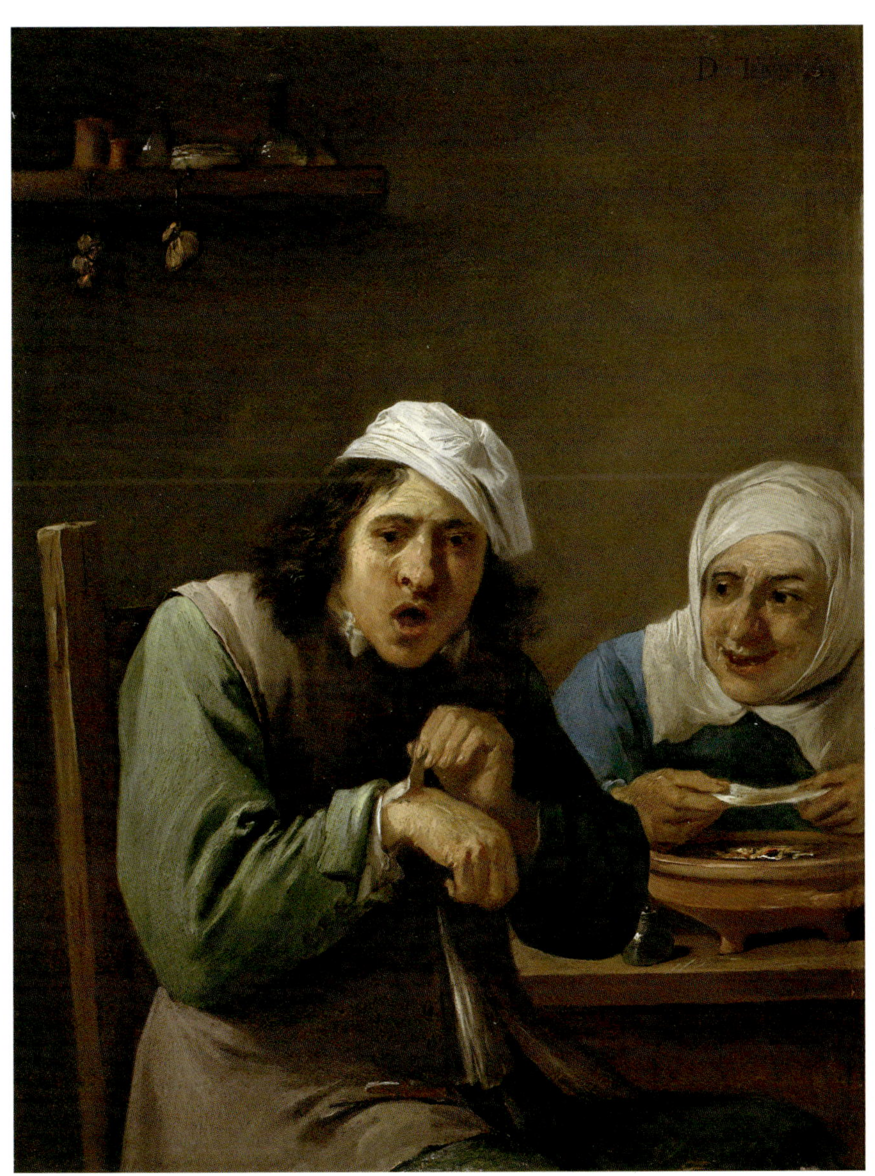

13

DAVID TENIERS THE YOUNGER
Antwerp 1610–1690 Brussels

The Five Senses: Sight

Oil on copper, 21.8 × 16.5 cm, signed
Sutton no. 67

The five senses are represented by five pairs of peasant characters, the central
figure in long half-length occupying the prominent position and the supporting
character adding depth to the composition. Taking up an ancient, ultimately
classical tradition with moral overtones often represented by abstract objects,
personifications and emblems, Teniers has characterized the senses through
the depiction of ordinary people of the Low Countries in everyday pursuits.
In *Sight* a young draftsman, possibly Teniers himself, pen in hand at a drawing
board, glances out of the picture plane, his bright eyes highlighted with points
of brilliant white. The rich red cap, yellow jerkin and blue tablecloth add emphasis
to the value of sight. In the background an old man, his rheumy eyes failing, holds
up a pair of spectacles.

David Teniers was the son of a successful artist from Antwerp, in the southern,
Catholic part of the Low Countries, then called the Spanish Netherlands, where
he remained all his life. Apprenticed to his father and married in 1637 to the
daughter of Jan Brueghel I, he achieved great fame and considerable material
success. Influenced by his father-in-law's family tradition and by an older
generation of artists like Adraien Brouwer, he drew on the subjects of peasant life
in kitchens and inns and in the countryside. Teniers was wildly popular within
his own country and his fame spread abroad in his own lifetime, as far afield as
Sweden, England and to the court of Philip IV of Spain. A popular artist with the
commercial dealers in Antwerp, he eventually became court artist to the Spanish
Governor, Archduke Leopold William, and moved to the capital, Brussels, in the
early 1650s. He was ennobled by his royal patron in 1663 and became the owner of
a prestigious castle, but his career was dependant on the success of the Habsburg
rulers, which faltered in the 1680s during the Nine Years' War with France, as did
Teniers's own fortunes in his final years.

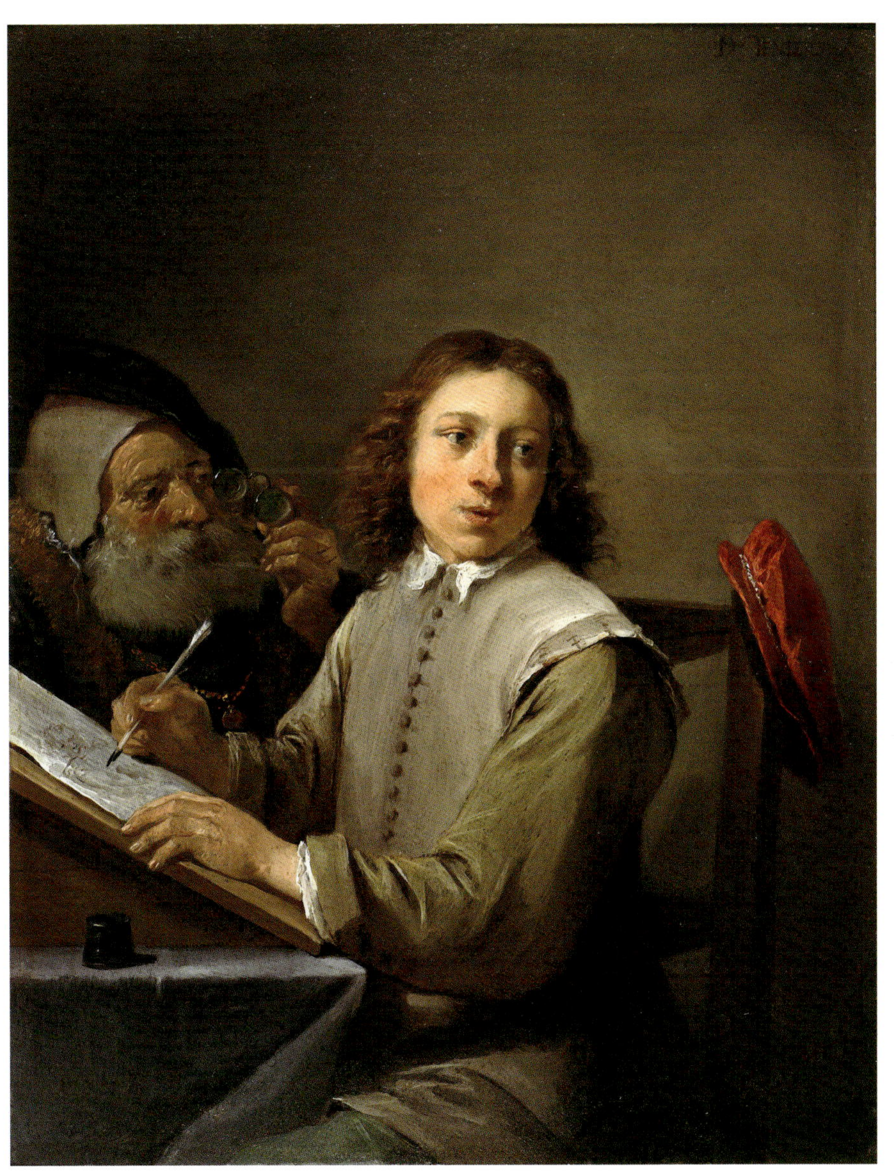

14

DAVID TENIERS THE YOUNGER
Antwerp 1610–1690 Brussels

The Five Senses: Hearing

Oil on copper, 21.8 × 16.5 cm, signed
Sutton no. 68

The set of *The Five Senses* was probably painted in the 1640s, while Teniers was
still in Antwerp providing works for the large and active art market. Gone are the
satirical and deprecating images of Brouwer and the Brueghels, replaced by more
accurate depictions of character and with a more positive feel. The bagpipe player
in *Hearing* has a fine fur hat, a rich blue coat with cuff buttons and a silver medal
tied to his instrument with coloured ribbons. The careful combination of pastel
colours gives a harmonious effect, with the hat set off against the dark, simple
background. The exceptionally smooth copper support allowed Teniers to paint in
minute detail. Fine lines of white paint delineate the sheet of music from which
the shadowy secondary figure is singing, for example.

A major difference between the northern, Protestant, democratic states of the
Netherlands and the southern, Catholic, Habsburg-ruled provinces of Flanders
was the nature of artistic patronage. In the north, the hugely economically
successful middle classes were avid buyers of modern pictures. Prints allowed art
to be disseminated and owned by all levels of society. In the south, an aristocratic
society, led from the cultural and administrative centre of an active and wealthy
court, still commanded the patronage of artists. Teniers's work satisfied a wide
variety of client groups. Rich merchants in Antwerp loved his slightly sanitized
and romanticized visions of the happy lives of peasants, while the courtly elite
loved his ability to depict their own everyday lives, their pursuits and pleasures.
Paintings of guardrooms, kitchens, gardens and halls and peasants at their
country dances – with no hint of war, famine or hard weather – were all popular.
Teniers's works for the Archduke Leopold, particularly his remarkable depictions
of the royal art collections, brought him fame and fortune.

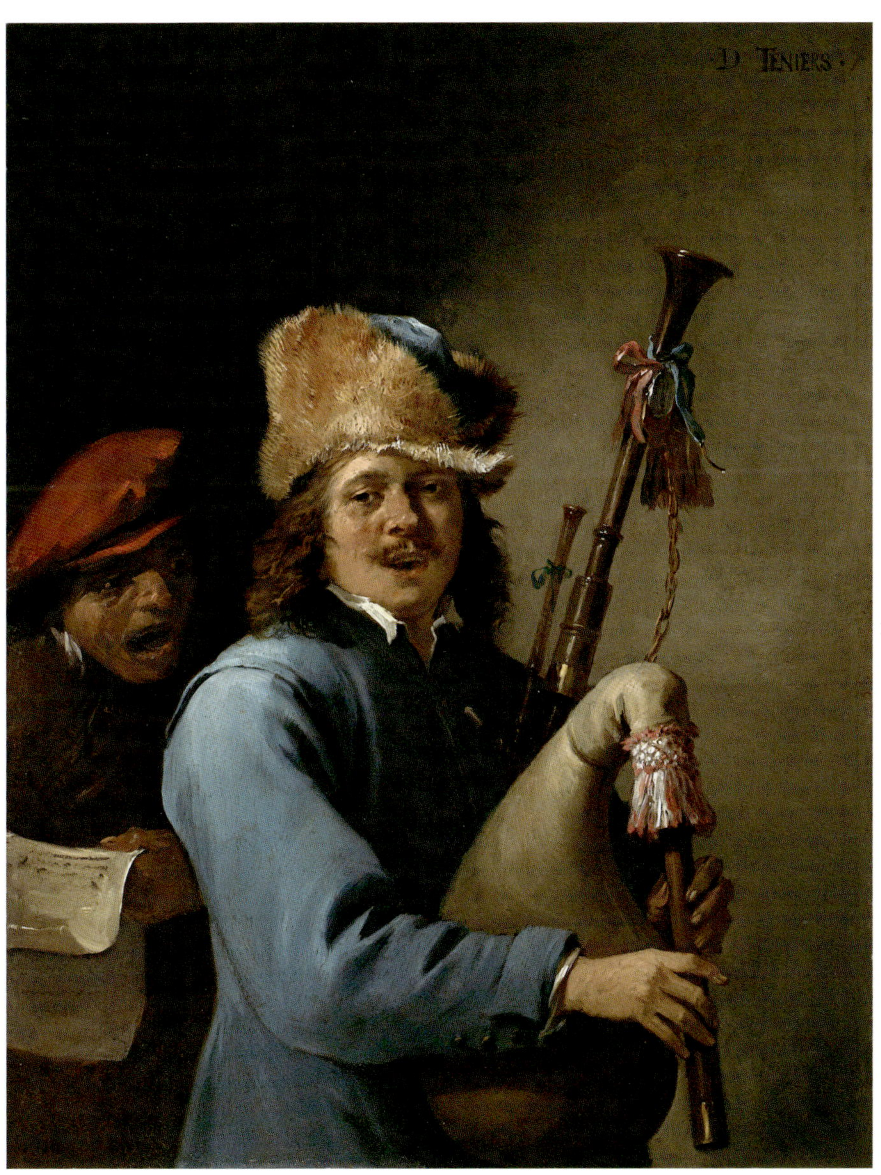
D TENIERS

15

The Five Senses: Smell

Oil on copper, 21.8 × 16.5 cm, signed
Sutton no. 69

Teniers loved to depict strong facial character and allowed for many interpretations in his works, which are rarely cruel and often humorous. His depiction of the sense of smell shows a hirsute and slightly anxious-looking gardener holding an earthenware pot of carnations, peering from under the brim of his jaunty hat at the woman behind him, to whom he has obviously just given a flower. She returns his look, holding the gift carefully between her fingers. Pink carnations (*Dianthus caryophyllus*) are famous for their heavy scent but also symbolize maternal love and marital fidelity, meanings that would not have been lost on Teniers's audience in the seventeenth century, when such symbolism both in art and so-called emblem books was hugely popular. The contrast of the subtle grey and black for the dress of the couple with the lush pink of the flowers and vibrant glaucus leaves is an example of what earned Teniers such great admiration. The cream-coloured hat relieves the monotony of the gardener's attire, and Teniers, with further subtlety, has given the ribbon round the brim of his hat a touch of the carnation's pink.

Though Teniers was able to paint on a large scale, his mastery of smaller formats was particularly valuable. He was commissioned to produce a large number of reproductions, on a miniature scale, of paintings in the collection of the Archduke Leopold at Brussels, as aids for the engravers working on an illustrated publication of the collection. These tiny works, often the only extant image of famous lost works, were particularly representative of Italian and Flemish artists, many of whom were Teniers's contemporaries, including Titian, Giorgione, Rubens and van Dyck. The Samuel collection's *Five Senses* are not the only set of this subject by Teniers to survive – there is a second slightly larger set at the Gallery of the Academy of Fine Art in Vienna – but these works have a particular subtlety and charm in their simplicity.

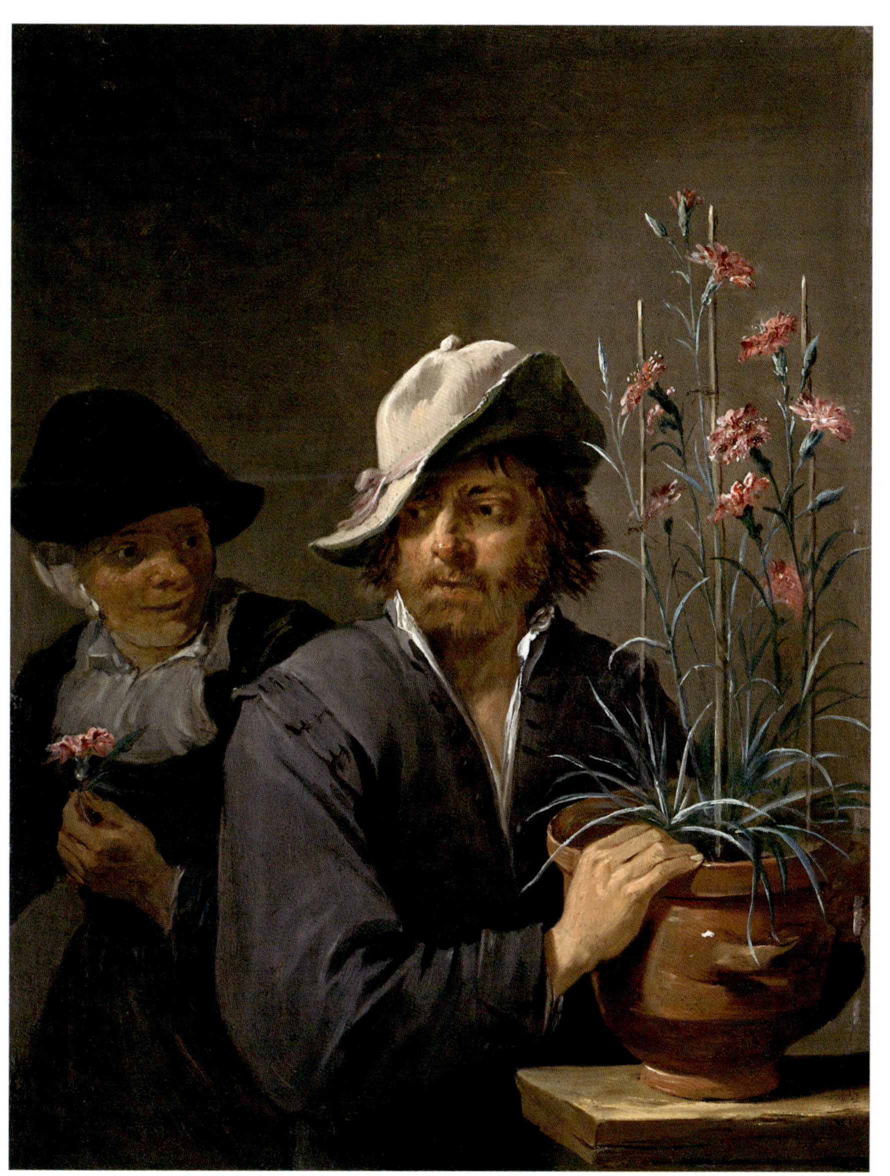

THE LONG PARLOUR

Used as a dining room, for meetings and receiving visitors, this room has changed little over the years. Indeed, bar the addition of a second fireplace on the north wall, matching and mirroring the original on the south, it looks much as it did in 1752. The impressive carved and plastered ceiling, heavily coffered, is particularly fine. The wall to the left as one enters was originally pierced with windows looking into the central court, and false fenestration has been retained. This leaves only tall, narrow spaces, matched by those between real windows on the long wall opposite, as places to hang pictures. The two fireplaces – of an elegant architectural design, with columns and broken pediments – also have spaces for pictures, but very high up and therefore somewhat difficult to see.

Though the room is not particularly suited to the hanging and viewing of pictures, smaller works from the Samuel collection are assembled here. The group of finely painted genre studies by Jan Steen, Gerard Dou and Jacob Ochtervelt are complemented by still lifes by Hubert van Ravesteyn and Jan Jansz van de Velde III. The tiny works on copper by Jan 'Velvet' Brueghel are easy to view on the window wall. However, it is the remarkably fine group of works by Adriaen van Ostade, four in number, together with by an important work by Nicolaes Maes, that make the collection here particularly noteworthy.

Leave the room by the door in the centre of the east wall

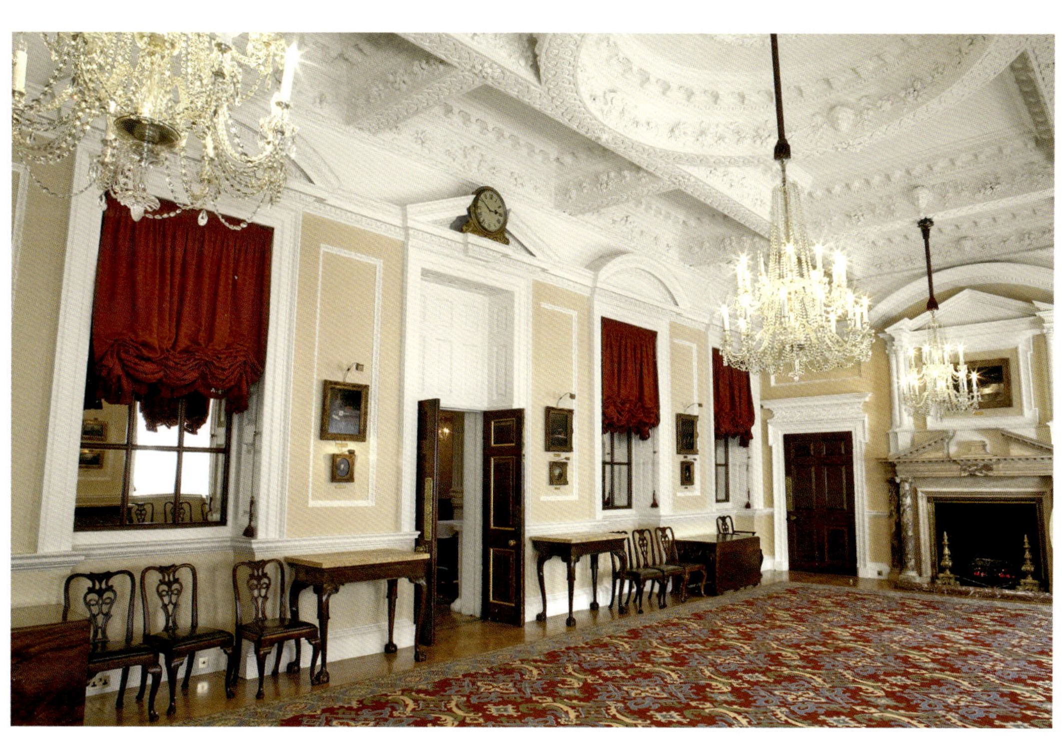

16

ADRIAEN VAN OSTADE
Haarlem 1610–1685

The Water Pump

Oil on panel, 45.3 × 36.9 cm
Sutton no. 51

"A marvel and a masterpiece" was how one nineteenth-century French critic
described this work. Adriaen van Ostade is best known as a painter of peasant life
and everyday scenes, usually interiors, that show, in a sometimes honestly brutal
fashion, the state of Dutch agricultural workers in the middle of the seventeenth
century.

Here, however, probably in the 1660s or 1670s and therefore at the mature
period of his life, van Ostade has painted a pure still life of immense sophistication
of composition and subtlety of colour and tone but with an elemental simplicity
that belies the art and craft of execution. The apparent squalor of the house,
with broken windows and detritus on the floor, is set against a rich feast of fish
in preparation for cooking, denying the poverty. An ancient pump, sheltered by
a sloping roof, is set against a brick wall in the corner of a court in which a vine
grows up to the eaves and a wooden stair spirals upwards. Lying on a board resting
across a hooped barrel are two haddock. Two more fish, already gutted and scored
for cooking, lie staring and open-mouthed on a deep red earthenware colander
on the floor. A cabbage leaf, some straw, bones and mussel shells indicate the
uses to which the water from the pump is put. A broken bowl, a twig brush, a
wooden water-dipper and a rough cloth all add to the scene, a temporary moment
of absence by the cook, brilliantly captured by van Ostade. The composition is
well balanced and the careful use of earth tones for the pump, walls and wooden
objects are in direct and elegant contrast to the silvery, reflecting fish, the red
ceramics and the deep green leaves above.

The Samuel collection has three more works by Adriaen van Ostade – from
all the most interesting periods of his working life and which reflect his better
recognized works of quotidian scenes – as well as one work by his equally talented
brother, Isack van Ostade.

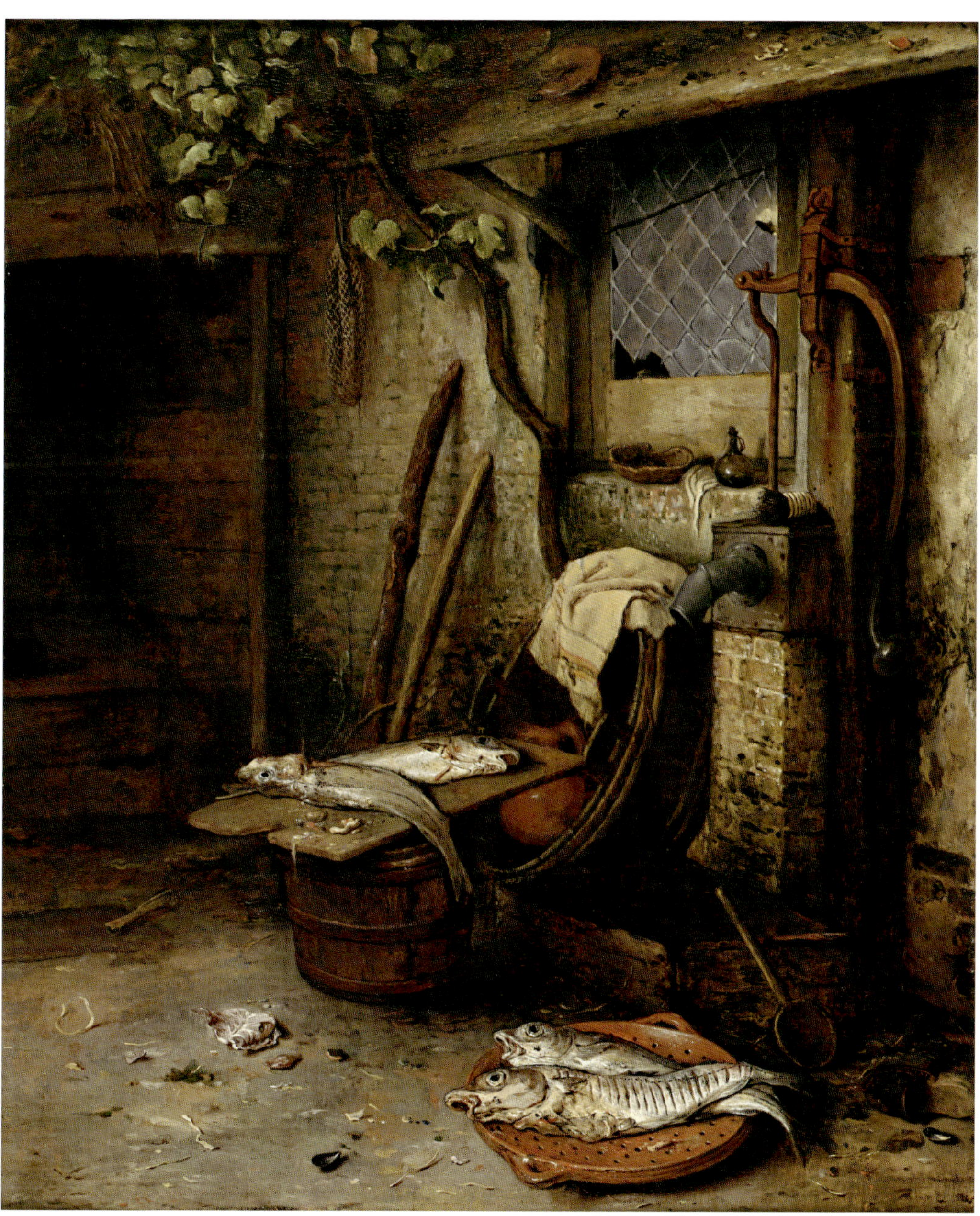

17

JAN STEEN
Leiden 1625/26–1679

The Sleeping Couple

Oil on copper, 18.7 × 24.5 cm, signed
Sutton no. 65

Taught by Adriaen van Ostade and married to a daughter of Jan van Goyen, Jan
Steen was a perpetual student of his craft, always seeking new inspiration from
the several artistic centres he moved between. Sadly, success in his lifetime eluded
him and stints as a brewer and an innkeeper also failed. (The subject of drink
and its effects was a constant theme of his paintings.) He was hard working and
prolific but it was only in the eighteenth century that his popularity rose and he
became greatly sought after in his home country, then amongst wealthy French
collectors and, finally, by the early nineteenth century amongst the influential
British collectors, whose taste formed the basis of so many public collections
today. This painting is one of Steen's most famous works, reflected in the number
of important collections it has passed through, including those of Napoleon's
uncle, Cardinal Fesch, and the Rothschild family in Paris. Steen's gift for narrative
was his greatest asset along with, on occasion, a technical skill in both design
and colour. His weakness was stylistic, in that he borrowed from so many of
his artist friends and from so many different schools that his quality and
consistency suffered.

Painted on copper and re-using a sheet previously engraved by another
artist, this work dates from the late 1650s or early 1660s. Steen's interest in space,
particularly within rooms, looking through doors and windows or across divides,
inspired him for the setting here, in which the massive stone table, set against
a brick wall with a balustrade on to a woody landscape, creates a number of
well-defined spaces that his two characters amply and naturally fill, in drunken
harmony. The subject can be interpreted in many ways. To the modern eye,
a couple dozing after a glass or two of wine can be seen as charming, a natural
pose of contentment. But to the Dutch eye it represented sloth, the evil of idleness
that drink brings, and had a deeply censorious element. The contemporary viewer
would have been scandalized by the indulgence.

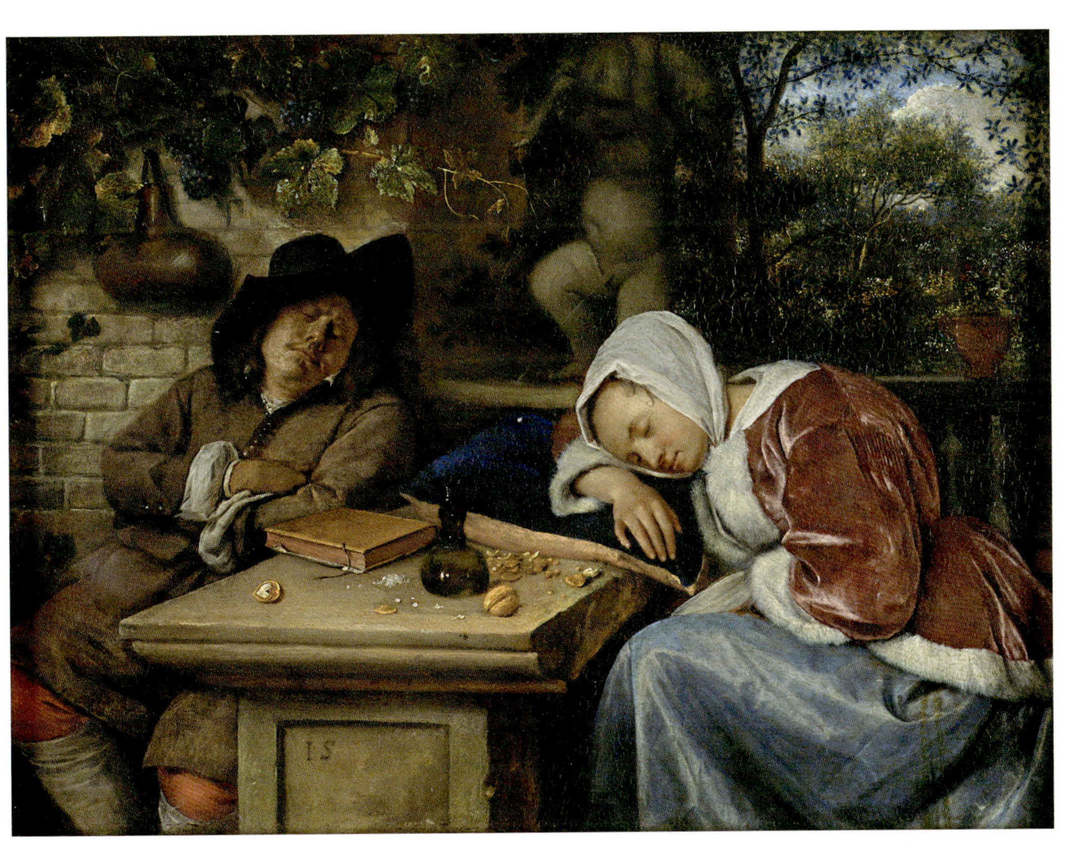

18

HUBERT VAN RAVESTEYN
Dordrecht 1638-before 1691

Still life with a stoneware jug, a glass and smoking requisites

Oil on copper, 43.1 × 35 cm, signed
Sutton no. 56

Works by van Ravesteyn are rare, the majority being tablescapes with drinking
and smoking utensils, a type invented by the Dutch. Though the artist is
comparatively obscure and his style old-fashioned for the date – this work was
probably painted in the 1660s – the painting is representative of an important
genre in Dutch art that Lord Samuel particularly liked.

The still life is supported by a wooden table with a barley-twist leg, partly
draped with a green cloth, dividing the neutral space into three, while the indirect
light forms a diagonal band from corner to corner. Lighter-coloured objects
and areas stand out against darker – the spills on the cloth, for example, and the
shaded side of the jug against the wall. The jug and glass are artfully arranged to
give verticality amongst the horizontal objects like the two pipes and the bundle
of spills. The two loose spills, one used, the other hanging by a thread from the
bundle and pointing towards the floor, reinforce a balanced, orthogonal structure.
So, though at first appearance the arrangement of the space, the light and the
objects themselves seems entirely natural, it is in fact highly contrived and
sophisticated.

These are not the objects of a peasant household. The pewter dish, the
earthenware brazier for charcoals and the spills are certainly quotidian, but the
long-stemmed pipes denote a bourgeois smoker. Such clay pipes were made
exclusively in Gouda. More expensive to make and more fragile than short ones,
they allowed the smoke to cool and taste less bitter. Similarly the tobacco packet,
propped up for all to admire, is a Dordrecht brand of imported tobacco, *Orientael
Verginis Toback*. The pewter-lidded jug, with its distinctive decoration stamped
into the surface and glazed in red and blue, is imported Westerwald stoneware
from Reiren, near Limburg in Flanders. Perhaps of more interest is the glass –
decorated with prunts with trails of glass, a form of decoration found only after
the appearance of Halley's Comet in 1658 – which is helpful in dating this work.

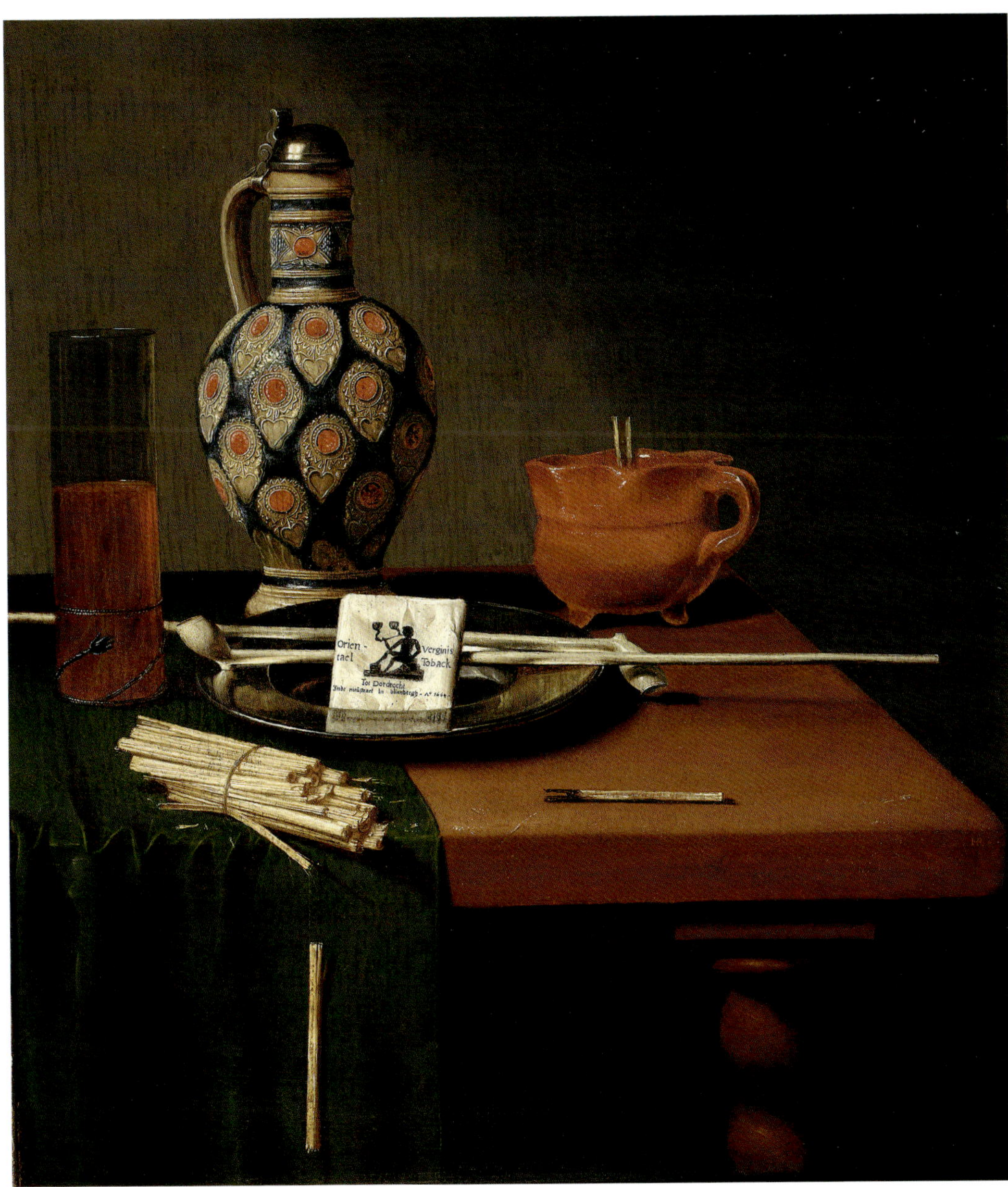
Orien-
tael
Verginis
Toback
Tot Dordrecht
Inde nieustraet In blienbergh · A° 1664

19

GERARD DOU
Leiden 1613–1675

Portrait of a young man

Oil on panel, 16.5 × 13.7 cm
Sutton no. 18

The leading member of the *fijnschilders*, or 'fine painters', of Leiden, artists of small-scale works of meticulous technique, Gerard Dou was the antithesis of artists like Frans Hals, for whom the paint itself became an implement in achieving effect. Invisible brush strokes and polished surfaces characterize Dou's work, and small-scale portraits such as this are common in his early oeuvre. He almost always worked on panel, eschewing the smoother surface given by copper. He trained in the studio of Rembrandt, spending three years with him before the master left his native Leiden for Amsterdam in about 1631, when Dou was not yet twenty years old. Nevertheless, the young artist quickly built up a highly successful – and lucrative – practice in these early years, largely painting small-scale portraits.

The influence of Rembrandt in this oval portrait of a young man is clear. The figure defines the space, lit strongly from outside the picture plane. With *chiaroscuro* effect, Italian in origin, the dark cap is contrasted against the lighter part of the background while the lighter hair and flesh on one side of the face are contrasted against the darker tones of the other. The touches of colour in the feathers and the row of buttons relieve the monotony of the narrow tonal range but they do not distract from the characterization of the face. It is only the small scale and the highly worked features – showing a fine understanding of flesh colours – that indicate that this is not a work by Rembrandt of the 1630s.

Dou's portraits show figures in repose. While they lack the animation of Frans Hals or the incidentals of costume and setting used by other Dutch portraitists, they do, we can assume, capture a likeness, as Dou was highly successful during his lifetime. He has also been much sought-after since, and this work passed through several distinguished Dutch collections in the eighteenth century before being acquired by Lord Samuel from his dealer of choice, Edward Speelman, in 1971, quite late in the collection's formation and rather an uncharacteristic purchase, as Samuel was not often enticed by portraiture. Probably some time in the nineteenth century this picture was turned from an oval into a rectangle with the addition of spandrels, now hidden by the frame.

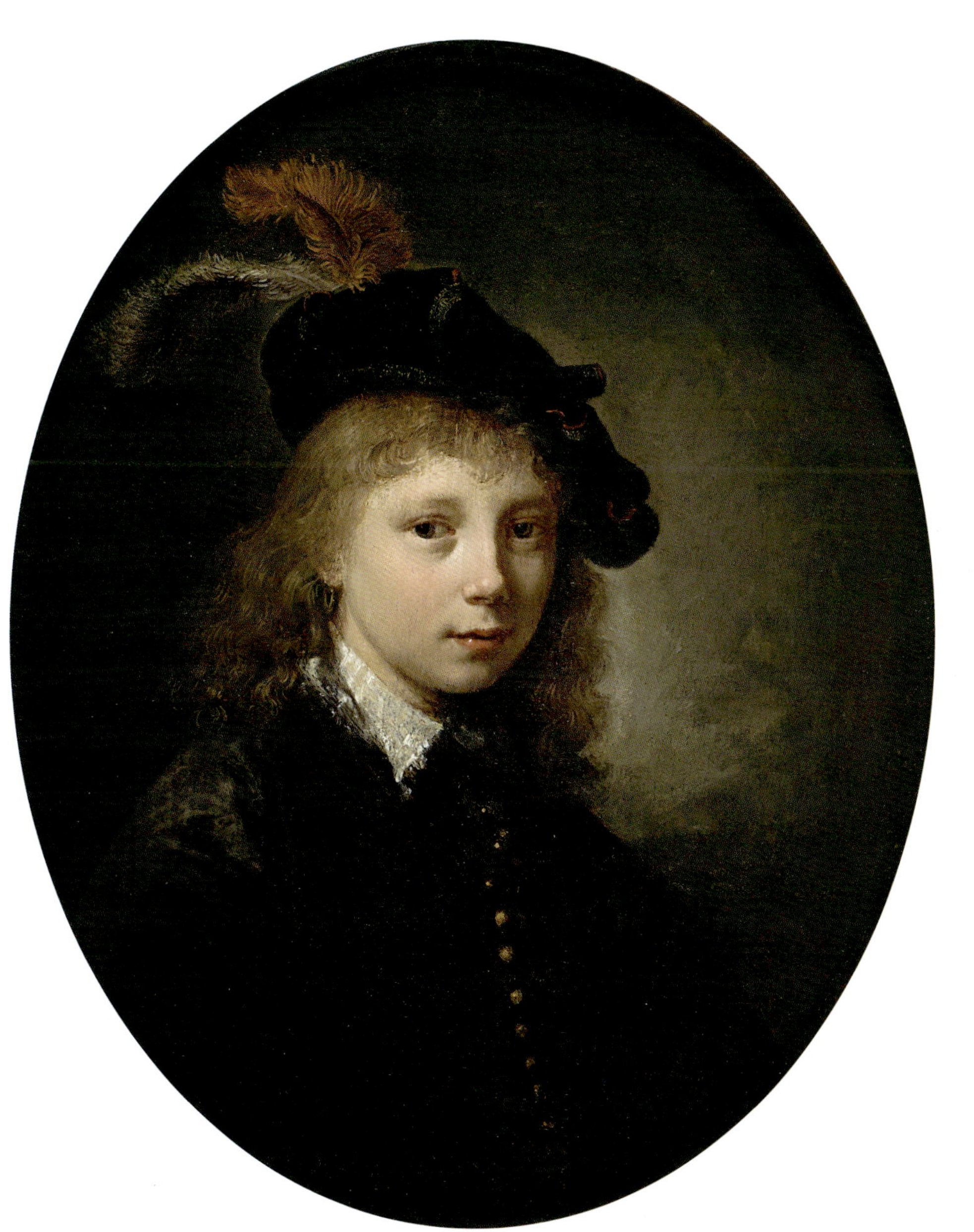

20

JAN JANSZ VAN DE VELDE III
Haarlem 1619/20–1663 (or later), Amsterdam

Still life with a glass of beer, brazier and clay pipes

Oil on panel, 40.1 × 31 cm, signed and dated 1649
Sutton no. 75

It is instructive to compare this still life of a glass of beer and pipes with a similar work on the same wall, by Hubert van Ravesteyn (no. 18). Though van de Velde uses the same component types, the composition is far simpler and the lighting effects less complex. The three zones (the table edge, tabletop and background) create a similar sense of depth, as does the return edge of the table, but the solid, dark background and the deep shadow beneath the table simply serve to highlight the tabletop itself. Diagonals are eliminated and the pictorial space is simply but effectively arranged by overlapping the objects – the glass of frothy beer before the pewter dish of tobacco, and the brazier, its broken rim revealing the glowing charcoal within, before the glass. An element of action is included in the gently smoking plug of tobacco, fallen from the pipe bowl and scorching the table, as others have done. Despite the apparent simplicity, compared with van Ravesteyn's more complex and colourful picture, van de Velde has achieved great subtlety that resonates with a modern audience for whom less is sometimes more.

Jan van de Velde was from a distinguished family of several generations of artists, engravers and draughtsmen, and his work is scarce but highly valued. He was clearly proud of his work, as the prominent, flourishing signature and clear date, while becoming part of the scene, also signify an artist well pleased with what he has done.

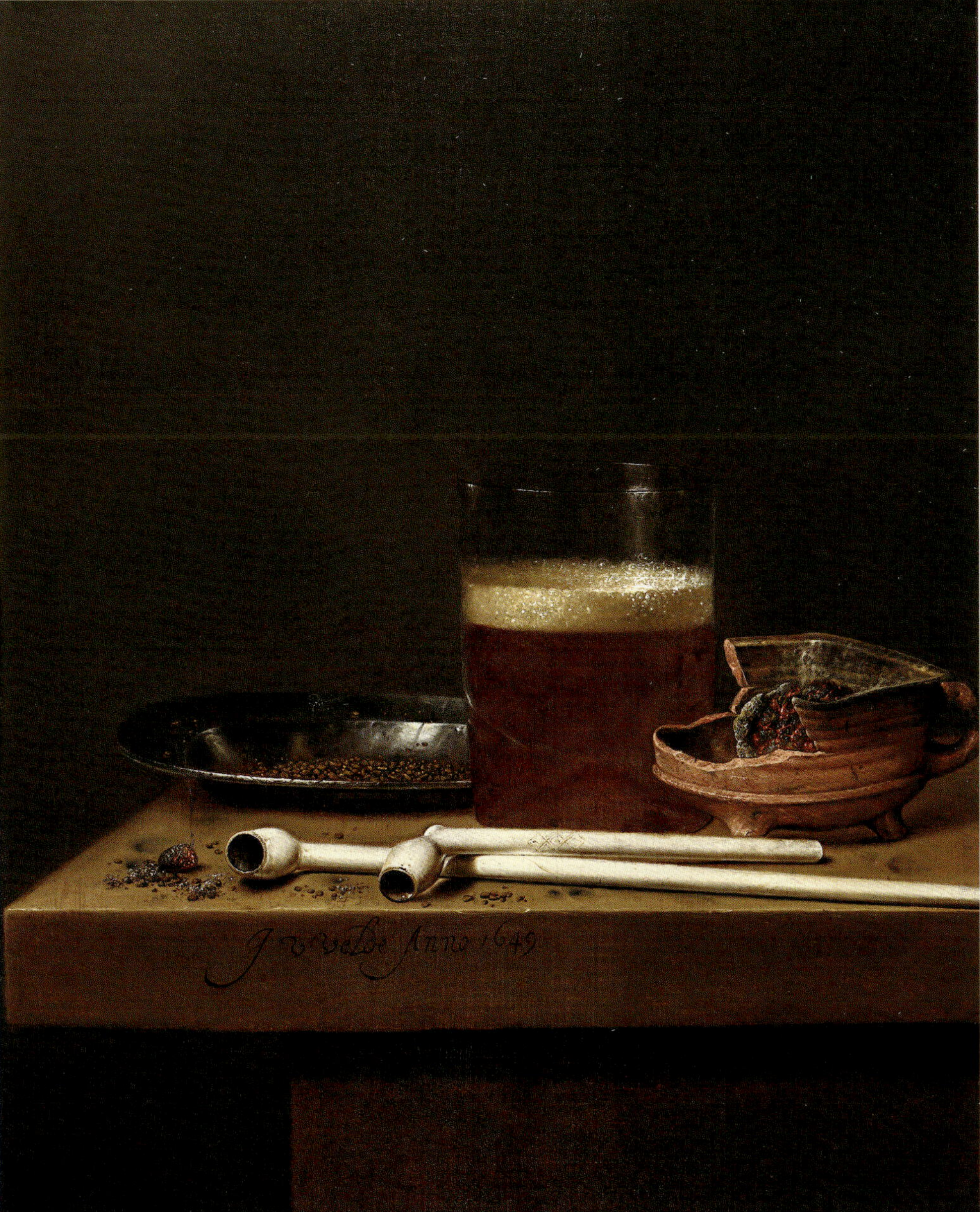
J. v. de Velde Anno 1649

21

ESAIAS VAN DEN VELDE
Amsterdam 1587–1630 The Hague

Winter landscape with skaters

Oil on circular panel, 17.2 cm diameter, signed
Sutton no. 74

Dispossessed from the Catholic, southern Low Countries, the Protestant van den Velde family moved in 1585 from Antwerp to Amsterdam, where Esaias was born two years later. Unrelated to the marine artists of similar name, these van den Velde were nevertheless a large band of painters, engravers and draughtsmen over three generations. By the second decade of the seventeenth century Esaias van den Velde was providing 'staffage' for the landscapes of a number of artists from Haarlem, where he was living by 1610. His own small landscapes – often in *tondo*, or circular, format and sometimes in pairs, with winter and summer being the obvious choice of theme – contribute to the development of Dutch landscape as a distinctive genre, inspired by Hendrick Averkamp in particular.

Van den Velde has used strong tones and the design technique of *coulisses*, or framing features. On either side of the foreground bold trees arch over to suit the shape of the panel. This device also translated into spits of land, stretches of water and buildings and was used extensively by Esaias's most famous pupil, Jan van Goyen, and his influence on landscape design lasted well into the seventeenth century. The figures are less anecdotal and interesting than those of Averkamp, though the use of reds and russets to enliven the otherwise drab tones of winter is effective. The greatest success here lies in the creation of depth. Painted with a clear understanding of the effect of ambient air on distance, the row of trees and buildings along the far river bank stand out in marked contrast to the defined trees and buildings of the foreground. This careful gradation is carried through to the sky, which is shown pale, almost white, at the horizon, rising to the delicate blue of winter at the top.

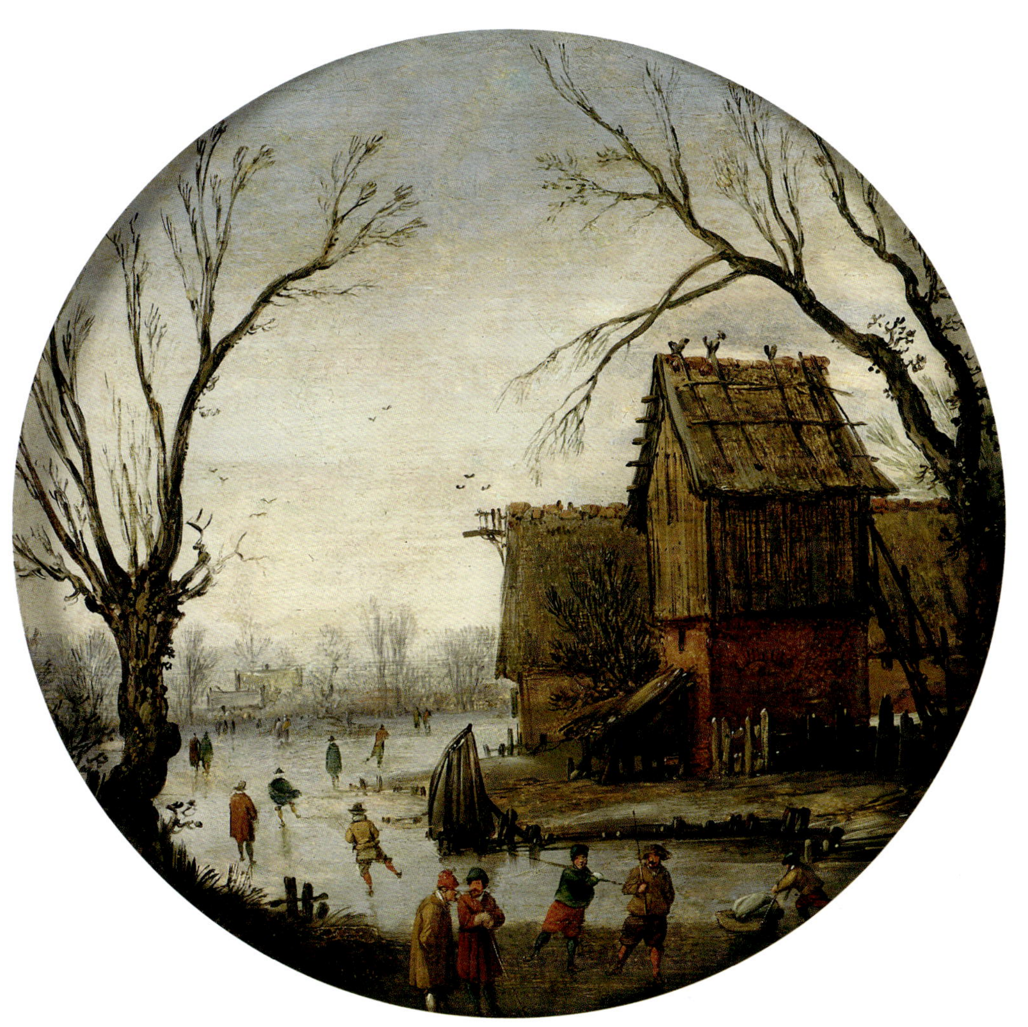

22

PIETER CORNELIS VAN SLINGELANDT
Leiden 1640–1691

Woman making lace, with two children

Oil on panel, 47.5 × 39.4 cm
Sutton no. 64

Of the generation of Dutch artists that takes us to the end of the seventeenth century, Pieter van Slingelandt, along with Frans van Mieris, was Gerard Dou's best pupil, carrying on the tradition of the *fijnschilders*, or 'fine painters', of the Leiden school. Immense and painstaking attention to detail and a smooth, refined finish were their trademarks. This work is a brilliant example of the type. The Samuel collection's work by Dou (no. 19) is a charming oval portrait, but he was better known for interior scenes very much in the manner of the present picture.

The darkened space allows the well-lit figures to stand out. From an invisible source to the left, light shines on the three faces, is directed across the floor and reflected in the decanter of wine on the mantel shelf. Details such as the tilted brass bucket of vegetables, the painted panels of the child's chair, and the objects on the table to the right are apparently carelessly arranged. Forming a pleasing group, they are all admirable in themselves but the whole lacks a sense of unity or meaning. Critics both contemporary and in the eighteenth and nineteenth centuries, when the works of Dou and his pupils were much sought after, admired the realism of the details and the accurate depiction of bourgeois life. However, the rather stilted compositions, whereby a number of still-life groups were individually artfully posed but did not necessarily form a cohesive whole, were seen as rather artificial in the twentieth century and their popularity declined.

Easy to appreciate and certainly skilfully painted, this work by Slingelandt was one of the earliest works bought by Lord Samuel from his dealer Edward Speelman, in 1958. It marked the unchallenging start of his interest in seventeenth-century Dutch genre painting.

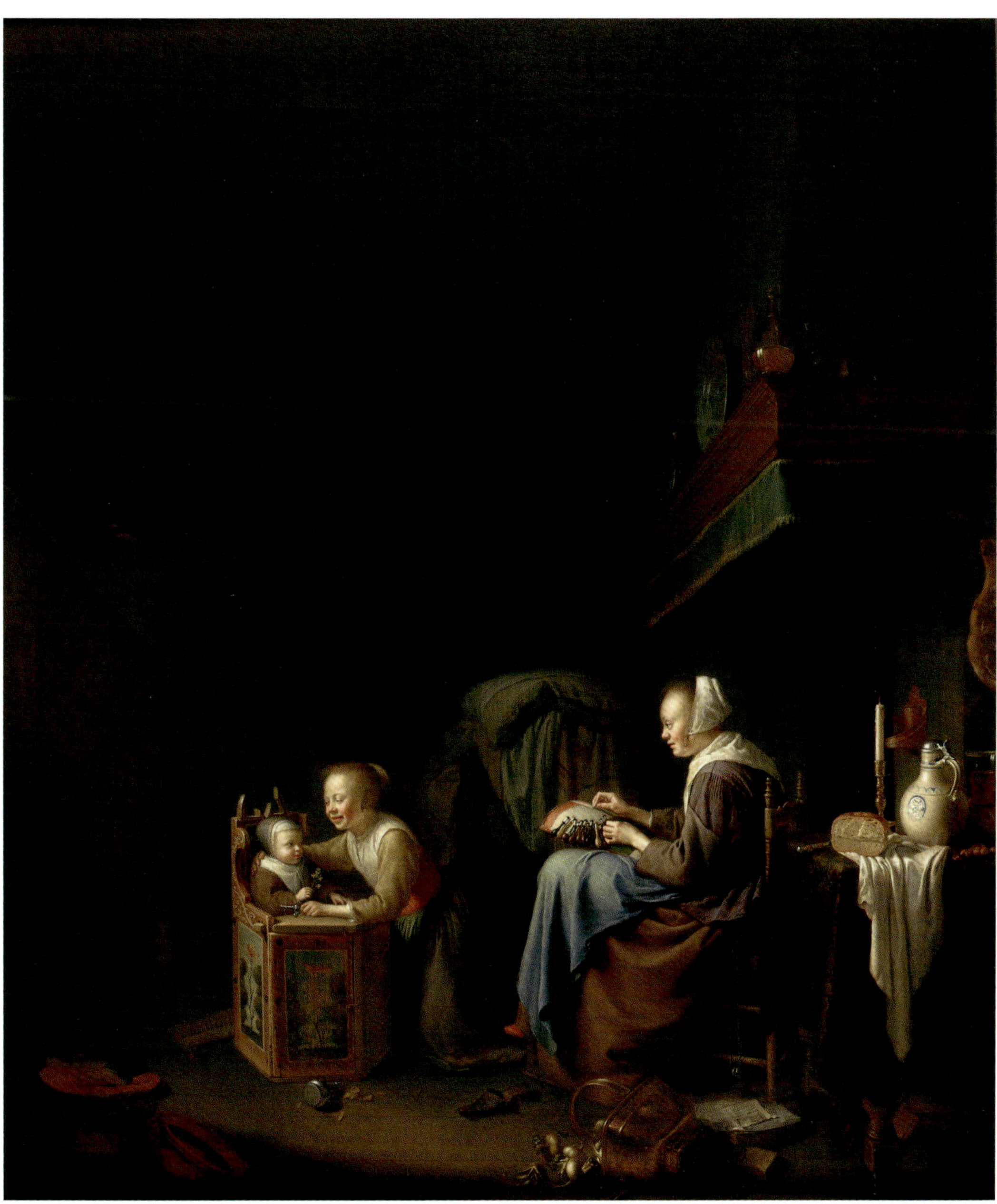

23

Copy after FRANS VAN MIERIS
Leiden 1635–1681

A young woman stringing pearls

Oil on canvas, 23.5 × 18.1 cm
Sutton no. 41

It is fully understandable why this painting was thought to be an autograph
Frans van Mieris, who, with Slingelandt, was the most famous of all the pupils
of Gerard Dou, the outstanding master of the Leiden *fijnschilders*. The technical
quality of the silver ewer and basin and the satin skirt is very high. Now, however,
the work is regarded as a copy of the original by van Mieris in the Musée Fabre in
Montpellier. It is of almost exactly the same dimensions, but the characterization
of the face of the young lady, particularly the shading, is more refined in the
original, while the brushwork of the Samuel example is broader and the shadowy
figure of the standing servant is coarser. The colouring in both is identical, so
clearly the copyist had access to the original. He chose to paint his version, unlike
the example in Montpellier, on canvas rather than on panel, which would have
allowed for a smoother and more refined finish.

It was not until Otto Naumann published his catalogue raisonné of the works
of van Meiris in 1988, a year after Lord Samuel's death, that it became clear that
the Samuel picture was a copy. However, this picture adds to our understanding
both of the work of the artist and – though the line between a flattering copy and
a forgery is sometimes very fine – the respect in which he was held.

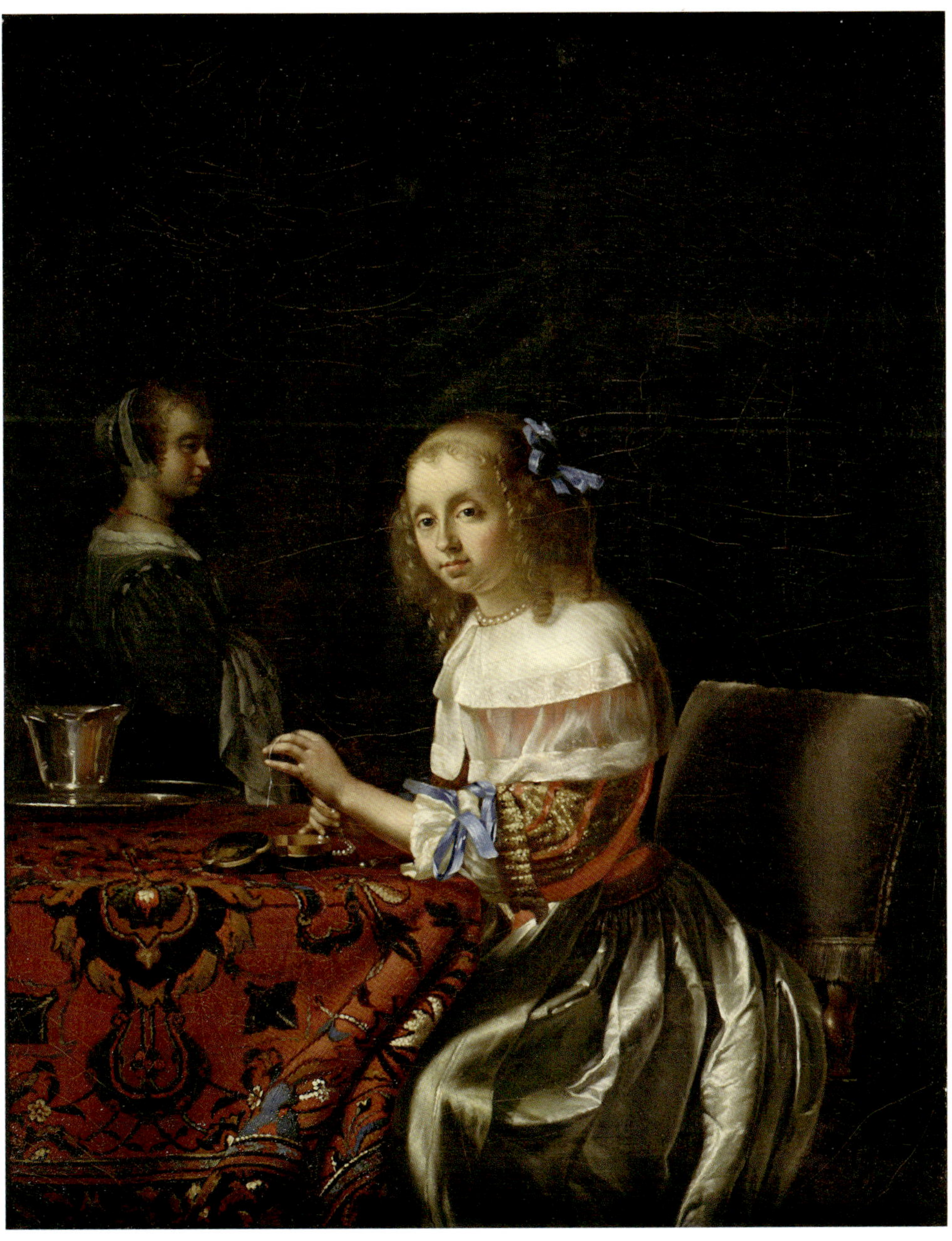

24

ADRIAEN VAN OSTADE
Haarlem 1610–1685

Peasants dancing in a tavern

Oil on panel, 53.4 × 72.4 cm, signed and dated 1675
Sutton no. 50

Far more typical of Adriaen van Ostade than *The Water Pump* (no. 16), this is a large work of his later period. Placed high over the fireplace in Mansion House and therefore difficult to see, it reflects the artist's changing attitude to the peasant revels that he often depicted – more than a dozen times over forty years. The theme, which brought him fame and wealth, gradually changed with time. Gone are the coarse, drunken and sometimes cruel characterizations of his earlier works. Here the scene, set in the large room of an inn, is boisterous but not out of control. The fiddler, standing on a stool at the back, provides the music for the jigging couple. Men and women, better dressed and looking more prosperous than those of van Ostade's works of the 1630s, fill the benches around the room. The space is complex, with stairs, doorways, the beamed roof and a variety of floorings creating an excellent sense of depth. At the front door, the landlord in a red cap doles out alms to a beggar, the moonlit landscape framed by the door arch. Children seated in the far left corner add to the homely, domestic atmosphere, with a floor littered with debris, scavenged by a dog.

The Netherlands had enjoyed an economic boom in the first half of the seventeenth century. With the country freed from the yoke of Spanish rule and made wealthy from trading around the world by sea and with Europe by her riverine connections, Dutch peasants were seen as living in a golden age of comparative wealth and peace. Van Ostade's ability to depict with insightful accuracy the lives of these peasants meant his works were very popular. To broaden their appeal and provide more affordable images, Ostade also produced many prints and a number of highly finished pen, ink and watercolour drawings, including one of the present scene (with only minor variations) which allows the finer details of the back of the room and the lofty wooden roof to be read more easily.

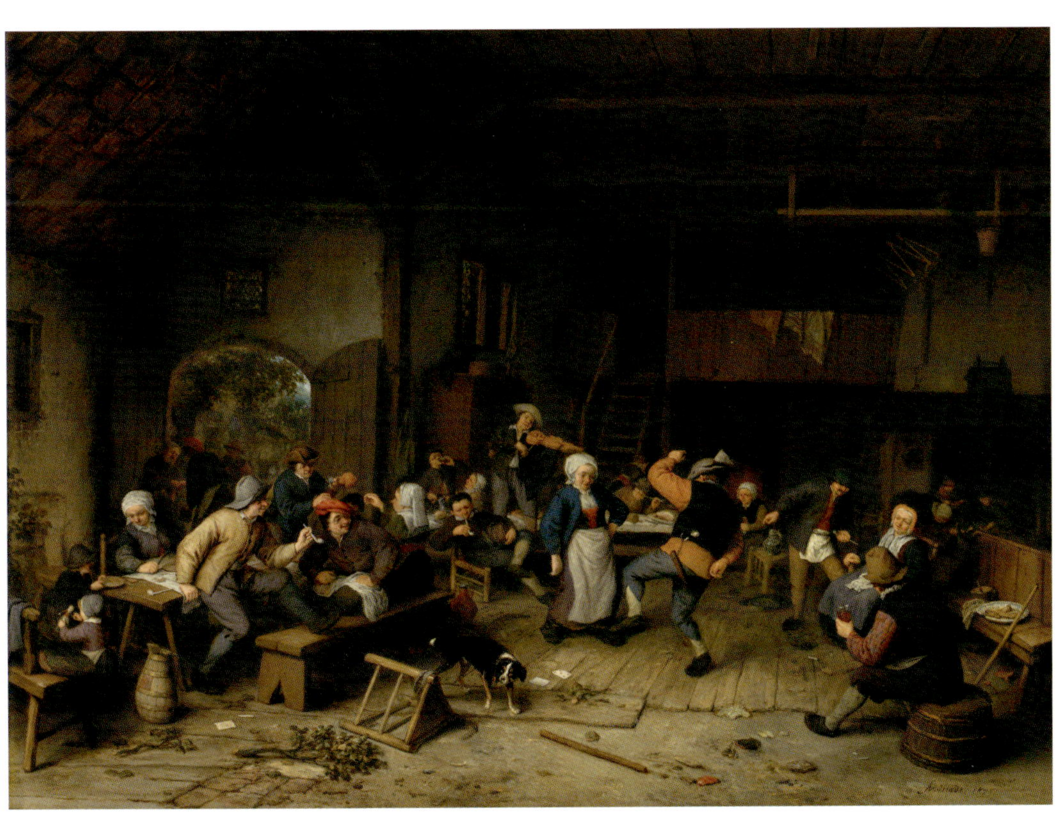

25

ADRIAEN VAN OSTADE
Haarlem 1610–1685

Tavern with tric-trac or backgammon players

Oil on panel, 30.2 × 25.3 cm, signed and dated 1669 or 1674
Sutton no. 48

The last of the works by van Ostade in the Samuel collection, dating from roughly the same period as the others, this painting was once in the same nineteenth-century aristocratic French collection as the one immediately above it. Though similar in size and certainly in subject, they have been regarded as a pair incorrectly. One of Lord Samuel's earliest purchases, this painting was bought from Edward Speelman in the early 1950s and it did not meet its putative 'pair' again until 1959. From van Ostade's finest and most admired period, the painting's narrow range of colours – browns and greys – are enlivened by areas of russet, red and blue, with the mauve of the quilted waistcoat of the central character providing a focus that brings the overall scheme of colours into a closer relationship. This coherence is further enhanced by touches of white in the clay pipes, in the flash of an undershirt between the waistcoat and breeches of the central character, in the gleam on the glass and the delicate pewter lid of the flagon standing on the floor.

The painting is rather abraded in the background, and the features of several of the figures are quite lost. A general thinning of the paint surface has revealed a *pentimento*, or change of design: the three-legged stool lying on its side in the foreground was once at a slightly different angle and closer to the legs of the main character. The staircase, rising and turning over the enclosed door that also allows access to the large shelf suspended from the ceiling, creates an effective depth of space and interest in the upper half of the picture. It frames the figures below and leads the eye towards the arched door and fireplace. The scene is lit from the left, from an invisible source suggesting daylight though a large window.

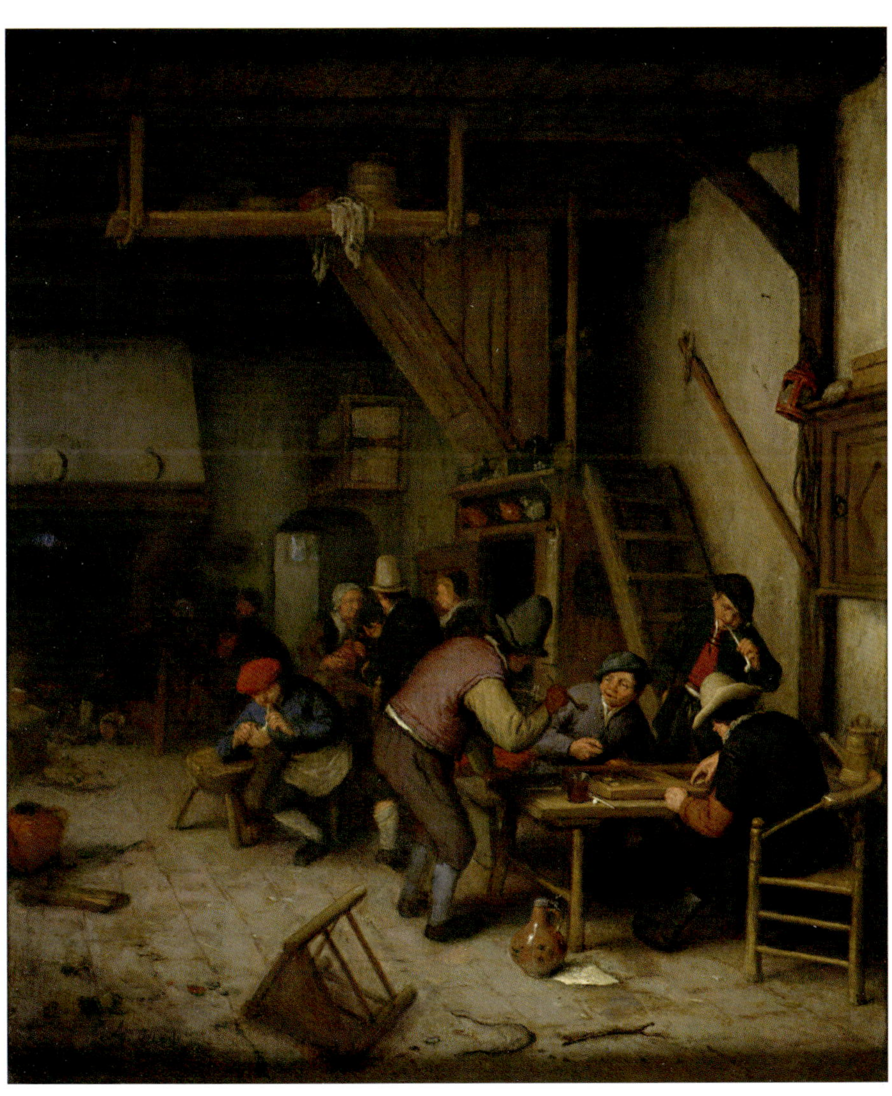

26

ADRIAEN VAN OSTADE
Haarlem 1610–1685

Village inn with backgammon or tric-trac and card players

Oil on panel, 31.5 × 26.6 cm, signed and dated 1674 or 1675
Sutton no. 49

Once regarded, incorrectly, as the pair to the next work, this painting is in better
condition, though the thinning of the paint with time has meant that some of
the features of the figures appear weak, particularly those in the background.
The principal occupations amongst the prosperous peasants at the table by the
windows are backgammon and card playing, while the group round the fire
smoke and chat to the landlord, who stands beside them with an earthenware
jug in his hand. A child holding something edible has attracted the attention of
a black-and-white dog that bears a striking similarity to the dog in van Ostade's
work over the fireplace (no. 24) and may well be the artist's family pet. A cage for
a bird with a small ceramic dish to one side, for feed or water, hangs safely out
of harm's way from the ceiling. A cord attached to a peg in the wall between the
windows would allow it to be raised and lowered. From a board on the back wall
jugs are hanging ready for the guests, an empty space where the one near the
seated man at the far left once hung. Details such as these would have delighted
van Ostade's patrons. Sunlight streams in through the elaborately lead-glazed
windows, attesting to the comparative prosperity of the innkeeper, and the
buildings and greenery glimpsed outside tell us that this is a country hostelry.

Gaming and smoking were commonly regarded as slothful and indulgent in
the Protestant Low Countries. How much van Ostade intended to make a social
comment in this and his other two scenes of peasant life in the Samuel collection
(nos. 24 and 26) is open to speculation. Despite not having any first-hand
knowledge of the lifestyle depicted, and despite the moralistic overtone, many
distinguished owners delighted in these pictures. In the eighteenth century,
however, English collectors felt – as articulated by the President of the Royal
Academy Sir Joshua Reynolds, influential artist and critic – that such crude scenes
were unworthy of consideration for a gentleman's cabinet of pictures. It was not
until the early nineteenth century that the taste for them, which continues to this
day, was revived.

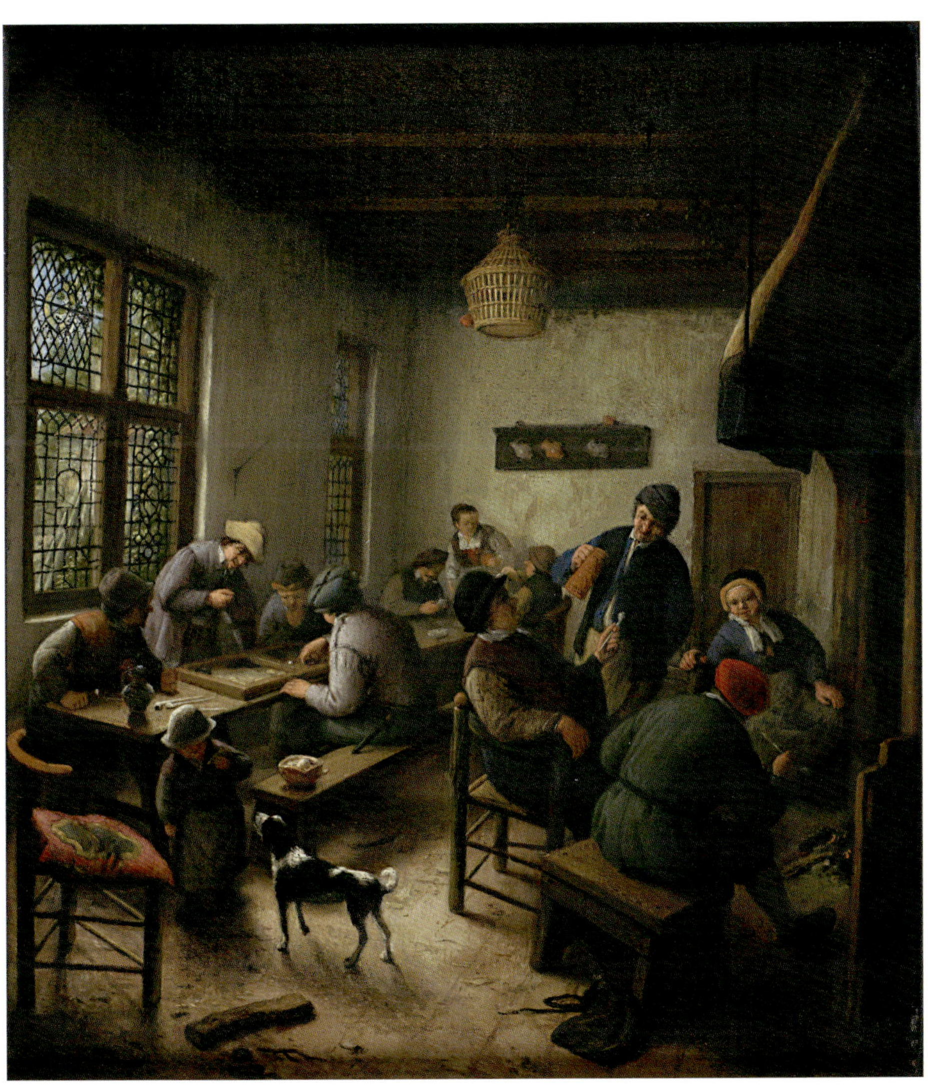

27

JAN BRUEGHEL THE ELDER
Brussels 1568–1625 Antwerp

River landscape with a village and a landing

Oil on copper, 20.9 × 32 cm, signed and dated 1612
Sutton no. 8

The Samuel collection has four works by Jan 'Velvet' Brueghel or a follower. Jan's father Pieter Brueghel I became famous for bridging the divide between the medieval mysticism of Hieronymus Bosch and the Baroque exuberance of Peter Paul Rubens. His allegories, often on a large scale, are set in dramatic landscapes and filled with incidents of contemporary peasant life. Jan was only a year old when his father died and it was his elder brother Pieter Brueghel II who continued painting, often indistinguishably, in his father's manner. Jan trained with his maternal grandmother, the miniaturist Mayken Verhult, in a different tradition of small-scale, meticulously painted works, mostly on copper, as with the four Samuel examples. Travelling widely while young, he spent at least eight years in Italy but by 1596 he had returned to his native Antwerp, where he married and his works quickly became much sought after.

The four works by Jan Brueghel at Mansion House represent only one aspect of his oeuvre – horizontal landscapes, crowded with figures of travellers and labouring peasants, highly detailed and well observed, with distant, atmospheric prospects. Lord Samuel abstained from collecting one important genre of Dutch and Flemish painting, of which Jan Brueghel was an early master – floral still lifes – saying his garden at his house in Sussex provided the real thing. Brueghel's landscapes were immensely popular and exported throughout Europe, notably to Spain, through the active art market in Antwerp. This brought him royal patronage and great wealth but also encouraged him to repeat successful compositions without much variation. The different dates of similar works allows a sequential stylistic development to be established. Dated 1612, this work is known in at least three other versions with the earliest extant, though probably not the first, dating from 1606. This river scene, with a ferry in the foreground that looks dangerously overcrowded with passengers and horses, may be a direct response to a voyage the artist made to Nuremberg in 1604 or to Prague in 1606.

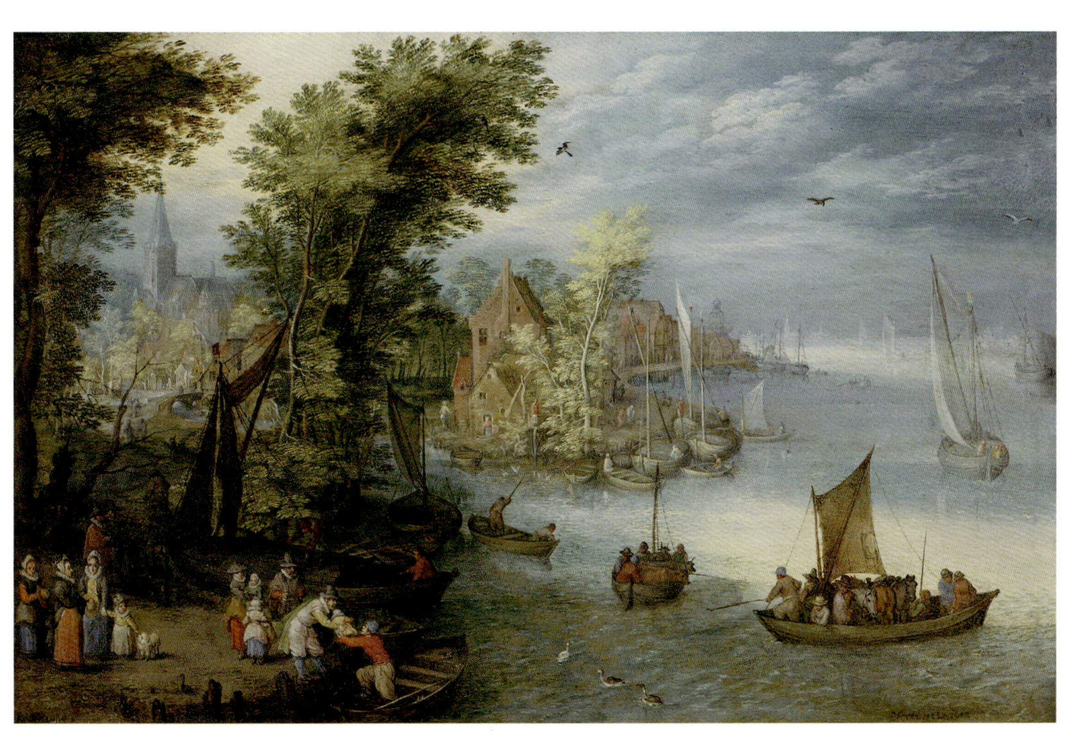

28

JAN BRUEGHEL THE ELDER
Brussels 1568–1625 Antwerp

Village landscape with figures preparing to depart

Oil on copper, 22.4 × 30.1 cm, signed and dated 1613 or 1617
Sutton no. 10

Painted quite late in Jan Brueghel's career, this work is one of several variants of the same scene produced over many years, exemplifying his continued use of a successful and established format. Brueghel began painting this type of deeply receding village landscape on his return to Antwerp from Italy in 1597. The early variants often included biblical references in slightly incongruous Flemish settings – *The Flight into Egypt* or *Mary and Joseph seeking Shelter in Bethlehem*, for example – but the figures became more incidental and secular as the complexity of the landscape increased.

The theme of halting at an inn to rest and change horses was to become common in later Dutch and Flemish painting, ultimately deriving from these quasi-biblical images by Jan Brueghel. This diagonal view, leading past an inn to a focus point on the horizon, placed three quarters of the way up the panel, had been established as a format by at least 1607, the date on an extant autograph example by Brueghel. The first version of this composition is unknown but it should be dated roughly to this period. Identified amongst the figure group about to enter the cart are Brueghel's wife and his daughter Paschasia, which provides a clue. The child, born in 1603, appears to be two or three years old, dating the original composition to 1605–06. (Paschasia's son was to be the artist Jan van Kessel I and her younger sister Anna was to marry another artist, David Teniers the Younger, in 1637.)

An ostler leads a horse towards the carriage with two horses already in harness, to make up the traditional Flemish threesome, while a groom brushes down a fourth horse tethered under the tree to the left. The other adults in the group may also be members of the Brueghel family and the black-and-white dog, seen in several of Brueghel's works, appears to be a family pet.

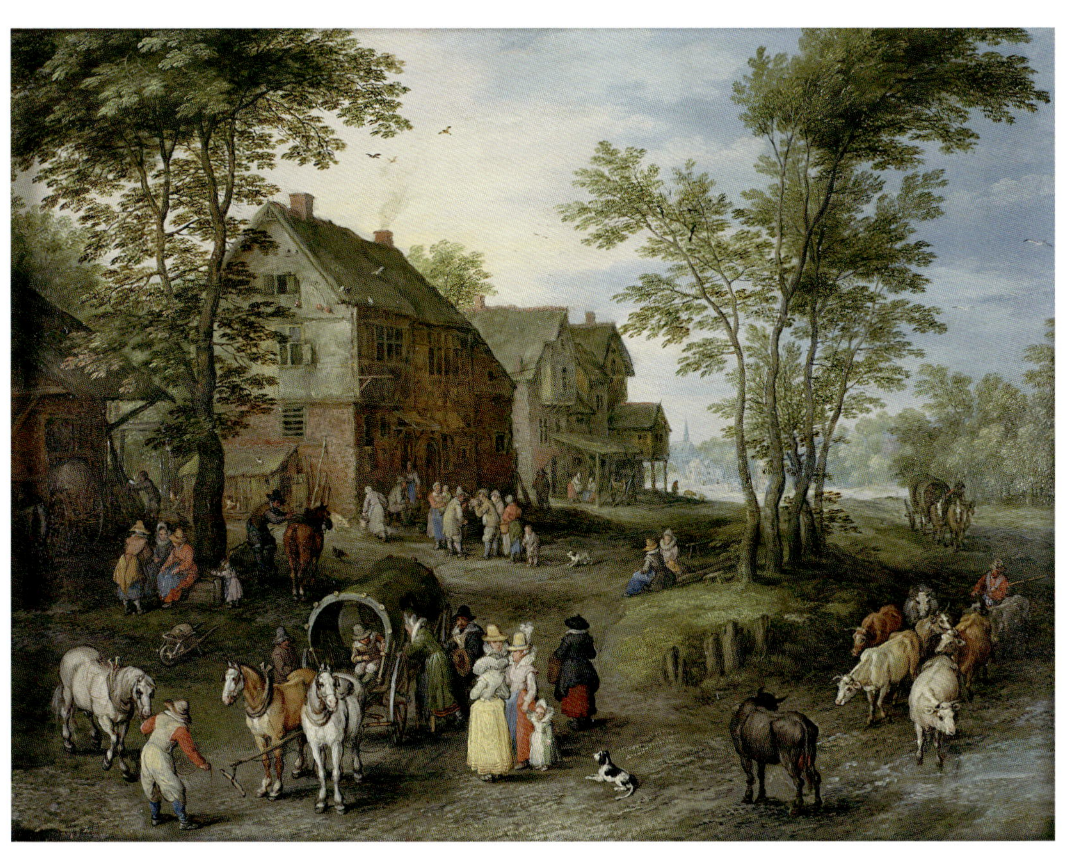

29

Follower of JAN BRUEGHEL THE ELDER
c. 1568–1625

The Road to the Market

Oil on copper, 24.1 × 31.4 cm
Sutton no. 11

This and the previous painting came from the famous collection of French
politician Prince Auguste-Louis d'Arenberg (1837–1924). Their dimensions, which
are almost identical, are familiar in Brueghel's work, but the execution in this case
does not show the skilled hand of the master. The curve of the main clump of trees
on the left reproduces the curve of those on the right in the autograph work with
which it has been paired for so long, but a casual comparison between the two
quickly reveals the inferiority of this work. The figures lack solidity, the colours
are less vibrant than one would expect and the trees in particular are thinner and
painted without a clear understanding of the effects of distance.

Competent, period copies of Brueghel's work are not uncommon as his pictures
were popular and were disseminated throughout Europe, where skilled imitators
and copyists abounded. The composition is certainly Brueghel's and several other
versions are known, though none is recognized as an autograph original. There
is also a drawing known certainly to be by Brueghel himself that gives the overall
composition of this painting but without some of the figure groups.

The building on the brow of the hill between the trees, with a kneeling figure
before it, is a wayside chapel. This may be a symbolic allusion to the pilgrimage
of life, while the variety of figure types represented may refer to various stations
in society: well-dressed, wealthy travellers ride fine horses and are accompanied
by a hound, prosperous peasant farmers with their laden carts make their way to
market, and poor men and women carry bundles and baskets on foot.

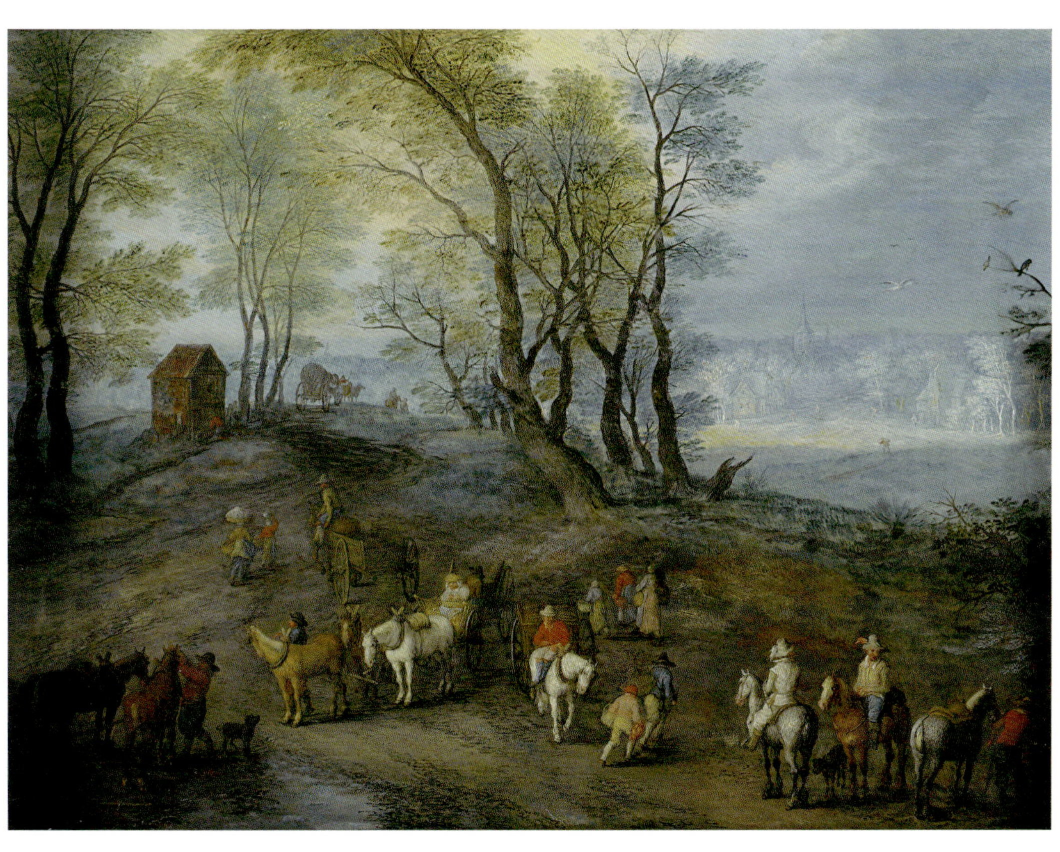

30

JAN BRUEGHEL THE ELDER
Brussels 1568–1625 Antwerp

Rest on the Way

Oil on copper, 21 × 32.2 cm, signed
Sutton no. 9

The last of the four works by Jan 'Velvet' Brueghel, this is painted, like the others, on copper. An expensive material used sparingly in the seventeenth century, originally by engravers for intaglio prints, copper is smooth and solid but soft enough to engrave into. Its weight makes it impractical for very large paintings but it is ideal for small-scale works, the smooth surface allowing the artist to paint with great delicacy, uninterrupted by the weave of a canvas or the uneven surface of a wooden panel. Works on copper are also less prone to damage, except along the edges, where they can be chipped or scratched. All four Samuel collection Brueghels on copper are in excellent condition.

The theme of travellers halting on an open road is one that Brueghel returned to many times, on each occasion developing the complexity of the landscape and the numbers and dispositions of the figure groups. The earliest known example of this composition is dated 1603, while a good, contemporary copy of the Samuel picture is dated 1612, which seems a reasonable date for this work.

The presence of several small changes to the composition, called *pentimenti*, mean this work can be regarded as autograph. They are clearly visible and indicate a change of heart by the artist in the course of painting, a change that would have been unnecessary if this were the work of a copyist. The most significant and easily visible *pentimento* is in the figure of the small girl carrying a basket and holding out her hand to a woman seated in a wagon. The shadowy outline of Brueghel's first version of this child can be seen directly in front of the present figure. Time has allowed the paint that covered up this first idea to become opaque and the white of her apron to show through.

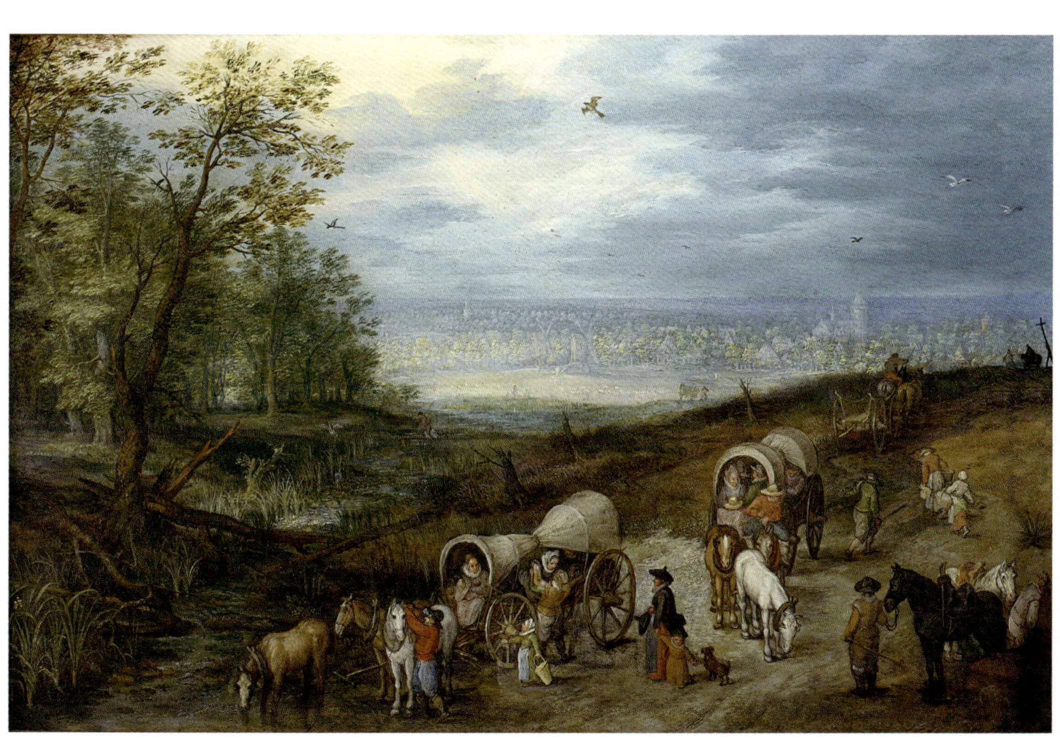

31

FRANS HALS
Antwerp *c.* 1582/83–1666 Haarlem

The Lute Player

Oil on panel, 17.8 × 18.1 cm, signed
Sutton no. 25

Formerly regarded as by a follower of Hals, this unusually shaped work is now
ascribed to the master himself. It is one of a group of three panels that show
children at musical pursuits, amongst the smallest works he painted. *Young boy
playing a violin* and *Girl singing from a music book* (private collection, Canada) –
of identical size to the Samuel painting, both also diamond in shape (unique
in Hals's oeuvre though not uncommon amongst Haarlem school artists) and
similarly signed in ligature – have long been considered as fully authentic works
by Hals. The eyes in the three paintings are either raised upwards or lowered
and the compositions are all weighted to the right-hand side. The fluidity of the
brushwork is emphasized by the smaller scale, directing attention to the swift
individual strokes with a small but broad brush, remarkable for their accuracy
and effectiveness. The lips of the young lutenist, for example, were strongly
defined in red before their shape was reduced with flesh-coloured paint in order
to emphasize the expression of concentration. The white points of the boy's collar
are pulled from thick strokes of paint, probably with the end of the brush, in a
manner found both in the related works and in many others by Hals.

An inventory of the effects of Willem Schrijver dated 1661 contained "Three
little paintings from the five senses painted by Hals". They appear again in
the posthumous sale of Willem's father Pieter Schrijver in Amsterdam in 1663,
when they were described as "Three special paintings of musicians by Hals".
Hals painted a portrait of Schrijver and his wife, his friends and patrons, in 1626
(Metropolitan Museum of Art, New York), roughly the suggested date of the three
panels. As part of a set of Five Senses, the three works can be cautiously identified
as Sight (the girl looking at her song book), Hearing (the boy with the violin,
his mouth open in song) and Touch (the boy tuning his lute and strumming a
chord). Taste and Smell, which would complete the set, are difficult to imagine
in the context of music, but might have worked well as a pair and therefore been
separated from the group.

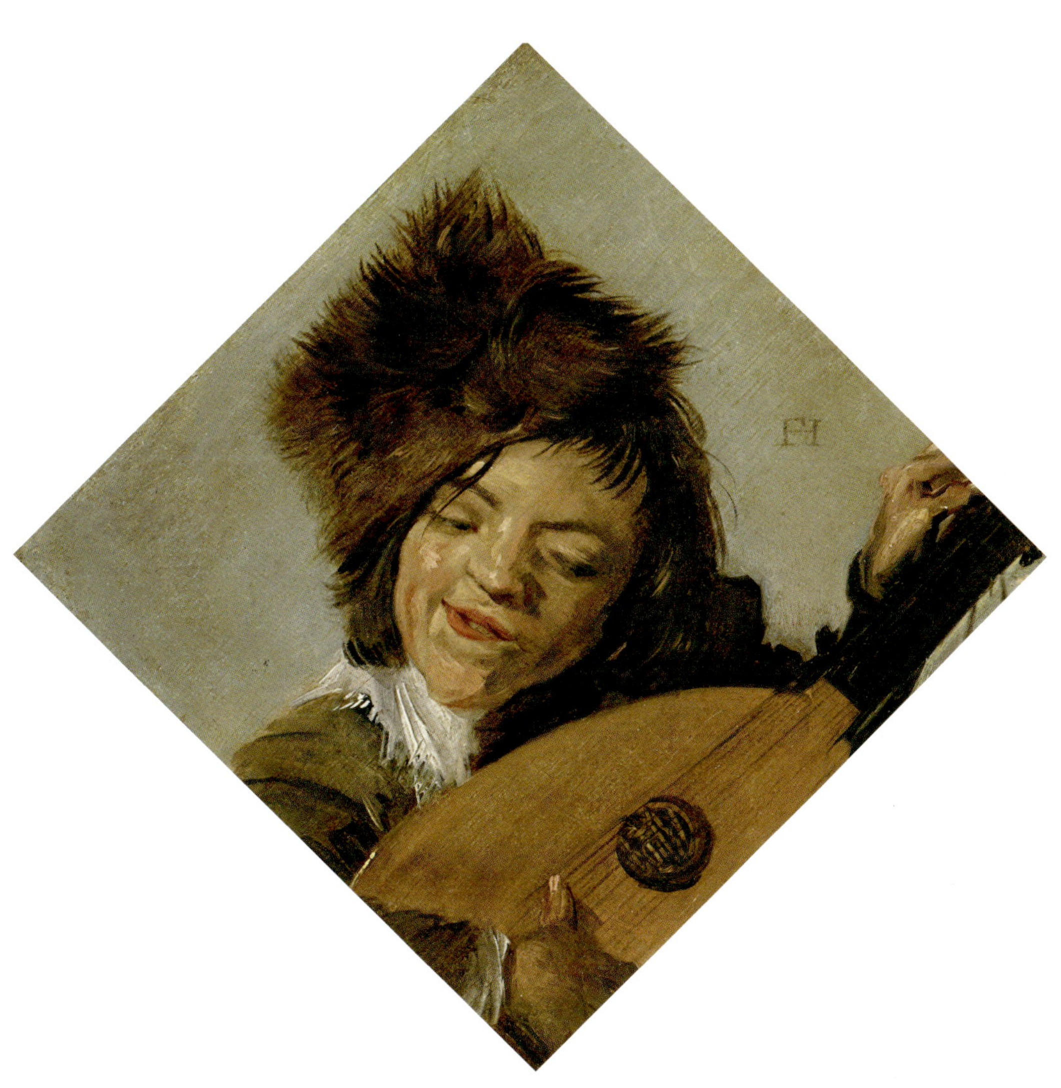

32

Copy after GABRIEL METSU
Leiden 1629–1667 Amsterdam

Young woman at her toilet

Oil on panel, 28.1 × 22.8 cm, bears a signature
Sutton no. 40

This is one of the very few paintings that Lord Samuel bought that has failed to live up to its reputation. This is a composition by Metsu that was well known and admired in the late nineteenth and early twentieth centuries and of which there are at least three versions, but the Samuel painting appears to be a copy, not by the artist. Regarded as one of the lesser masters of seventeenth-century Dutch genre painting, Metsu may have trained in the studio of Gerard Dou in Leiden, though he was closer in style and content to Gerard ter Borch. While more fluid and less hard and enamel-like in style than the *fijnschilders* of his native Leiden, Metsu was just as refined and elegant. Small-scale, simple compositions were a favourite, as in this copy, the design of which we can usefully comment on, if not the execution. Celebrating female domesticity, the young woman seated at her mirror is marked by a quiet, introspective tone of admirable sincerity.

Cautious collectors of Old Master paintings in the eighteenth and nineteenth centuries often preferred Dutch and Flemish works above those of the Italian or Spanish schools because they were easier to authenticate as originals over copies. While copying in itself is not reprehensible, if it is done deliberately to deceive the work becomes a forgery. It is impossible to tell nowadays if a painting such as this was meant as a fake. It was bought in 1959 with thirteen other very fine pictures from the collection of the French wine-merchant Etienne Nicolas, a great collector in the 1920s and 1930s, who gave two magnificent Rembrandts to the Louvre. It is a compliment to Lord Samuel's tutored skill as a connoisseur and to his advisors that so few of his pictures have failed the test of time. This work is a pleasing image, nevertheless, and, to judge from the number of known versions and copies, it has long been greatly admired. It still has an important role to play in our understanding not only of the work of Metsu but of the creation of collections and the history of taste.

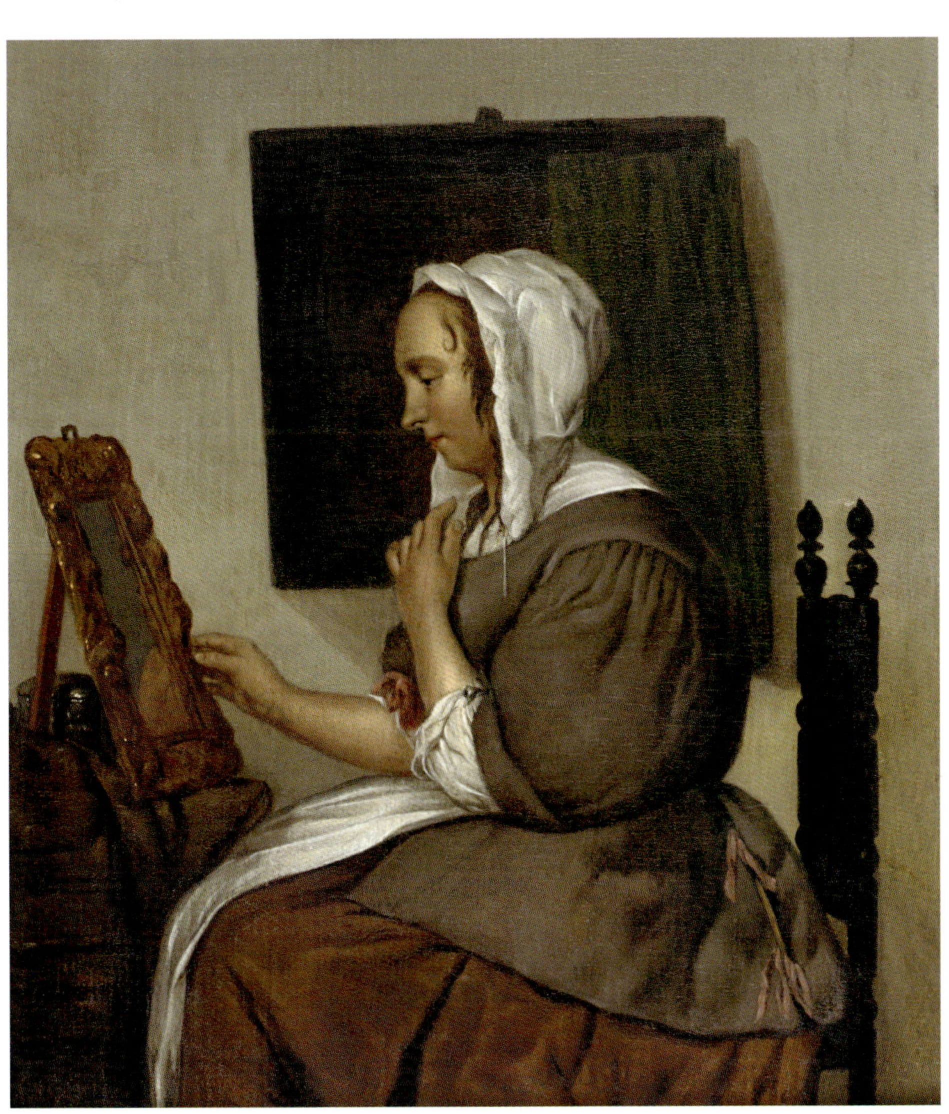

33

NICOLAES MAES
Dordrecht 1634–1693 Amsterdam

An eavesdropper with a woman scolding

Oil on panel, 45.7 × 72.2 cm, signed and dated *1655*
Sutton no. 37

Hung high up over a fireplace and therefore difficult to see, this is undoubtedly one of the most imaginative and charming of the interior genre scenes by Maes and is one of three works by him in the collection at Mansion House. Conceived as a painting within a painting, the scene is surrounded with a *trompe-l'œil* frame of ripple-carved ebony, as typically found on paintings of the period. To the right hangs a blue-green curtain on a brass rod, commonly used to protect precious paintings at the time and seen not only in the Metsu copy that precedes this picture but also in the Pieter de Hooch hanging in the Salon (no. 37), in which a grand gilt framed painting on the wall over the door is shown similarly protected. Maes's interest in the depiction of space is not confined to the concept of a frame-within-a-frame. The spiral staircase and the view up and into the far room emphasizes complex spatial relationships from the foreground to the distant window. The elaborate still life to the left and the half-hidden chair with a stoneware jug hanging above it all add to the three-dimensionality of the space depicted.

The subject of a maid eavesdropping on her mistress (who is scolding someone – presumably an errant husband – in the room behind) carries greater emphasis not only by the finger raised to the maid's lips that enjoins the spectator to remain silent, but also by the fact that the scene is partly hidden from view by the curtain. The viewer becomes complicit in the events. Servants were often the butt of derogatory social comment in the Low Countries in the seventeenth century, being seen as idle, feckless and disrespectful, but here the tables are turned. The rueful smile on the maid's face shows delight that she is, for once, not the object of her termagant mistress's ire. This is one of six works Maes did on the theme of eavesdropping, a new, creative approach to anecdotal genre subjects; all were painted between 1655 and 1657.

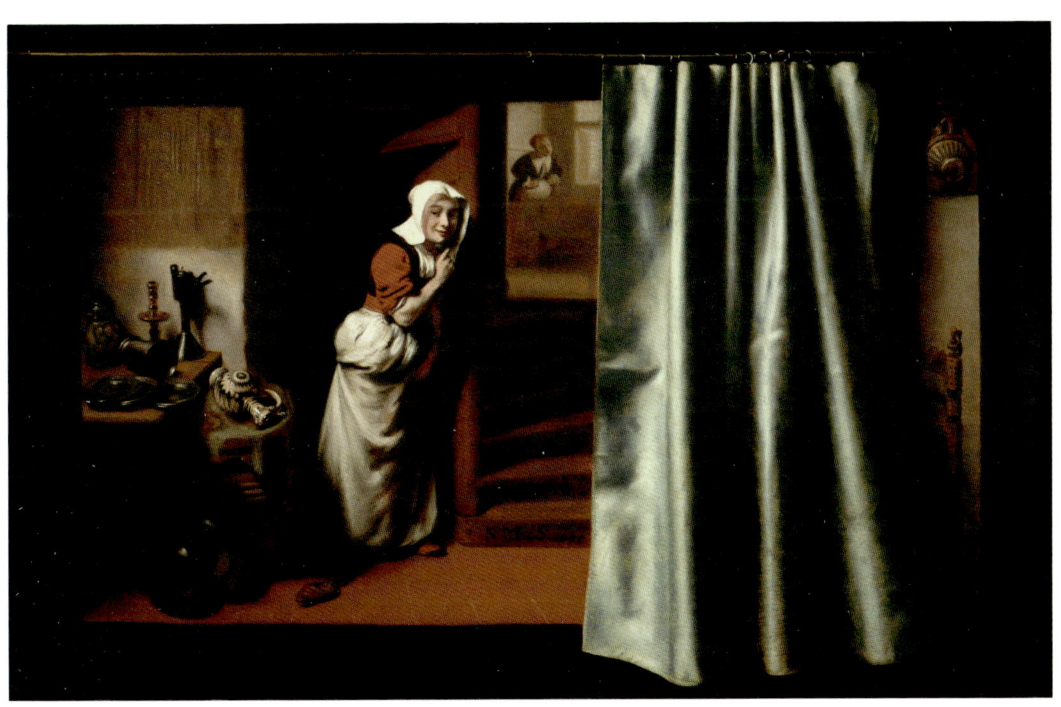

THE SALON

Originally an open court in the centre of the house, the Salon was covered over by George Dance the Younger in 1795. The ceiling was replaced by Bunning in 1861 and again in the major refurbishment of 1991–93. The colonnades at either end were introduced in the nineteenth century and mark the balustrade of the original court that surrounded light-wells illuminating the ground-floor offices. The mid-eighteenth-century architecture was relieved, almost as an afterthought, by the contemporary addition of magnificent wood-carved and plaster decoration in the Rococo style in the form of giant reliefs of elaborate trophies. The wood carving was done by John Gilbert, and George Fewkes executed the stucco with Humphrey Willmott.

On the left, beyond the Vestibule, was the original front door, while on the right, through the screen of columns, lies the principal reception room of Mansion

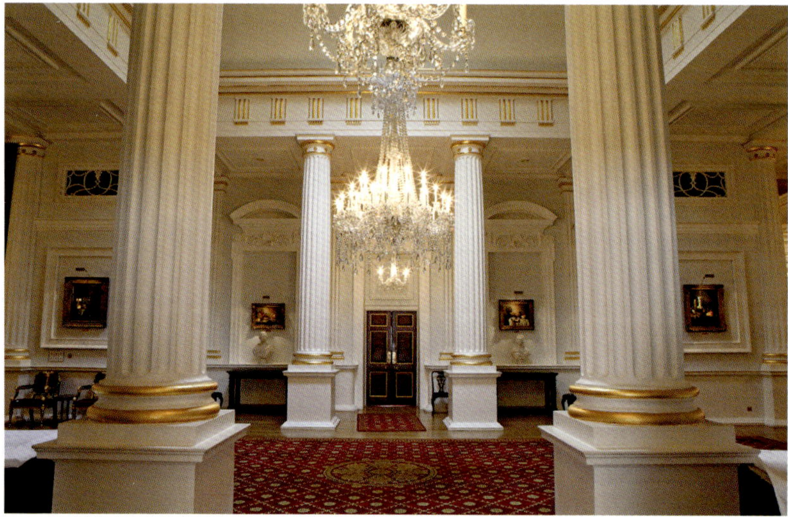

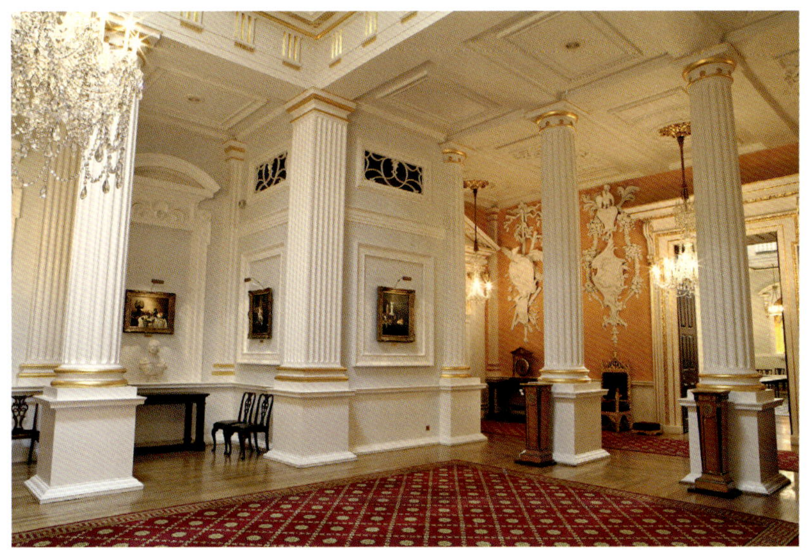

House, the Egyptian Hall – so called not because of any Egyptian theme to the decoration, but because the arrangement of the columns was taken from a design for a hall in the Egyptian manner by the Roman architect Vitruvius. The design was introduced to England by Lord Burlington in the early eighteenth century via the designs of Palladio.

The columns and recesses with their blind Kentian frames give little wall space for pictures other than tall, upright spaces around the centre of the room, but here hang a fine group of genre paintings – two more by Nicolaes Maes, a second work by Jan Steen and the still lifes by Pieter Claesz and Willem Kalf. The full-length but small-scale portrait by Gerard ter Borch, which is unrelated to any other work in the collection, is also here as it can hang in comparative isolation.

Leave through the door on the opposite side of the Salon

34

Follower of JAN VAN KESSEL I
c. 1626–1679

A still life with fruit and flowers on a table

Oil on copper, 30.3 × 53.3 cm
Sutton no. 35

The attribution of this picture has always been problematic. Painted in the manner of Jan van Kessel I, an Antwerp artist of flowers and allegorical still lifes, it cannot be compared directly with any autograph works by him. Since it was first published, in the 1920s, it has been variously ascribed to Jan van Kessel himself, Joris Hofnaegel and Jan Brueghel I, which is the attribution under which Lord Samuel acquired it in 1964. This circle of Flemish painters is the most likely area to look for this elusive artist, as the small golden tazza filled with flowers to the right of the composition is directly drawn from a design by Brueghel, whose daughter Paschasia was Jan van Kessel's mother. Osaias Beert and Jacob van Es, working in this manner and in Antwerp, and Isaac Soreau, a German, have also been proposed as influences on the artist. Recently a new master, called the Pseudo van Kessel, has been created to account for other works that share with this its distinctive style and singular composition.

Viewed from a high angle, the wide table, littered with dishes, a flagon and glasses, is set for two people, as suggested by the two knives and the two glasses of wine at the back on the left, one a *roemer* of white, the other a tall flute of red. The meticulous detail is complemented by a wide variety of textures – of fruit, flowers, metal and even fur – on the exotic guinea-pigs and the charming red squirrel next to the flagon. Unnaturally evenly distributed over the tabletop, the dishes and larger fruits just overlap, giving depth to the composition, reinforced by placing smaller and flatter objects at the front of the table, with larger, taller items at the back. The high viewpoint allows each item to be seen almost completely, but the strange, almost aerial perspective gives a disjointed view overall.

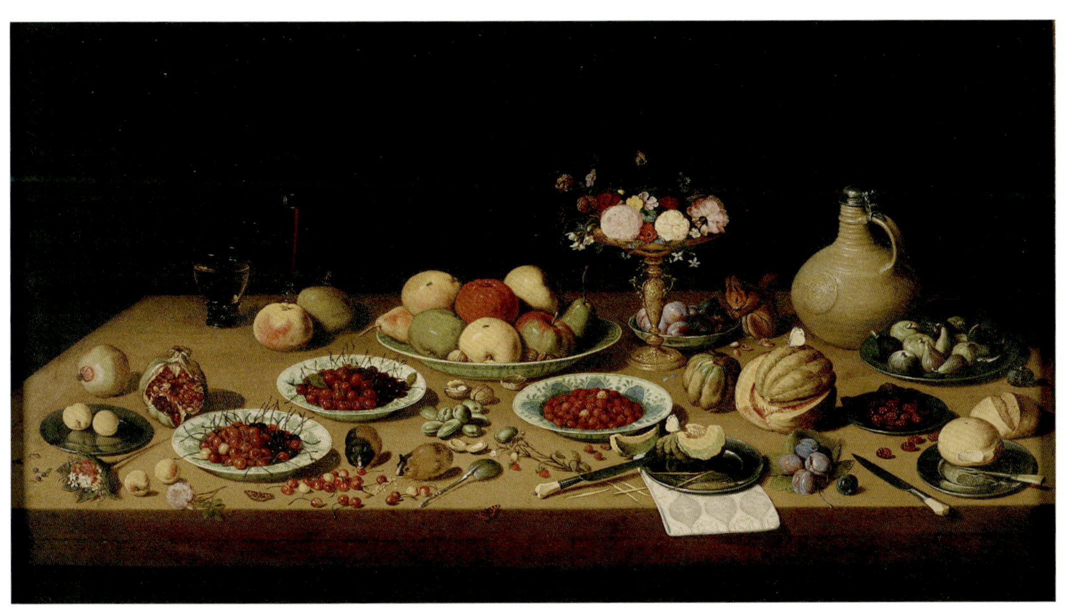

35

NICOLAES MAES
Dordrecht 1634–1693 Amsterdam

A woman selling milk

Oil on panel, 55.9 × 41.9 cm, signed
Sutton no. 39

This, the second work by Maes in the Samuel collection, follows the moralizing genre we met earlier but in a manner that might not be as easily understood today as it was in the seventeenth century. A pretty milkmaid, whose appearance and profession should alert the viewer be on guard, has deposited her polished can and wooden bucket on the ground to ring at the door of a house for custom. Dressed in the red and black of Amsterdam's official street-vendors, she turns to look at the viewer in a manner that would certainly have been regarded as brazen, too direct and too lingering for the modesty her age requires. Her distraction allows a small dog to plunge his head into the bucket and drink the milk she should be guarding. The moral, clearly understood by the contemporary viewer, is that anything desirable left unattended, milk or a pretty girl, will attract a predator.

Maes has used *chiaroscuro* to emphasize the three protagonist elements – the maid's head, which is in contrast to the shadowy door, and the dog and the milk can – which together form an elongated pyramidal composition of great elegance and strength. The picture plane is shallow, being no more than a few inches of pavement and the narrow step before the door, but is cleverly extended by a sliver of landscape with the gables of distant houses to the left. The composition is strengthened by the limited palette, set off by the rich red underdress, indiscreetly revealed by lifting and tucking away the sober black apron.

A pupil of Rembrandt in Amsterdam in the early 1650s, Maes returned to his native Dordrecht by 1653 but moved back to Amsterdam in 1673 and lived there for the rest of his life. His genre scenes, including the three in the Samuel collection, were produced within a short period of time, between 1653, when he left Rembrandt's studio, and 1660, when portraits monopolized his output and brought him commercial success.

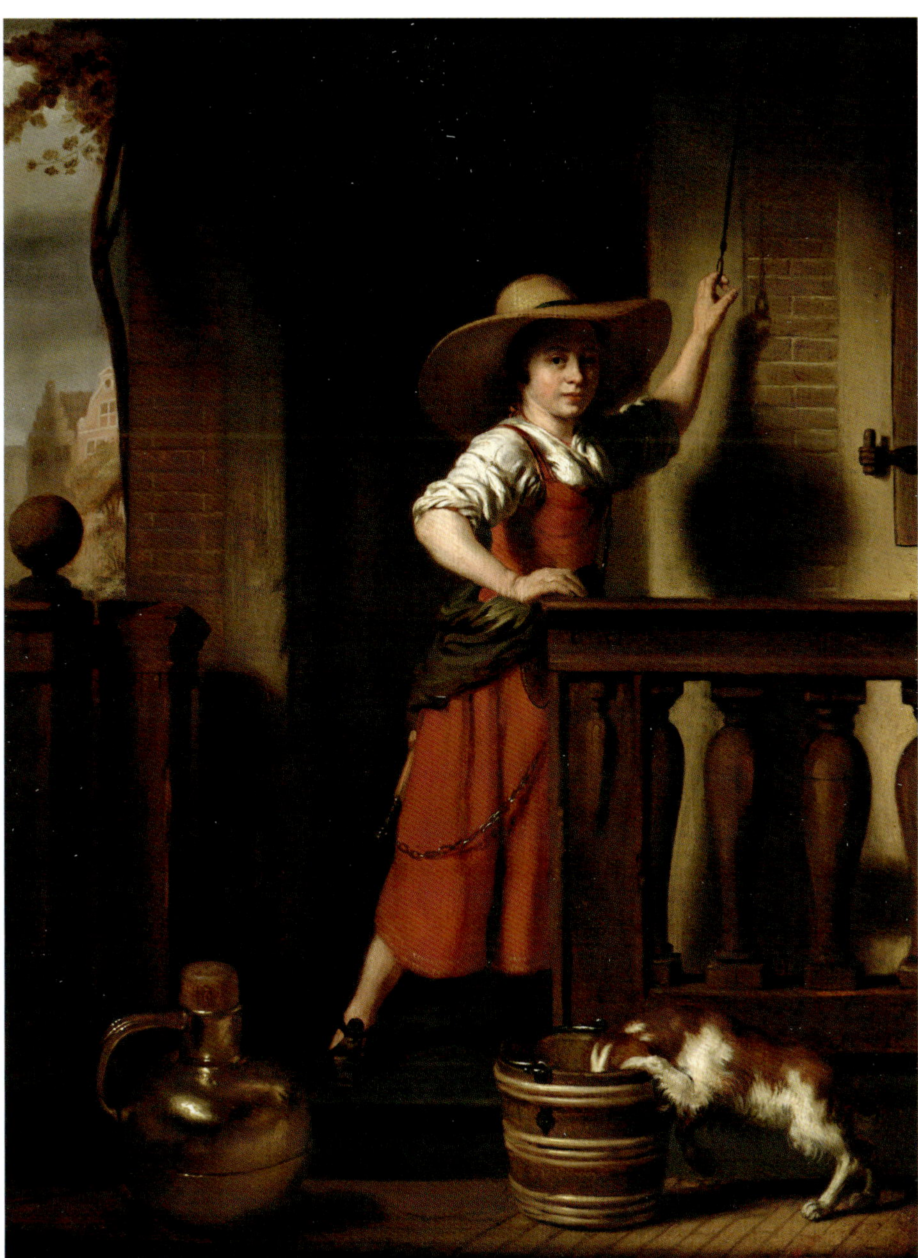

36

JAN STEEN
Leiden 1625/26–1679

Musical company

Oil on canvas, 64.7 × 51.6 cm, signed
Sutton no. 66

This is a wealthy household. The harpsichord, the rich upholstery, a parrot, the armorial stained glass in the round window and the view into a courtyard garden all set off the luxurious dress of the daughter of the house, whose behaviour with a love-lorne suitor is about to be discovered by the soberly clad approaching adult. Though at first glance this picture can be read as an essay in elitist pastimes, subtle hints that point to Steen's habit of moralizing abound. The parrot, while now resting freely on a perch, could easily be returned to its cage. The youth stretching for the lute hanging on the wall cannot quite reach, like the young man in his desires. The beautifully painted jug, the flask and glasses of wine, symbols of licentiousness, point to possible problems ahead, while the dog, a readily understood symbol of both fidelity and lust, licks itself.

In his depiction of space, Steen has been influenced by an earlier generation of artists including Nicolaes Maes and Pieter de Hooch. Though not complex, the strong architectural elements of floor, windows and door with a view through all help create a firm space, with the jug in the right foreground acting as a 'stop' to the composition in an otherwise blank area. Steen links his figures in subtle ways. Blue ribbons of the young man's doublet reflect the blue of the girl's bodice, for example, and shadows mask all the faces but that of the girl.

Steen's work was not popular in the eighteenth century, being regarded as unworthy and lacking in decorum by influential critics like Sir Joshua Reynolds, who nevertheless admired his technique and use of light. A nineteenth-century writer described Steen as "an inexplicable mixture of science and license, of profundity and frivolity". This work, which has been dated from a good, contemporary copy to the early 1660s, must have appealed to Lord Samuel for its touching sentiment, superb execution and magnificent design – science and profundity.

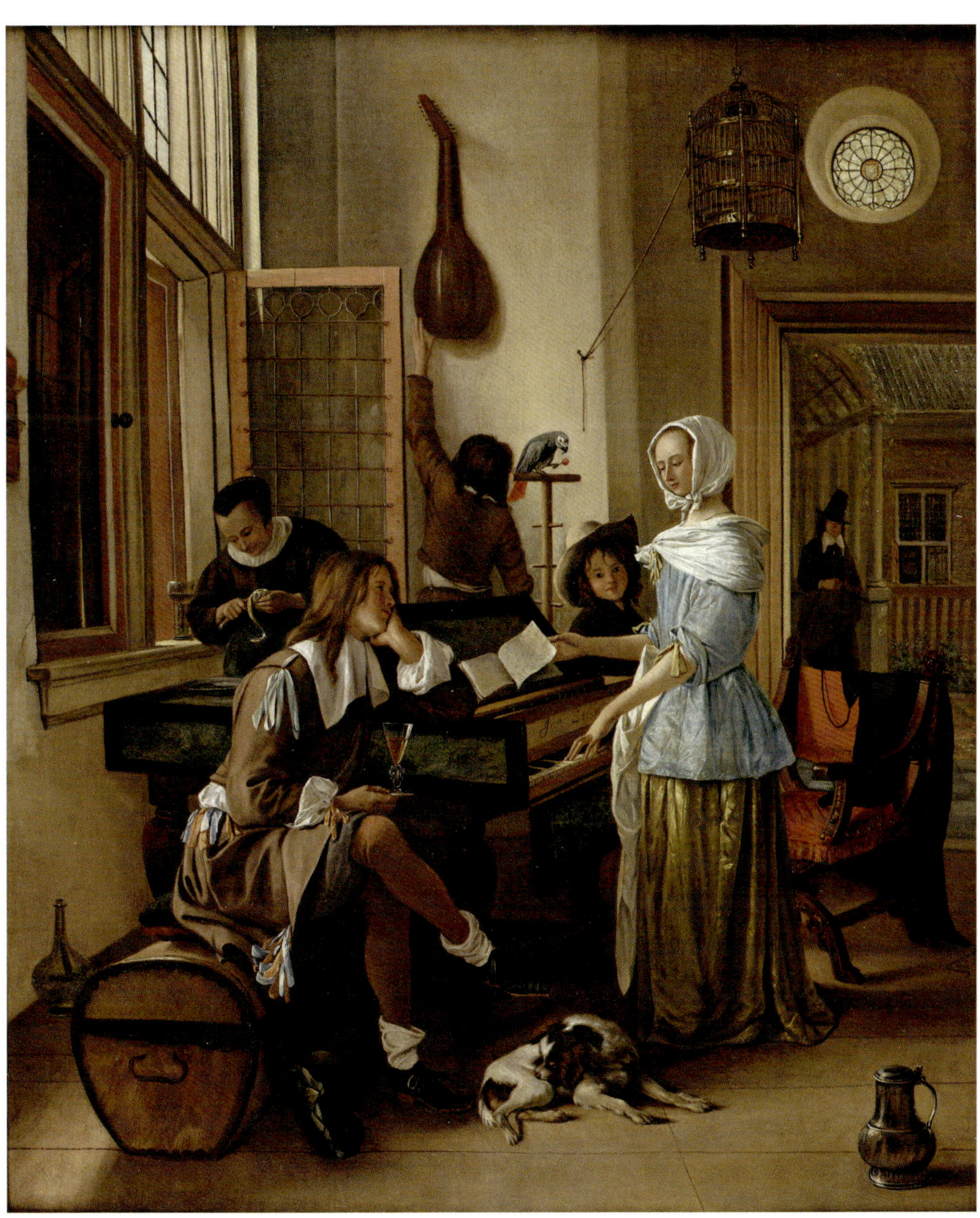

37

PIETER DE HOOCH
Rotterdam 1629–1684 Amsterdam

Interior with a woman knitting, a serving woman and a child

Oil on canvas, 74 × 63.8 cm
Sutton no. 33

From the dark, rich palette this work can be dated to the 1670s, when de Hooch had moved from Delft, where he had begun his career, to Amsterdam. The distant spire seen through the open door is loosely based on the city's Westerkerk. The broad brushwork, large scale and richer subject-matter are typical of this late period. The elegant interior – the Turkish carpet used as a table cover, the parrot brought from exotic lands and the Oriental ceramics displayed on the *kast*, or wardrobe, itself made from rare imported woods – reflects the prosperity of Amsterdam, the major trading and social centre of the United Provinces. The richly dressed seated lady, her feet warmed by the brazier box containing hot coals or charcoal, presents the ideal of domestic virtue. She is offered a pie with a flower set upright in it by the child. Her house is neat and well cared for, she is usefully occupied at knitting and she is a good mother and mistress in a house full of love, exemplified by the painting hanging over the door of Venus and Cupid, which has a curtain half drawn over it for modesty and discretion.

De Hooch loved complex light sources, reflections and effects. Here light streams into the outer room from the garden but also falls diagonally from the window on the left, glinting on the brass birdcage, the vases on the *kast* and the small mirror. He used a string, pinned in the canvas just to the left of the servants head, to establish the simple set of orthoganals for the perspective of his picture.

Unfortunately this large work has suffered somewhat over time. De Hooch used inferior quality paints and often painted very thinly using many layers of tinted varnish, which, over time, have worn badly. De Hooch's work declined in later life and he died in poverty in a madhouse.

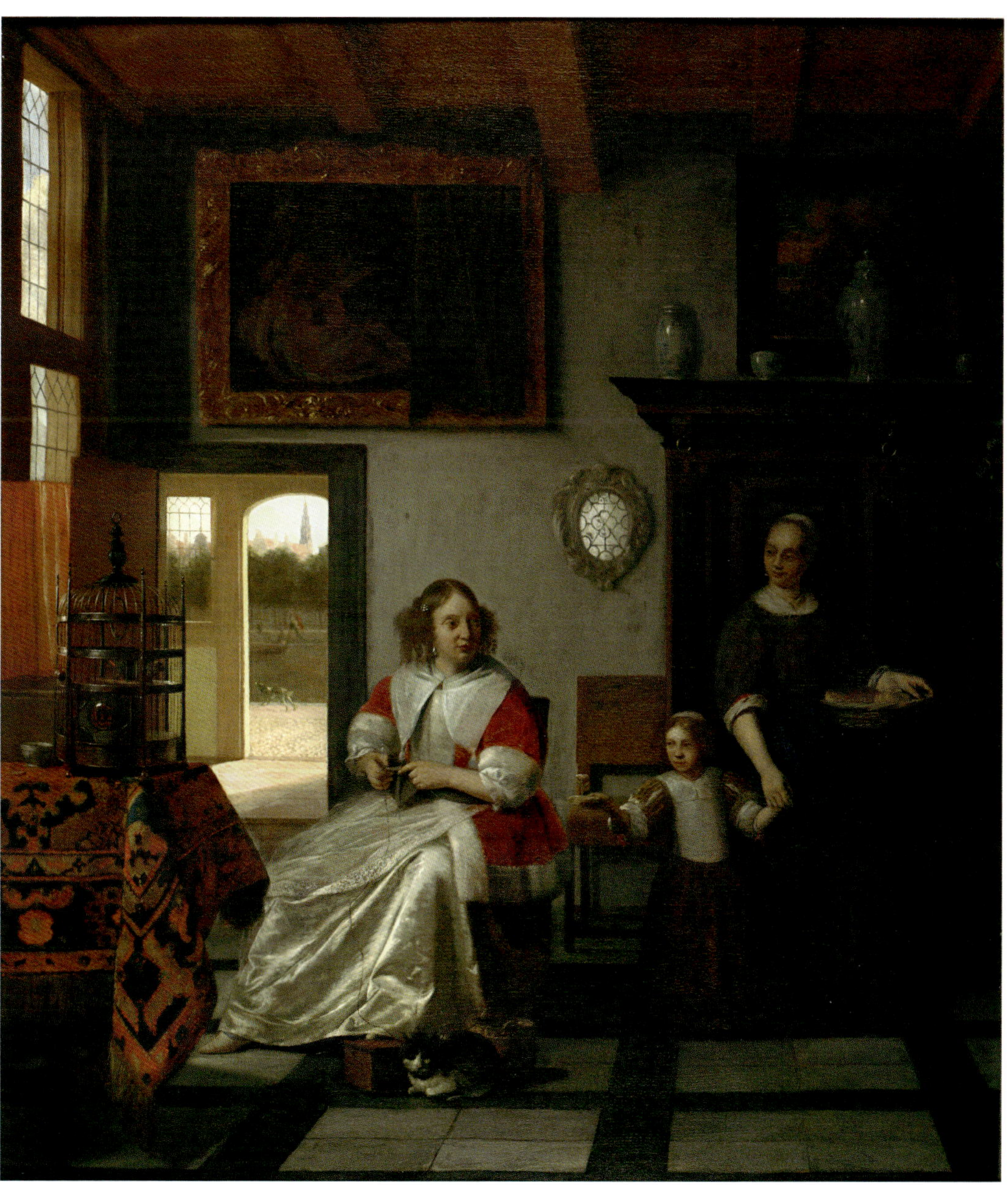

38

A young woman sewing

Oil on panel, 55.6 × 46.1 cm, signed and dated *1655*
Sutton no. 38

In Deep Thought was the title of this picture in the nineteenth century. The two other works by Maes in the Samuel collection tell rather different stories of young women in domestic service (nos. 33 and 35). Here the maid works with quiet concentration, giving her full attention to the sewing as she gently lifts the edge of the white cloth and pulls the needle and thread away. Light streams down from an unseen window. Her hair is drawn back and neatly covered, her black apron lifted just enough to reveal the red skirt with modest touches of red undergarment at her cuffs. Though this painting is simple in subject and design, details like the *soldertein*, or low dais, with which drafts and cold floors could be avoided, the wainscotted wall, the chequered floor and the map suspended above the maid's head all create an impression of calm, ordered space, in keeping with the work in hand. The small notes of paper stuffed beneath the frame of the wainscoting lends the scene an intimate and informal air – this is a place of work, not entertainment.

Like many Dutch seventeenth-century genre paintings, more can be read into a scene should it be sought. The chair beside the maid is no ordinary seat, being made of finely turned, exotic and expensive ebony. On its tapestry cushion rests a lace-making pillow with polished bobbins of different woods reflecting points of light. The industrious maid is merely a seamstress and the owner of the lace-making pillow must be her mistress. To a contemporary viewer the fact that the maid continues with her work in the absence of her mistress would be seen as admirably virtuous.

Maes has signed and dated the work by carving his name on the front of the dais, making it part of the scene. The fact that the N is in reverse adds to the sense of informality and simplicity. The influence of his master Rembrandt in the design, soft execution and use of light is obvious.

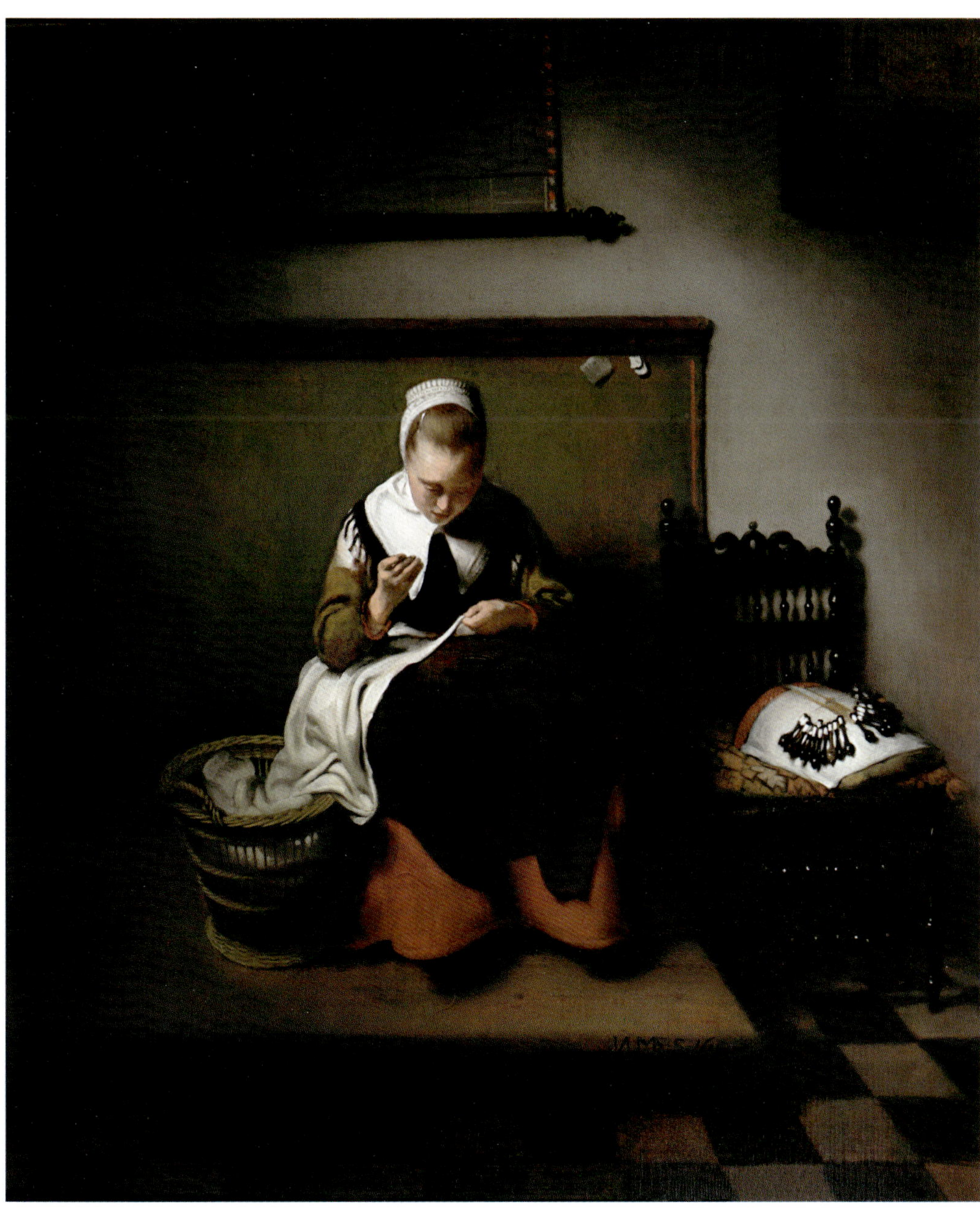

39

PIETER CLAESZ
Steinfurt 1597/98–1661 Haarlem

Still life with a jug, herring and smoking requisites

Oil on panel, 45 × 65.5 cm, signed and dated 1644
Sutton no. 15

It is easy to understand why Lord Samuel would wish to have two examples of still life by the same artist (nos. 39 and 40), similar in dimensions and tonality, in that they represent two very different types of the same subject. Both are *ontbijtjes*, or breakfast pieces, as opposed to *banketjes*, or banquet pieces, and are simple, everyday meals. This example is more rustic in its content than the other but no less sophisticated in design and execution. Bread, beer and a grilled herring comprise the principal ingredients. The pewter plate, brass tobacco-box and horn-handled knife emphasize the simplicity of the meal and mundane nature of the scene.

Herring, whether salted, smoked or pickled, was a major source of protein for Dutchmen in the seventeenth century, when preserving food for the winter months was vital. Also a great source of revenue, herrings were exported by Dutch merchants throughout Europe, particularly to Catholic Poland. Developments in the preparation of salted herrings at sea – so that the fish were not completely eviscerated, thereby aiding the curing process – meant delicious Dutch herrings became widely popular.

The viewing points of this and the second work by Claesz are low, so depth is created by overlapping and foreshortening. This painting can be usefully compared to the work by the follower of Jan van Kessel in this room, in which the viewing point is much higher, allowing the objects to be seen in their entirety.

Though he always seems to have signed and often dated his works, over a hundred of which are known, Claesz is an elusive artist. Originally from Germany, he lived all his adult life in Haarlem. Otherwise we know very little about him. Like the landscape artist Jan van Goyen and like Aelbert Cuyp in his early works, Pieter Claesz used a very limited range of colours and tones to create his works. His use of browns, russets, greys and shades of white to achieve the effect of truthful depiction is highly skilled and deceptively simple. In the background the brushstrokes are left visible self-consciously, to remind the viewer that the apparently real objects of the still life were in fact created by art.

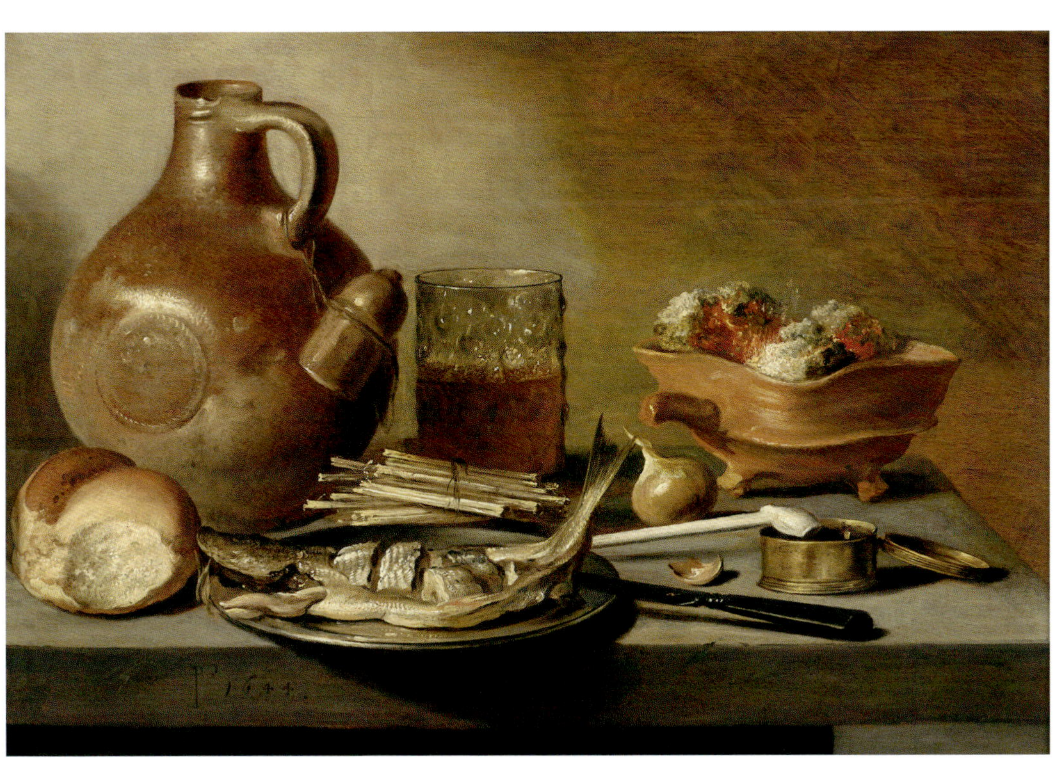

40

PIETER CLAESZ
Steinfurt 1597/98–1661 Haarlem

Breakfast still life with roemer, meat pie, lemon and bread

Oil on panel, 55.2 × 65.2 cm, signed and dated 1640
Sutton no. 14

This second work by Claesz is similar in form to the first but the meal is
substantially different, with more luxurious food and drink and finer objects
and utensils. Set on a linen cloth, the central pewter dish holds a mincemeat pie,
the pastry crust dusted with powdered sugar and broken open by a silver spoon
to reveal the raisins and slices of lemon within. Served with white wine in a large
roemer (a second glass is upturned behind), the pie is accompanied by walnuts,
hazelnuts, a finely peeled and sliced lemon and a white bread roll. A beautiful
knife, presumably used to peel the lemon, has a handle of mother-of-pearl
alternating with squares of ebony, each set with a silver rosette. To the left is an
open watch, the key dangling from a blue ribbon over the table's edge. The knife
and watch, from their frequent appearance in Claesz.'s work, must have been
personal objects of the artist's. A finely tooled leather case that sheathed the knife
is often included in his pictures.

These are rich men's utensils and rich men's comestibles. Lemons and sugar are
expensive imports. The knife and watch are also valuable. While it is tempting to
see these works as merely aspirational – their audience was the wealthy middle-
class of provincial towns like Haarlem for whom such meals were regarded as
treats but obtainable nonetheless – there may be a subtext on the passage of time
and human vanity in pleasurable pursuits. The bread and wine may refer to the
Passion of Christ, particularly as the bread depicted is made from the finest white
flour, rather than the heavy, dark rye bread from the average Dutch dinner table.

The contrast between the two works by Claesz reflects the range of the artist as
well as Lord Samuel's predilection for refined, unostentatious still lifes, of which
he had seven.

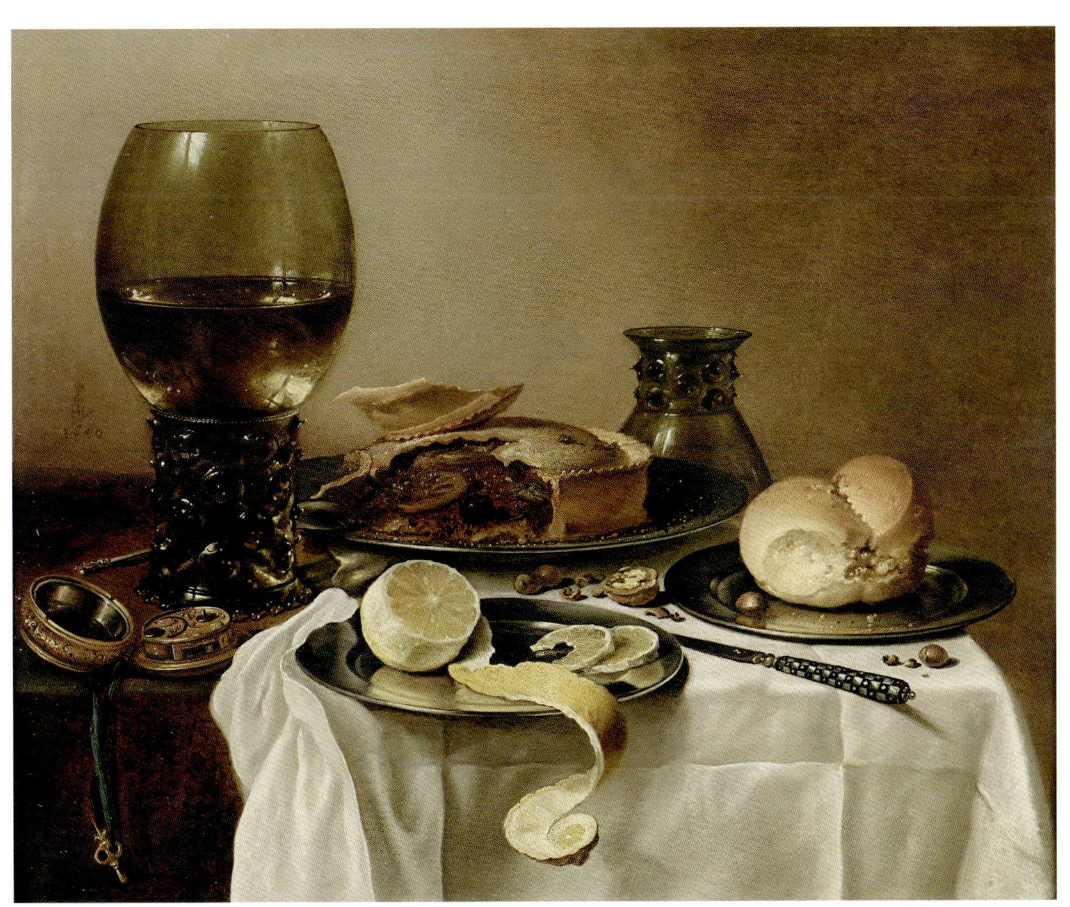

41

JACOB OCHTERVELT
Rotterdam 1634–1682 Amsterdam

A lady and maid choosing fish

Oil on canvas, 69.3 × 57.7 cm
Sutton no. 47

Ochtervelt trained alongside Pieter de Hooch in the studio of Nicolaes Berchem but their debt was clearly to Ludolph de Jongh, an early proponent of interior scenes in the school of their native Rotterdam. Ochtervelt moved to Amsterdam in the early 1670s, roughly when the present picture was painted, and remained there, in comfortable but not luxurious circumstances, until his death. He was quickly forgotten. It was not until the nineteenth century, when interest in Dutch paintings was growing, that he was identified as a painter in the manner of Pieter de Hooch, albeit with less sophistication in his use of space and colour. Indeed, this work was thought to be by de Hooch when it was first recorded, at a sale in 1893.

Octervelt's use of space in this work is a clue to his authorship. His contemporaries began to develop views from rooms into courtyards, gardens and beyond, through doors and windows, at angles and in corners, as elaborate settings for narrative figure groups. Octervelt's spaces are simple, often only the corner of a room, and never progress beyond an open door, usually viewed from the hall of a fine house. The solid, blocky draperies of the figures are also distinctive, as is the theme of visiting tradesmen and servants. In that respect this work, in which a maid servant brings a basket of fish to her mistress for inspection, is typical of Ochtervelt. The mistress, seated quietly in the sunshine, has put down her needlework. Dressed in a fine red jacket trimmed with white fur and a spotless apron edged with a band of lace, she turns her kindly face to the drably dressed and modest servant. The scene exudes virtuous housekeeping, social order firmly in place. Only the fact that Ochtervelt has placed the light source on the right of the picture rather than on the more orthodox left-hand side distinguishes the composition, in that the Western eye naturally tends to read an image from left to right, as with the written word.

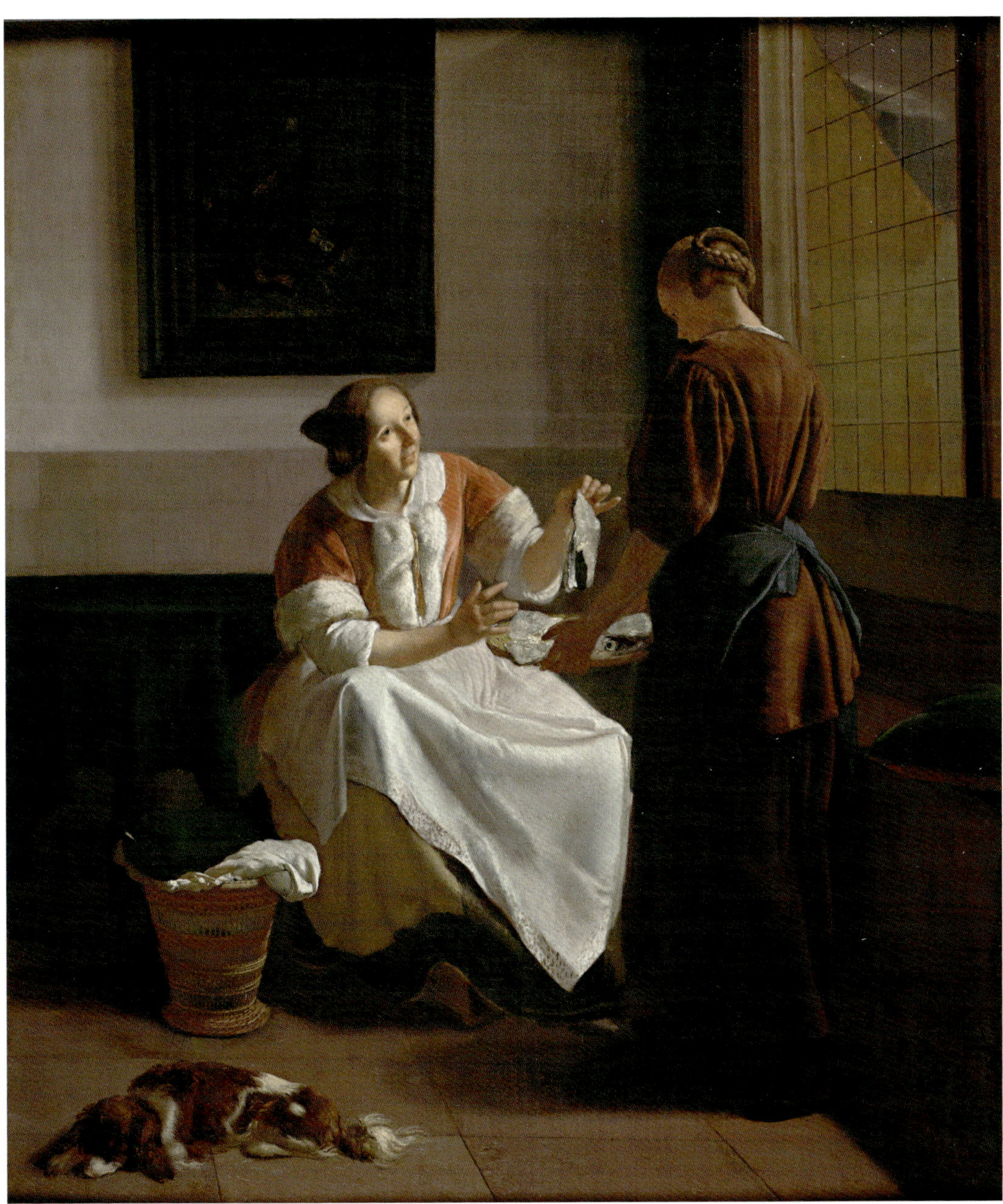

42

WILLEM KALF
Rotterdam 1619–1693 Amsterdam

Still life with a pilgrim flask, candlestick, porcelain vase, glasses and fruit

Oil on canvas, 72.5 × 59 cm, signed
Sutton no. 34

Perhaps the finest of the later generation of Dutch seventeenth-century still-life painters, Kalf spent several formative years, from 1640 to 1646, in Paris, where this picture was probably painted. He was a member of a group of Dutch artists there who were to be more influential on than influenced by the French school of painting. Kalf developed a skilled proficiency in the depiction of luxurious objects – ostentatious, sumptuous still lifes called 'pronkstilleven' – whereby the objects are shown merely for their richness, rarity and diversity of colours, forms and textures. He always denied that they carried any moral or hidden meanings.

A silver flask lies on its side. Called a 'pilgrim bottle', its form derives from the leather flask carried by travellers on a strap or chain, transformed into a rich accessory in silver. Behind it is a columnar candlestick also in silver and a Chinese blue-and-white porcelain vase, probably from the period of the Ming Emperor Wan-li, which both give a strong vertical emphasis to the design. Though Chinese in origin, the tall-necked bulbous vase derives from an Islamic metalwork prototype, epitomizing the many cultural themes brought together by contemporary European trade. The two pieces of glass are a drinking vessel with an elaborate, bifurcated stem, and a rare 'ice glass' covered bowl. Both are in the *façon de Venise* but probably made in Amsterdam or Antwerp rather than a Venetian glasshouse. The technique of a crackled surface was achieved by plunging the hot glass into water, just enough to fracture the surface lightly but not shatter it. On the far right lies a knife with an almost identical handle to that seen in the Pieter Claesz still life (no. 40), so probably a popular and fashionable model. The objects are set off by the orange and the peeled lemon – exotic, luxury fruit – and a tasselled and draped curtain above. A self-portrait of the artist, soberly suited and hatted, can be seen in reflection in the silver pilgrim bottle.

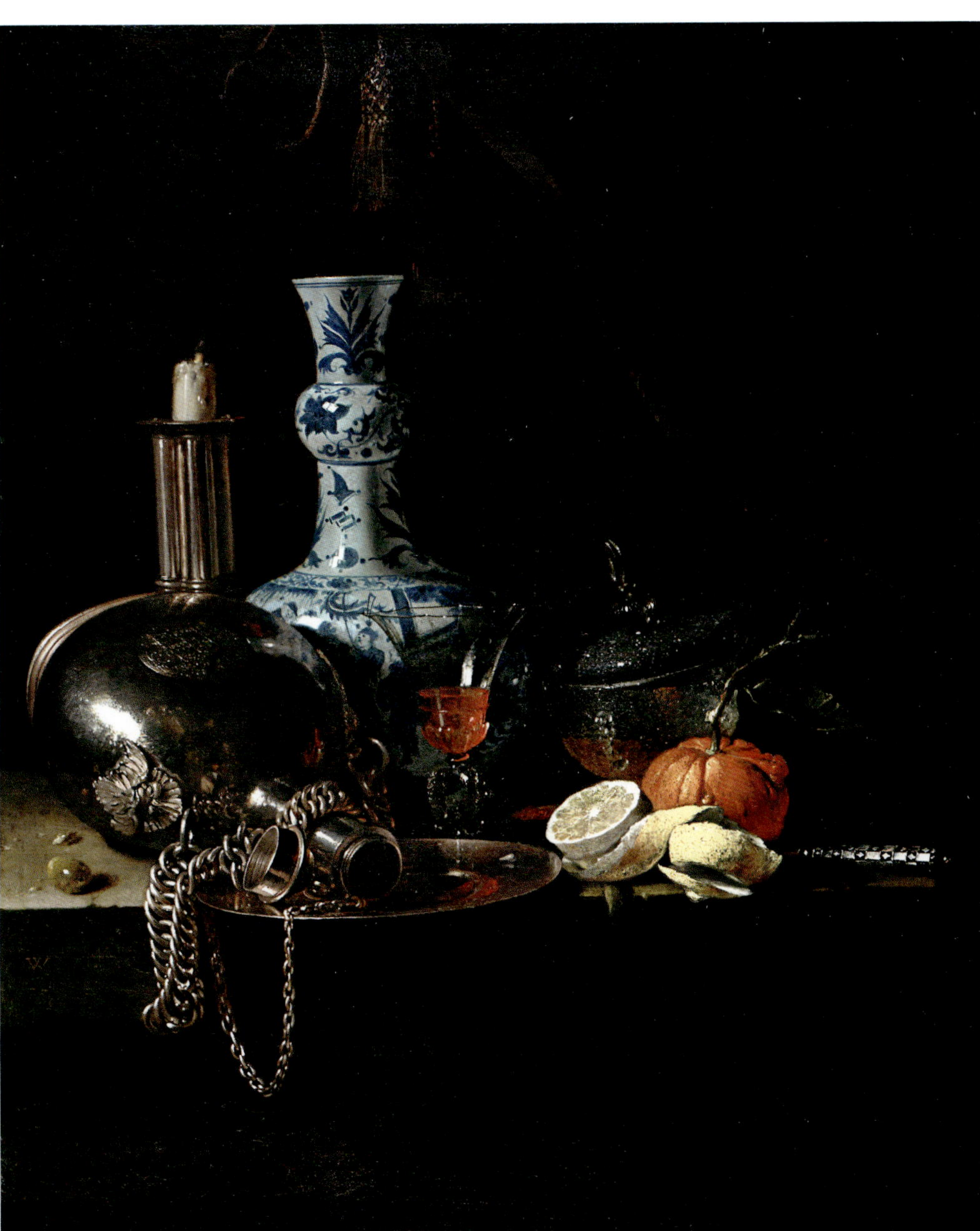

43

GERARD TER BORCH
Zwolle 1617–1681 Deventer

Portrait of a man in his study

Oil on canvas, 72.7 × 55.5 cm, signed?
Sutton no. 7

Lord Samuel was not overly fond of portraits and this work by ter Borch is
a rare example of the genre at Mansion House. Precocious son of a painter,
ter Borch studied with the artist Pieter de Molijn and then travelled widely,
to England, France, Italy and Spain. He settled in the eastern Dutch city of
Deventer, producing a large number of skilled and sophisticated figure groups
in domestic interiors. He was deeply influential on the work of Pieter de Hooch
and Gabriel Metsu, but his production changed in the late 1660s, when he moved
to Amsterdam and started working primarily on small-scale but full-length
portraits, of which this is a typical and fine example.

With a barely defined, neutral space as the setting, ter Borch concentrates
on the character of his sitter. In his genre scenes he avoided definitive action,
preferring to use a more psychological approach to give subtle depth and
meaning. Here he achieves this aim in the direct, unabashed gaze of the sitter,
clearly a sober, well-read and educated man, probably a merchant – certainly
well travelled, to judge from the map of Europe that hangs behind him. The dog,
asleep, representing fidelity, and the sombre dress of the sitter add to the air of
calm responsibility, but a recorder in front of the writing lightens the mood and
the flash of red breeches is the touch of colour needed to give a feeling of some
worldliness. That this was important to the artist and probably the sitter as well is
revealed by a *pentimento* at the knee that extends the amount of red on view.

The map is Joan Bleau's *Europa recens descripta*, first published in 1613, reprinted
with the decorative border in 1630 and rarely out of print until a fire destroyed
Bleau's printing works in 1672. Bleau was the official cartographer of the Dutch
East India Company and this portrait may well show one of the company's
merchants.

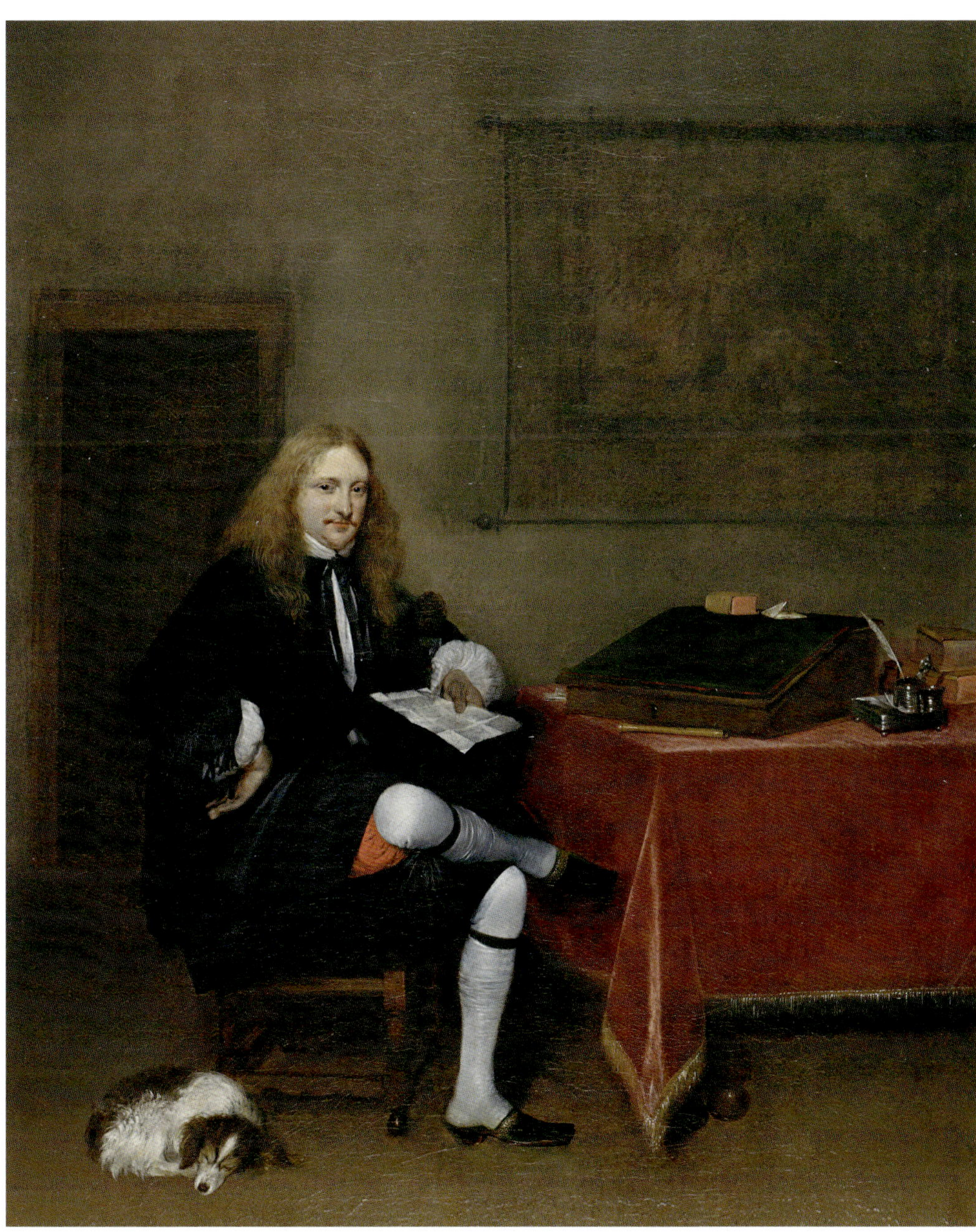

44

JACOB OCHTERVELT
Rotterdam 1634–1682 Amsterdam

The Oyster Meal

Oil on canvas, 53.5 × 44.5 cm
Sutton no. 46

This second work by Ochtervelt reveals the influence of a number of his
contempories, not least Gerard ter Borch – in the magnificent technical display
in the representation of textiles – and Frans van Mieris in the composition.
The young lady leaning back and at an angle to the picture plane is pressed by her
male companion to take an oyster from the octagonal dish. The hands and arms
of both figures interweave delightfully, presenting any number of meanings:
the languid hand, the hand that tightly holds the foot of the suggestively angled
glass, the hand that proffers the dish and the hand raised towards the pretty
face. The leaping dog points directly to this line of interchanges. Ochtervelt has
used deep shadows and selective light accents to define his spaces. The inanimate
objects are used to the same end by foreshortening, all being placed in receding
positions. The composition is marked by his usual simple, low-viewpoint setting
of a floor and two walls.

The meaning of the scene is clear. Oysters and wine, with their aphrodisiac
and inhibition-releasing effects, the unmade bed in the loft above and the dog
excitedly pawing the woman's leg are all easily read. The implication of the
cross around the neck of the remarkably well-dressed woman is less clear to the
modern eye. It was a popular notion in the Protestant Low Countries that Catholic
girls, easily absolved from their sins by confession, were more ready to become
prostitutes. Once we have made this connection, or rather this assumption,
small details emerge, like the revelation of a pert bosom and the striking fact that
though richly clad she lives in what seems to be a fairly modest setting – and not
least the fact that her sleeping quarters are in the loft above her head. It is a scene
that is a trifle naughty but not enough to be vulgar.

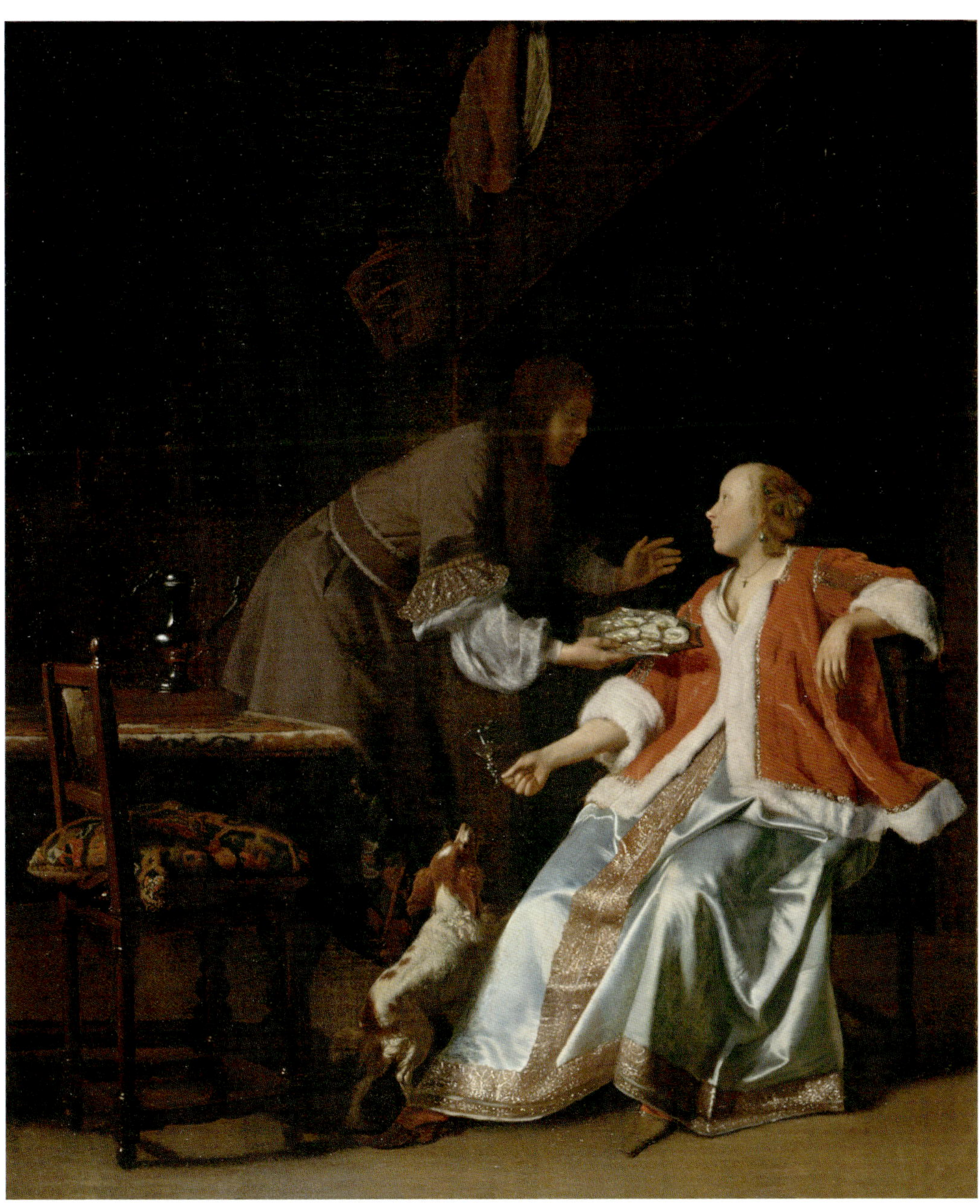

45

FLORIS VAN SCHOOTEN
Active in Haarlem 1612–1655

Still life with beaker, cheese, butter and biscuits

Oil on panel, 39.5 × 57.5 cm, signed
Sutton no. 63

Lacking, perhaps, the dignity of a Claesz, the grandeur of a Kalf or the sophistication of a Ravesteyn design, this late work is by van Schooten is admirable in its restraint, simplicity and crisp execution. Prolific but provincial – he lived his entire life in Haarlem – van Schooten was successful if somewhat predictable. His style changed with the times and this *ontbijtje*, or breakfast piece, reflects the influences of younger Haarlem artists like Pieter Claesz towards simpler compositions in almost monochrome palates. The tall, engraved, flared pewter goblet stands on a pewter plate, its dull tones reflecting the light source to the left and what may be the artist's reflection on the right. Two cheeses, biscuits, nuts, a knife and curls of butter lie on a linen cloth with a simple embroidered edge. The darker cheese, from Texel, was made with sheeps' milk, to which their dung was added. The honest, plain fare of a prosperous but not wealthy home is epitomized by the dish in which the butter rests – Dutch earthenware in blue-and-white tin glaze, imitating the vastly more expensive Chinese export porcelain, its quotidian nature revealed by the hint of red clay at the rims.

The still life, though seen as a distinctively Dutch type of picture, was developing across Europe in mercantile communities besides those of the North Netherlands, in Antwerp, Paris and Milan. Rather than acquiring historical and mythological works or portraiture, rich traders – not usually associated with military or courtly life or with pretentions to education – bought still lifes as decoration or aspirational symbols. Though not presented in chronological or stylistic order, the Samuel collection's group of still lifes represents an interesting cross-section of a trope instantly recognizable as Dutch and seventeenth-century and widely recognized as a major contribution to the development of painting.

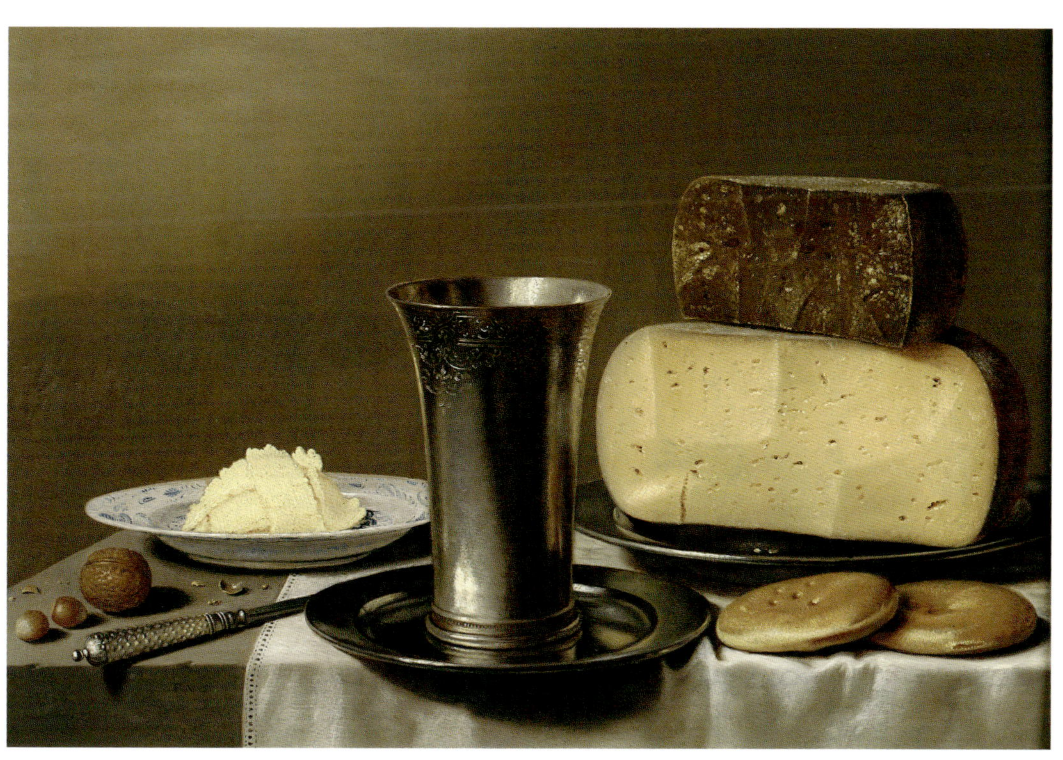

THE NORTH DRAWING ROOM

The remodelling of the central court by Dance in 1795 allowed the interior walls of this and the adjoining South Drawing Room to remain blank, ideal for hanging pictures. Although it was remodelled again in 1822 the bulk of the Samuel collection landscapes, marines and architectural pictures are displayed here very much in the manner of an eighteenth-century collector's cabinet. The arrangement is achieved by centring the pictures on the largest work, in this case the Salomon van Ruysdael, with pictures arranged by size around it. The three larger pictures in the lower register are amongst the finest landscapes in the collection and represent three entirely different styles: from left to right they are Jacob van Ruisdael's *Castle of Bentheim*, the classical and atmospheric river landscape with cattle by one of Harold Samuel's favourite artists, Aelbert Cuyp, and a very rare winter scene by Jan van de Cappelle. There are two works by Cuyp at Mansion House, but Samuel originally owned four more.

This hang, done in 1993 by Vivienne Knight, curator at the Guildhall Art Gallery, presents works by related artists together and takes account of similar and complementary subjects, therefore working well in art-historical terms as well as presenting a pleasing overall effect. Smaller works hang on the lower registers, where they are more easily seen. The pale aquamarine colour of the walls harmonizes with the strong reds of the carpets and the upholstered furniture, called the Nile Suite. Supplied in 1803 by John Phillips, Upholsterer to the City of London, it is of imitation rosewood, carved and gilded with anchors, swords and coils of rope, which may signify Nelson's victory at the Battle of the Nile in 1798 or refer to the City's maritime connections.

John Gilbert provided the white marble fireplace, and the grisaille roundels of 1774–75 above it are by Edward Edwards. The narrow site means the neighbouring buildings are very close and, though facing east, these rooms get little natural light.

Turn right into the South Drawing Room

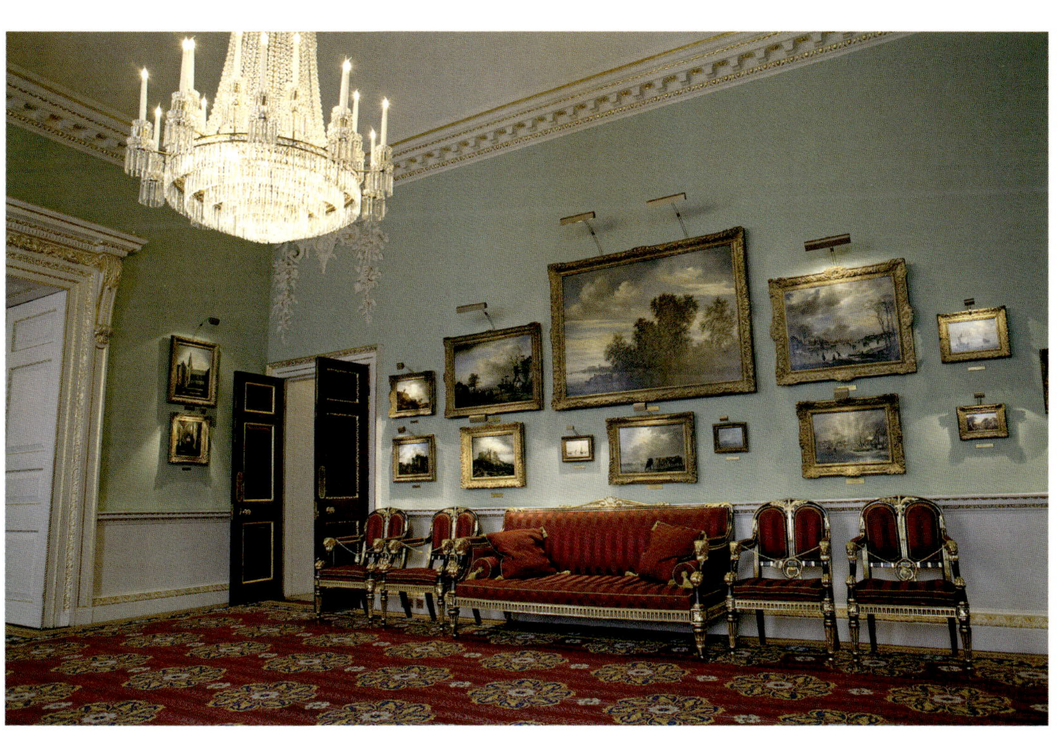

46

PHILIPS WOUWERMANS
Haarlem 1619–1668

Landscape with grey horse and figures by the wayside

Oil on panel, 30 × 39.8 cm, signed
Sutton no. 84

The two works by Wouwermans at Mansion House give opposing views of one of the finest painters of the Dutch school in the seventeenth century. Eschewing the Italianate figure groups of Honthorst and Bloemaert, Lord Samuel may also have found much of the work of landscapist and horse-painter Wouwermans too baroque and flamboyant for his sober taste. The later of his two acquisitions, this small painting is dateable to early in Wouwermans's prolific career and seems closer to Samuel's recognized taste. The son and brother of artists, Wouwermans studied in the studio of Frans Hals, though there is no evidence of this in his style. He travelled a little, probably no further than Germany and never to Italy itself, but sunny southern skies and vivid colours were to become synonymous with the lavish horse-filled scenes of hunts and battles, smithies and stables of his later career.

Here he is in sombre mood. Dividing the picture plane diagonally in two, he achieves depth in this strangely empty scene of muted tones by placing the grey horse entirely within the foreground and the cattle beyond the near horizon. Low hills, sketchily painted, enhanced by the defused light, add to the overcast feeling of the scene. Wouwerman's technical skill as a young artist in his mid twenties is already evident in the line of white on the grey horse's chin, the reflected clouds in the murky water and the touch of red in the garment carried by the female figure. The flying birds add to the enormity of the lowering sky, while the pose of the cow, in the act of bellowing, adds a mournful touch. Less becomes more and the picture, though small in scale, achieves a monumentality that is striking.

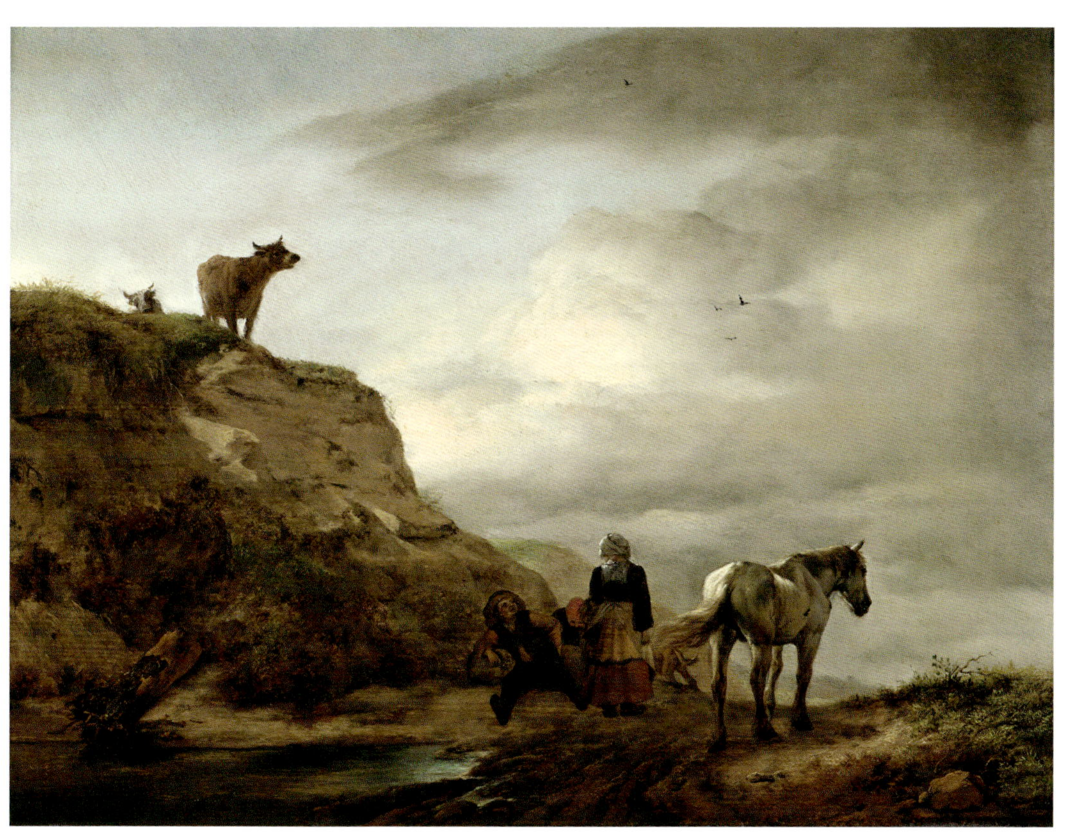

47

JAN VAN DER HEYDEN
Gorinchem 1637–1712 Amsterdam

An imaginary town gate with triumphal arch

Oil on panel, 31 × 37.5 cm, signed and dated 1663
Sutton no. 27

The Samuel collection contains no less than seven townscapes, a rare genre in Dutch art of the seventeenth century and so constituting a highly important group. Jan van der Heyden and Gerrit Berckheyde are the recognized masters of this field and Lord Samuel clearly loved the meticulous attention to detail, precise depictions both of real places and, as in this picture, of *capricci* that drew on a number of elements of recognizable architecture, placed in an imaginary setting. As a type the *capriccio* developed quite late in the seventeenth century, deriving from the background studies of urban settings in figurative works, like the views from interiors in the work of Pieter de Hooch or in Gabriel Metsu's street scenes. Van der Heyden's townscapes are painted largely on panel, the smooth surface of which is ideal for the detail with which blocks of stone and the individual bricks are rendered.

The strange-looking building in the centre rear of the picture is a Roman triumphal arch, seen in profile. It has been turned into a home by the addition of a pitched roof and chimney stack. The ruined Gothic tower, gabled buildings on the left and pedimented stone shrine on the right are such disparate elements that the artist must have used drawings made on his travels up the Rhine into Germany or drawings and prints made by others on their travels to Italy.

Though the architecture and beautiful sunlit clouds are by van der Heyden, the elegant figures strolling past the beggars, the young man leaning on the parapet, admiring the view, and even the dog in the left foreground are introduced by Adriaen van de Velde, who often painted 'staffage' for landscapes by his friends and colleagues.

When he died van der Heyden had seventy of his own works still in his possession but he was nevertheless a rich man. It is unclear whether he achieved his prosperity from painting or from his work designing fire-fighting equipment and overseeing the street lighting in Amsterdam that he invented.

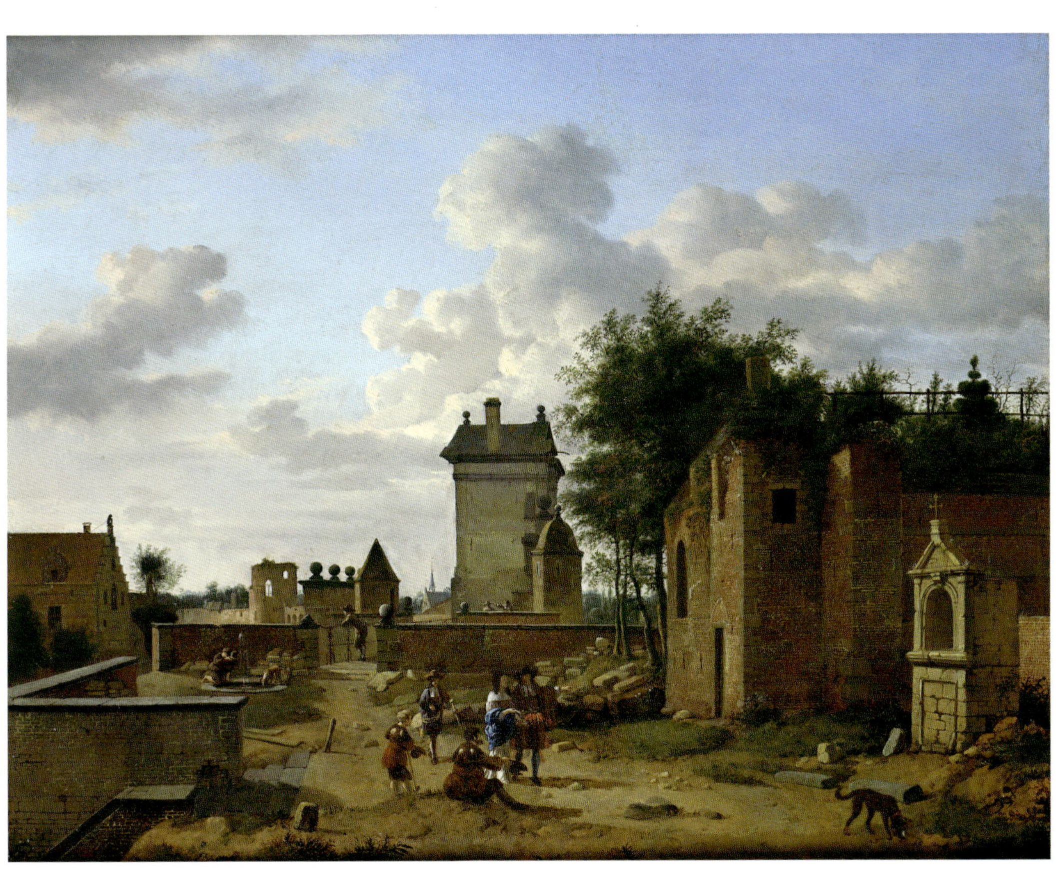

48

PHILIPS WOUWERMANS
Haarlem 1619–1668

Landscape with kermis (or *The Rustic Wedding*)

Oil on canvas, 59.2 × 85 cm, signed
Sutton no. 83

This is one of Wouwermans's finest paintings. In a wide, light-filled landscape, with a river and distant mountains wreathed in clouds, an aristocratic party on horseback have halted by a rustic inn for refreshment. Two horsemen are accompanied by a lady, riding side-saddle and carrying a parasol, to whom the landlord offers a sparking glass of red wine. Taking place to the left is a *kermis*, or rustic entertainment, from which a bagpipe player leads a ragged procession, headed by a dancing couple clearly the worse for wear. The themes of the rest at an inn and the peasant carnival, here combined, were well-established in Dutch and Flemish painting.

Close inspection of details will be rewarded. Crowded with incident and accident, the juxtaposition of high and low life is both charmingly observed and brilliantly executed, without envy or scorn. The composition is excellently balanced. The light falling on the lower right-hand corner is mirrored by the grey clouds in the top left. The grey horse with its brilliant-red saddle-cloth – framed by a tree and a building, outlined against the clouds – acts as a forcible focus point. The two groups of buildings and trees at different distances frame the scene on either side, without appearing to be contrived.

The subtle combination of genre scene and landscape, despite its Italianate feeling of light, clearly appealed to Lord Samuel when he acquired this work in 1959, making it one of his earliest purchases. It is hardly surprising that it was greatly admired in the eighteenth and nineteenth centuries, holding prized positions amongst the Dutch pictures of the distinguished collector Gerard Braamcamp in Amsterdam in the 1770s and in the large and famous collection of the connoisseur, collector and designer Thomas Hope by the 1820s. Samuel bought it, along with several other works, from the collection of Sir Alfred Beit, a South African millionaire, through his dealer Edward Speelman.

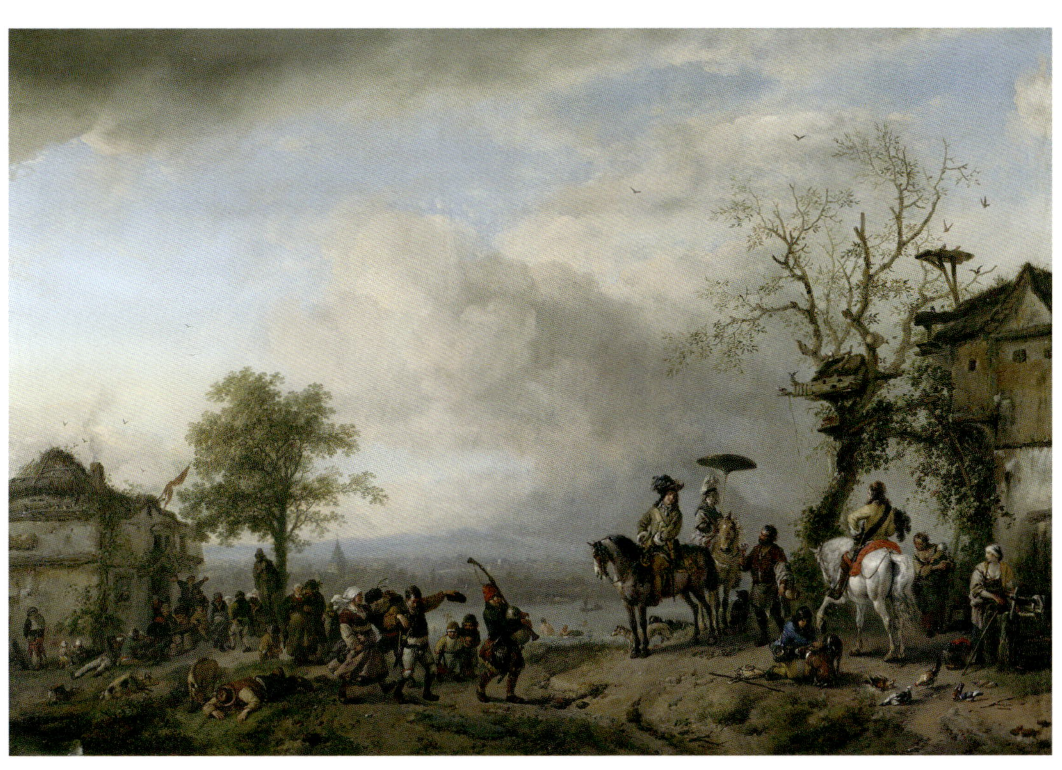

49

JACOB ISAACKSZ VAN RUISDAEL
Haarlem 1628/29–1682 Haarlem

The Castle of Bentheim

Oil on canvas, 38.8 × 46.5 cm, signed
Sutton no. 57

Bentheim Castle, seen from a low viewpoint that emphasizes its strength, grandeur and antiquity, stands on a rocky eminence. Cob-built cottages of timber and plaster cluster beside a sandy road at the foot of the hill. The ridge on which the castle sits falls away into the distance, where a windmill breaks the skyline. Though the depiction of the castle is accurate, the reality of this ancient site, which is actually on a low ridge of the plain of Westphalia in western Germany, is very different. In 1650 or 1651, as a very young man, Ruisdael visited the castle with his friend Nicolaes Berchem. Inspired by the patina of building styles and materials and the grandeur of the setting, he made paintings of it no less than fourteen times, usually as the centre of far larger landscapes. This small work may be one of his earliest depictions, testifying to an already well-developed skill, and the model for several of the later, far larger works. Jacob had studied landscape painting with the skilled but pedestrian Cornelis Vroom and his own uncle, Salomon van Ruysdael, but his precocious talent and quick development meant his distinctive style was well formed by the time he travelled to Bentheim.

Ruisdael is regarded as the greatest of all Dutch seventeenth-century landscape artists and his views of Bentheim the most demonstrative of his skills. He masterfully combined topographical accuracy with purely imaginative landscape. The combination of colours in the old stonework and warm brick are mirrored in the tiled roofs of the cottages below, all set against the rich greens of trees and sandy heath. The tiny touch of red on the seated traveller acts as a focus. The light, unusually falling from right to left, lands selectively on the walls, as the passing clouds cast shadows on the brick gables and the keep, adding greatly to the sense of depth and variety of architecture. The flock of birds adds still more to this depth and gives scale.

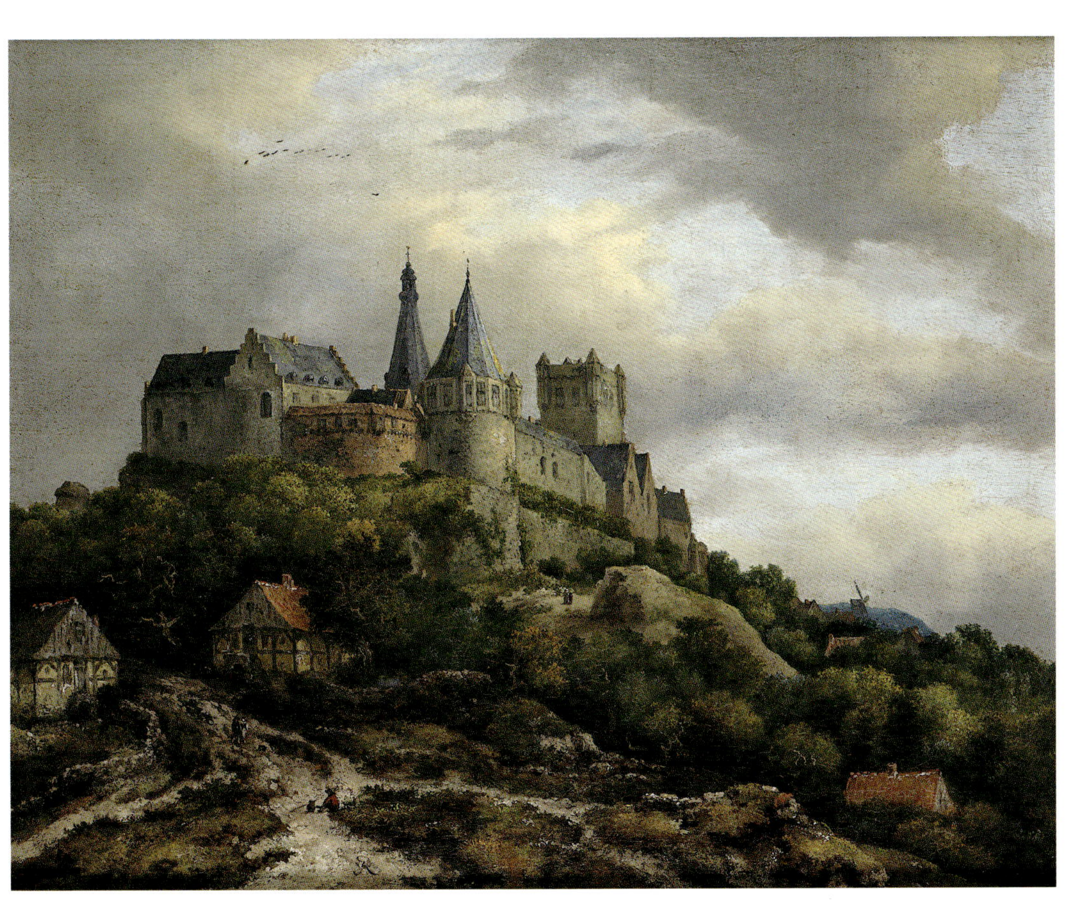

50

SALOMON VAN RUYSDAEL
Naarden 1600/3–1670 Haarlem

River landscape with ferry boat

Oil on canvas, 111.5 × 151 cm, signed and dated 1650
Sutton no. 62

Talented teacher and uncle of Jacob van Ruisdael, Salomon was a member of the
artists' guild of Haarlem from 1623. His early work recalls landscapes by Esaias
van den Velde but his work in the 1630s became more 'tonal', no doubt influenced
by his friend and rival Jan van Goyen. His later period, in the 1640s and 1650s, saw
the introduction of more colour and greater use of figures, always on or beside
the quiet, sandy-banked waterways of his native heath. River landscapes – never
stormy, always calm, often with ferries or small boats, cattle and passengers
in river traffic – were Ruysdael's speciality. His colouring is distinctive, with
highlights of red, white or black often used to add emphasis. Having established a
popular formula, Dutch artists rarely risked great changes in style or format and
Salomon van Ruysdael was no exception. Though clearly a successful and prolific
artist, he had a second occupation in dealing in the blue dye indigo, used in textile
production.

Dating from Ruysdael's mature period, the scene is set on the bank of a wide
river. Only at the very left-hand corner, beyond a great house with a free-standing
keep, a water wheel and a very distant church, can the horizon be seen. The well-
wooded wedge of bank, shading a road with wagons and horsemen, is reflected
in the still water. High cirrus clouds stream across the sky, adding to the strong
horizontals of the composition, while the taller cumulonimbus clouds mirror the
outlines of the leafy trees along the bank. A flat-bottomed punt ferries cattle and
peasants towards the shore, the cattle clearly content with the mode of transport.
A white cow, reflected in the water, gazes benignly into the distance while her
neighbour scratches her head on the edge of the boat. Such scenes of agrarian
plenitude, prosperous and ordered, not only appealed to the artist's many clients
but have maintained their popularity to this day.

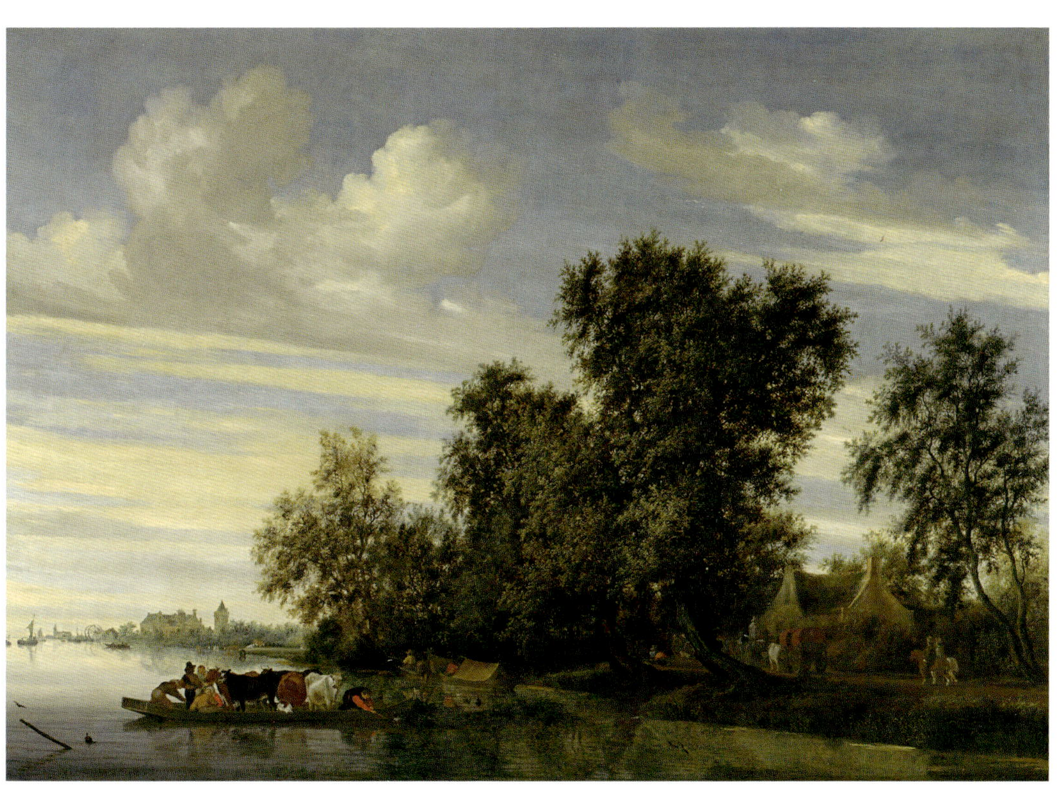

51

SALOMON VAN RUYSDAEL
Naarden 1600/03–1670 Haarlem

Sailing boats on a river

Oil on panel, 20.9 × 28.3 cm, signed
Sutton no. 61

This tiny picture, the smallest recorded work by Salomon van Ruysdael, achieves monumentality in terms of design and a masterful fluidity of execution, despite the size. Probably dating from the mid 1640s, when the influence and rivalry of his friend Jan van Goyen was at its height, the entirely tonal composition is lightly, even roughly executed. The space is defined primarily by the far bank, which divides the picture horizontally into a third of river and two thirds of sky. Ruysdael was a sky painter of the first order and it is the sky and its reflection that are the chief attractions of this work. A church and cottages are reflected with the wooded shore in the still water. A small strip of land in the foreground acts as a frame, or *repoussoir*, defining the river's width, which is further shaped by two spits of land at either side, adapting what at first sight appears to be a simple river running across the scene into a wider and more complicated waterway.

A warm, golden light suffuses the scene. Barely defined clouds are painted with swift, visible brushstrokes. These and the light-blue sky reflect in the still water, where a breeze just fills the sails of the boats and stirs their flags. To create the water, Ruysdael has dragged a brush laden with paint across the panel, leaving heavy lines of impasto that give an excellent indication of the passage of the rowing boat from right to left, disturbing the reflection of the larger sailing boat. Dabs of paint, almost in shorthand, define the figures and distant boats. The muted red of the flag and the hint of russet on a figure in the rowing boat add the required focus of colour in an otherwise monotone painting. Ruysdael achieves a view of calm, sedate activity that would have resonated as a subject with his contemporaries and still delights the modern viewer with the timelessness of skilled artistry.

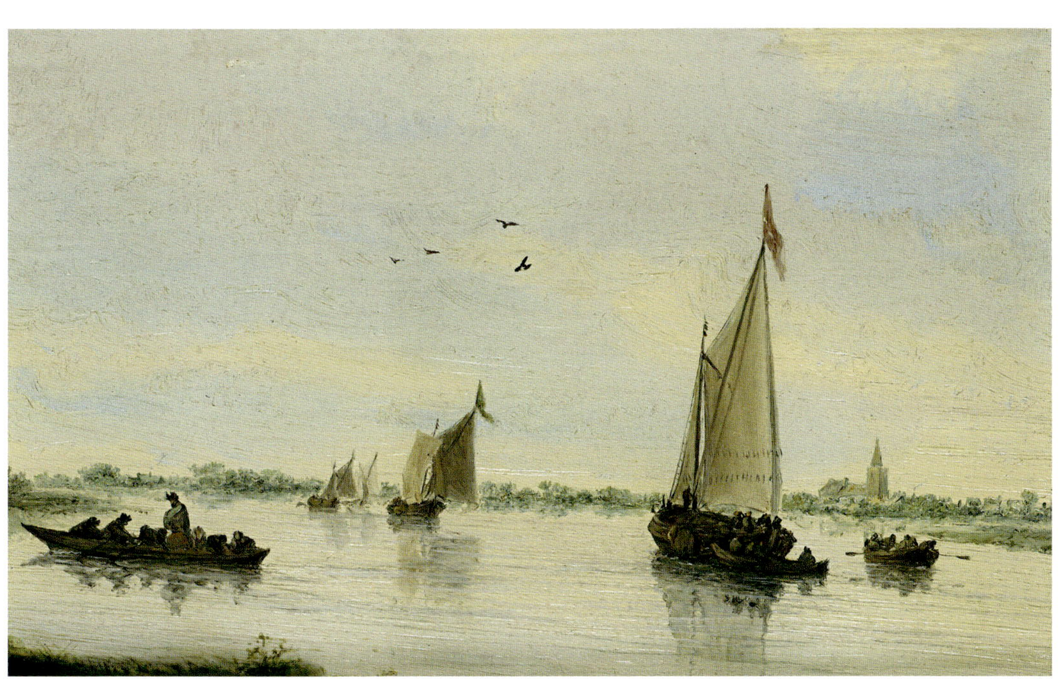

52

AELBERT CUYP
Dordrecht 1620–1691

Cattle by a river

Oil on panel, 38.3 × 55.2 cm
Sutton no. 17

Nothing is more evocative of Dutch landscape painting in the mid seventeenth century than Aelbert Cuyp's images of cows at the water's edge. The golden glow of an evening sky over streaming clouds gently lights the standing fecund kine, gazing limply, reflective and reflecting, while heavy-laden sailing boats pass by. Eugène Fromentin, artist and critic, observed that Cuyp "contributed more than anyone to enlarging the basis of local observation upon which his country's art unfolded".

Cuyp developed the theme of cattle sitting and standing in or beside water in the early 1650s, both on a monumental scale and in more compact formats such as this. His earlier paintings featured a high bank with standing and seated cows and bulls, human figures and other animals, but these gradually gave way to mere groups of cattle and flowing water, as in this example. Here the lowest viewpoint possible allows the undulating outlines of the cows' ears, horns and rumps to run parallel with the horizon and the river. When this work was discussed by Sutton soon after the Samuel collection was presented to Mansion House he was ambivalent about its autograph status. Since then and as recently as the major exhibition on Cuyp in 2001, it has been accepted as fully authentic. Standing as the work does later in Cuyp's development of the format, the design and the variety of colours and attitudes of the cattle had been perfected, which may account for the lack of freshness detected by Sutton. The work was engraved in 1767 and from the print we can see that the painting may have been slightly cut at the bottom.

Though Cuyp had a few contemporary followers, whose work is easily detected by their weak composition and technique, later works in his manner tend to be exact repetitions of known paintings rather than versions with differences. This picture, though following the general design of a group of other works, includes details not found amongst them, the floating leafy log in the foreground for example, indicating the hand of the master.

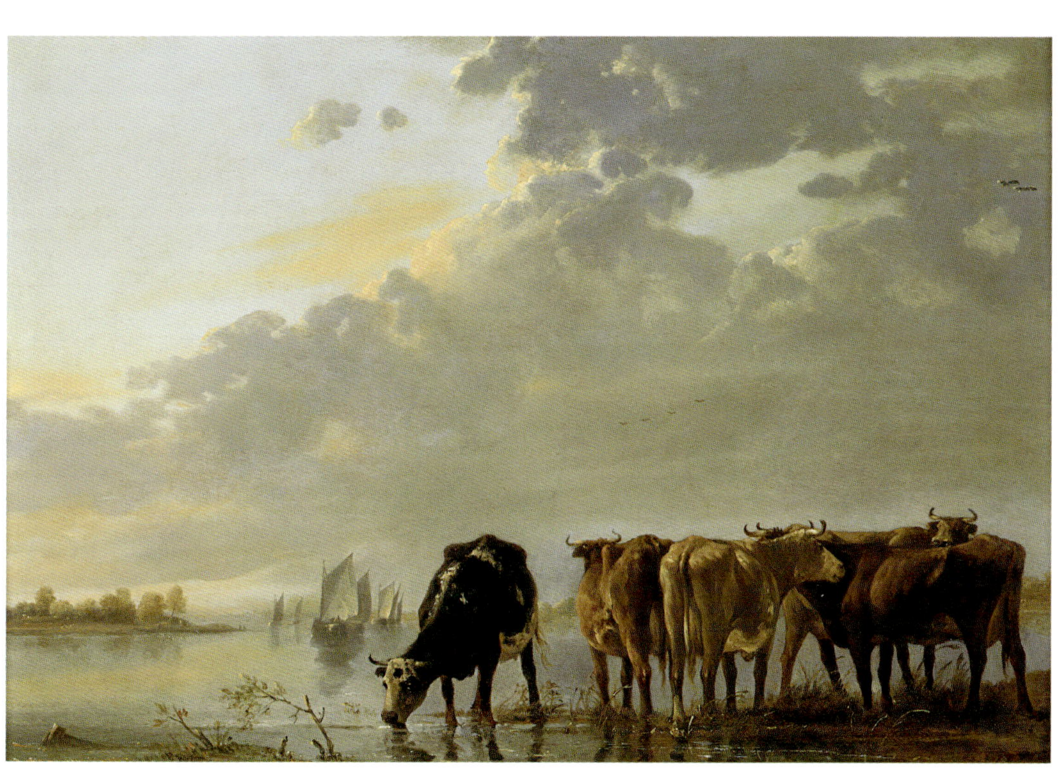

53

JAN VAN GOYEN
Leiden 1596–1656 The Hague

Winter landscape with a horse-drawn sleigh

Oil on panel, 14.6 × 17.9 cm, signed and dated 1645
Sutton no. 20

Native of Leiden, where he received his early training, van Goyen moved to
The Hague in his mid thirties. He travelled extensively throughout the United
Provinces and was working from the house of Isaac van Ruysdael, father of Jacob
and brother of Salomon, at Haarlem in 1634. Salomon became a friend and rival in
the art of landscape. The two works by van Goyen on the Red Staircase show his
debt to his early mentor Esaias van den Velde and the development of the 'tonal'
style of his later works.

This small winter landscape of 1645, painted when van Goyen was settled in
The Hague, can be usefully compared to Ruysdael's tiny river landscape nearby,
of roughly the same date. The low horizon divides the panorama, giving more
emphasis to the mass of pinkish-cream cloud cover, reflected in the ice below.
A subtle *repoussoir* is provided by the darkly shaded stretch of ice at the very front.
Strong horizontals – particularly a raised causeway from which a horse-drawn
sleigh descends, its occupants outlined against a lighter patch of cloud – divide the
land and water into bands of light and dark. Depth is created by the subtle use of
several small uprights – two posts on the causeway, a distant church tower on the
left, a windmill on the right and more buildings on the far horizon – that lead the
eye into the pictorial space. The tonal effect, achieved with a limited range of grey,
brown and the soft pink of the evening sky, is relieved by touches of reds and blue
– on the jacket of the woman in the sleigh, the hat of the man in the punt in the
left foreground and on the breeches of the man kneeling in the centre. *Kolf* players
complete the scene, but the overall mood is somehow melancholic.

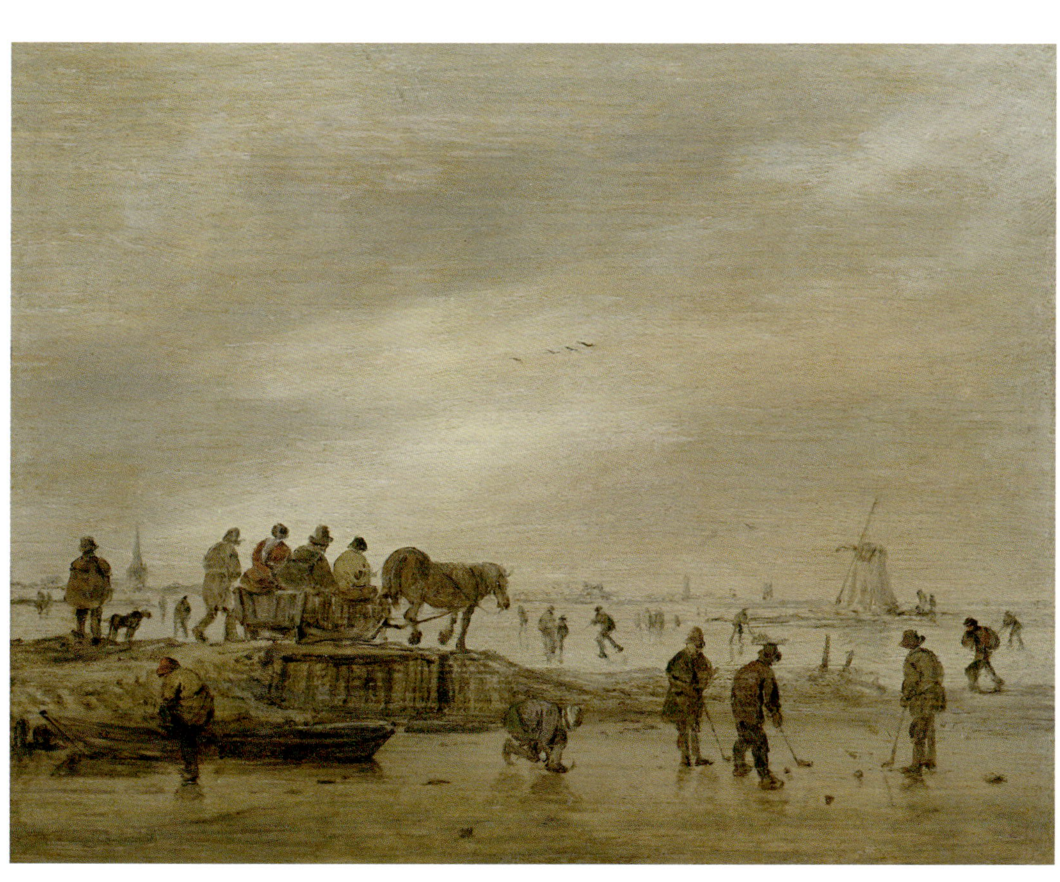

54

AERT VAN DER NEER
Amsterdam 1603/04–1677

Winter landscape with figures on a frozen canal

Oil on canvas, 61.5 × 74.5 cm
Sutton no. 42

Lord Samuel's great love of Dutch seventeenth-century winter scenes reaches its apogee with this large and colourful work by van der Neer. His winter landscape on the Red Staircase is subtly monotonous in palette, while here there is far more direct, local colour, particularly the striking red of the jackets, socks and shirts of several of the figures. In the sky the pinks and yellows of the distance give way to several shades of brilliant blue, reflected in the ice below and all set off against the dark trees and frosted reeds. A touch of blue can be seen in the washing hung to dry on the fence of a cottage on the left. The trees and buildings recede alternately, left and right and diagonally across the scene, towards a church on the left and a windmill on the right, in a well-established convention of *coulisses*. There is merely the smallest hint of a flat horizon line in the far distance. Van der Neer's subtle skill at blending the distance into the middleground and the middle into the foreground has matured, with a fabulous technical understanding of differential calculus that expresses atmospheric changes in space. Peopled with well-wrapped idlers and single skaters, the game of *kolf* occupies no less than a dozen of the figures, who include the man in red, prominent in the foreground, whose ball has entered the rough of the reedy bank.

Dating from the mid 1650s, this work displays van der Neer's mature style and mastery of design. Viewed from a high vantage point at the centre of the stretch of water, the scene is framed with land on either side and across the front. Critics have lamented this last feature, which infringes the naturally straight course of Dutch waterways. Despite the early lessons absorbed from the Camphuysen brothers on the choice of subject and on the identifiable time of day and from Jan van Goyen on the monotonal palette of his middle years, the clearly dominant influence is Nature herself.

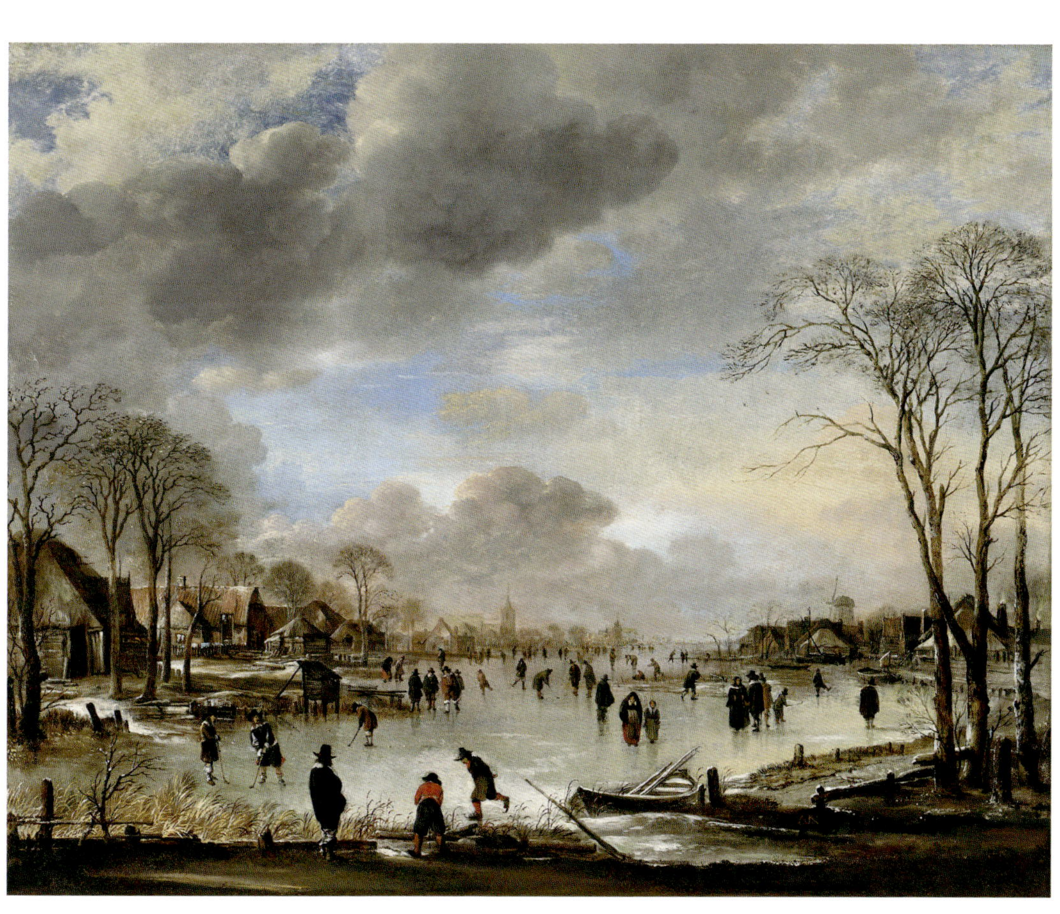

55

JAN VAN DE CAPPELLE
Amsterdam 1626–1679

Winter landscape

Oil on panel, 36.5 × 49.7 cm, signed
Sutton no. 12

Continuing the theme of winter landscapes, this is a rare subject in van de Cappelle's oeuvre. Independently wealthy – he inherited a profitable dye works – van de Cappelle was self-taught, a contemporary noting that he had "learnt painting for his own pleasure". If this is true, he was naturally skilled and greatly talented. Free from commercial constraints, he was able to please himself in choice of subjects and style of execution. His collection of art comprised over 200 paintings and 6,000 drawings, many by Amsterdam's leading artists, but his own style and ability was well developed before their acquisition. Despite his proximity to Aert van der Neer in Amsterdam, he owned no paintings by the older artist – a comparative failure and living in poverty at his death. The owner of a yacht, van de Cappelle could study the crowded ports and river-mouths of Holland, perfecting his magnificently constructed and finely observed shipping pieces, always in calm weather, filled with accurate detail.

His known period of activity as an artist was brief, the dated works covering the short span from 1649 to 1663. In the mid 1650s he turned to winter scenes, of which a mere dozen or so survive, with this example probably dating to about 1652–54. He has treated the inland waterway – lined with trees and buildings, devoid of local colour – in the same manner that he used to show large groups of shipping becalmed. The strong verticals, which draw your eye right and left and right again, and isolated diagonals – particularly of the logs and the snow-bound boat – create orthogonal movement, all in a limited palette of grey and white, set against the stunning blue of the ice. A vestigial *repoussoir*, the logs on the ice and isolated patches of snow, demarcate the foreground as the eye is lead upstream towards the distant bascule bridge. Depth is created by the varying scale of the trees and buildings, by their juxtaposition, overlapping and receding. There is only a hint of a horizon as water mingles with the leaden, snowy sky. Unlike those of the busy scenes by Averkamp and van der Neer, the figures in this masterful evocation of winter seem incidental, hurrying about their chilly business.

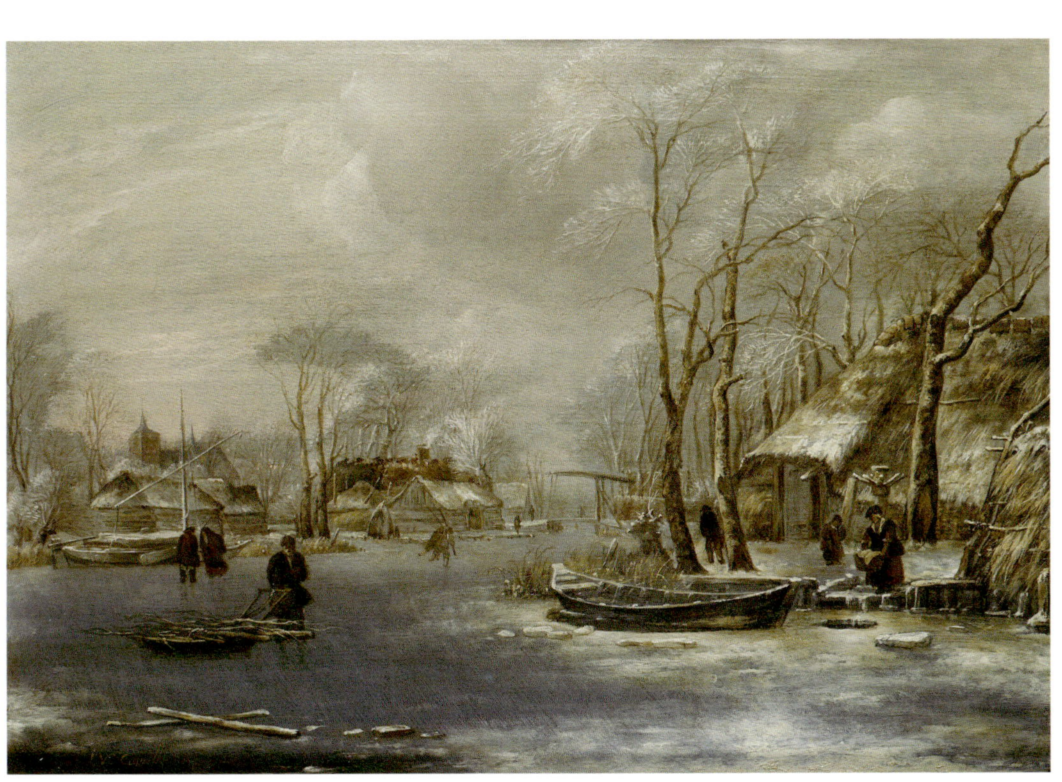

56

WILLEM VAN DE VELDE THE YOUNGER
Leiden 1633–1707 London

A hoeker alongside a kaag at anchor

Oil on panel, 20.9 × 28.3 cm, signed
Sutton no. 79

The son of a marine artist of the same name, Willem van de Velde the Younger
lived and worked in Amsterdam until around 1672, when he moved with his father
to London, entering the service of Charles II and his brother the Duke of York,
the Lord High Admiral. The Elder was responsible for the drawing and obsessive
accuracy of the designs, while the Younger applied the paint and achieved the
atmospheric settings. Dating from the early 1660s, so painted while still in
Amsterdam, this work – set in a flat calm under magnificent, luminous, billowing
clouds – is one of four by van de Velde the Younger in the Samuel collection.

In 1990 Michael Robinson, curator of paintings at the National Maritime
Museum at Greenwich, published his exhaustive two-volume catalogue of the
works of the father and son. Such was Robinson's understanding of seventeenth-
century ships that he could identify the slightest deviation or mistake in their
representation, then assess the extent to which the works were by the masters,
done with studio assistance or merely by a follower. He detected hands other than
van de Velde the Younger's in many works, including this one, blighting them
with the suffix 'and studio'. In this work, on the ship firing a salute "the fore
topmast yard, which is lying on the top and not on the cap of the lowermast"
is apparently the tell-tale sign of an assistant's hand.

Robinson's approach, while presented in good faith and with the certitude of
long, thorough study, gives little attention to the practicalities of studio practice,
merely mentioning that Cornelis van de Velde, Willem van de Velde the Younger's
son, was the principal assistant. The idea that van de Velde would have left crucial
details in small-scale works to the hands of assistants, who then mis-painted,
is highly unlikely. If, as Robinson suggested, the attention to detail and full
understanding of ships on the part of the master was so great, then surely such
a blunder would have been instantly recognized and corrected? The finest details
were often painted last and most delicately, therefore the first to be abraded and
lost. Clumsy restoration is the most likely cause of apparent errors in the depiction
of rigging. This is certainly a work entirely by the master.

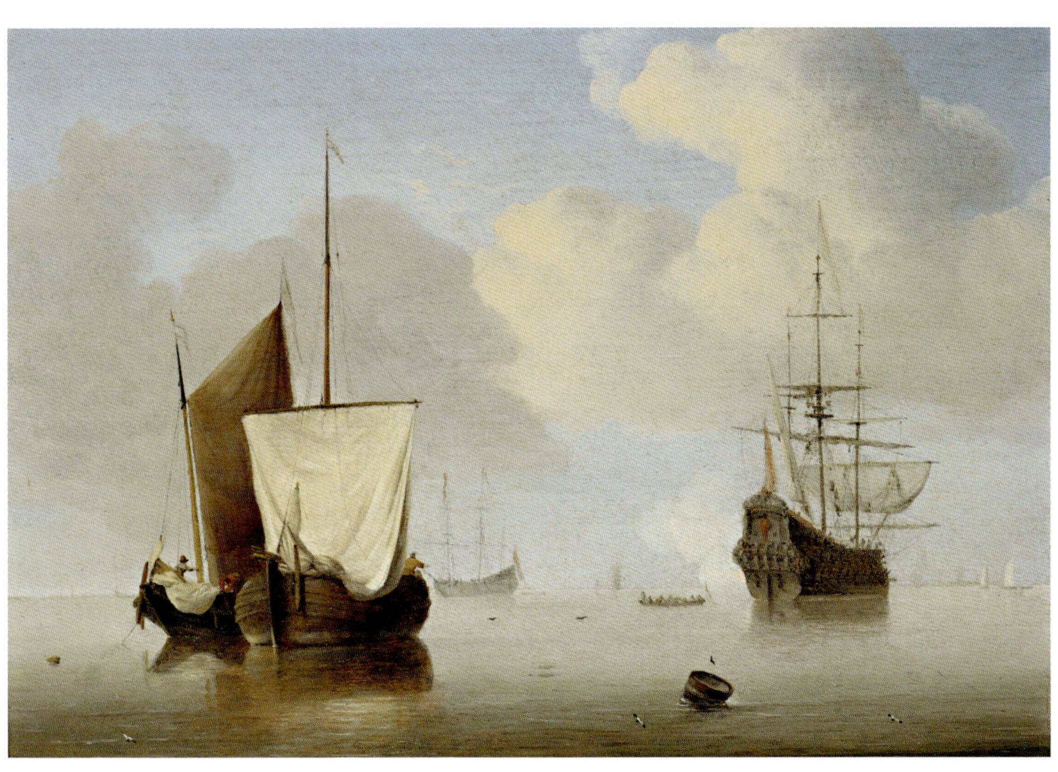

57

JAN VAN DER HEYDEN
Gorinchem 1637–1712 Amsterdam

A fortified moat or canal

Oil on copper, 11.4 × 17.5 cm, signed
Sutton no. 30

Bought in 1956, so at the very start of the formation of the Samuel collection, this work had previously belonged to Geoffrey and Dorothy Hart, who had sold their house, Wych Cross Place in Sussex, to the Samuels two years before. The Harts collected Dutch pictures and also used Edward Speelman as their dealer. When this work first appeared at auction in 1731 it was one of a pair and the two pictures remained together until a sale in 1864, when they were sold separately.

The scene, though entirely fictitious, is drawn from a number of architectural elements that van der Heyden would have seen on his travels through the Low Countries, notably in Utrecht and Arnhem, but the resemblance is largely passing. Moated towns and cities like this one abounded, and the gabled house to the left is entirely generic. In a country with few sources of building stone, brick was the primary building material. The technical skill in rendering these bricks and mortar in fine detail is a distinctive characteristic of van de Heyden's work, as is the beautiful light reflecting from the distant, yellow clouds and mirrored in the water. This, combined with the blue hills on the horizon, give the picture an Italianate feel, intentionally echoed by the Roman-style tower, also in brick.

Van der Heyden used his imagination to adapt and recreate settings by changing scale and materials and altering significant details to make *capricci* that were pleasing and plausible. The earlier artists who had begun the fashion for townscapes in the 1640s and 1950s – Jacob van Ruisdael, Jan Wijnants and Ludolph Bakhuizen in particular – had now been superseded by Gerrit Berckheyde and van der Heyden. Though similar in many ways, Berckheyde and van der Heyden, both well represented in the Samuel collection, present very different ideas in their townscapes. Van der Heyden was not a true architectural painter and was not always site specific, rather he was a painter of urban views. He sometimes asked artist friends to provide the 'staffage', though that is unlikely in this work given the small scale.

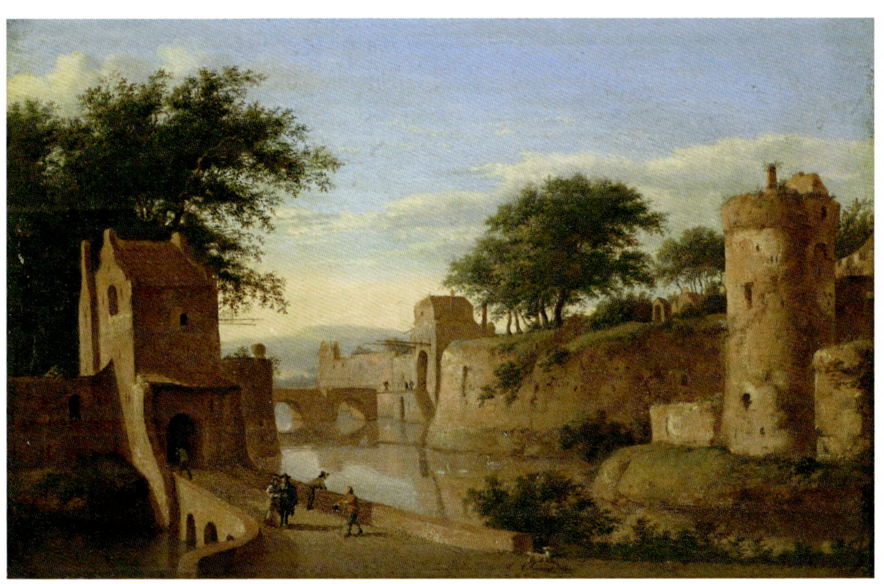

58

Imitator of AERT VAN DER NEER
18th century

A canal in winter

Oil on panel, 26.3 × 37.8 cm, signed
Sutton no. 45

All collections have mistakes, some greater than others. This picture is the only true failure in the Samuel collection. It presents a fair approximation of what a composition by van der Neer should look like, with all the correct attributes – a winter canal scene with the distinctive strip of land in the foreground, a rather high viewpoint and a single perspective vanishing point on the horizon in the middle of the scene. Figures in traditional winter pursuits populate the ice, but something is wrong.

The uniformly even tone of yellows and russet-browns shows little variation and no sense of atmospheric change from the foreground to the far distance. Totally unmodulated, the colours of the landscape, ice and sky have no subtlety. As the work has been signed with the putative artist's initials and since no composition of this design is otherwise known, it must be seen as a fake rather than a copy. It is unlikely to have been painted in the seventeenth century, which would have redeemed it somewhat by being a period picture, but is most likely to date from the eighteenth century.

The position of this painting in Mansion House hang reflects its status. It has a firm and important place in the Samuel collection, however, illustrating a pitfall that lies open for even the most cautious, experienced collector.

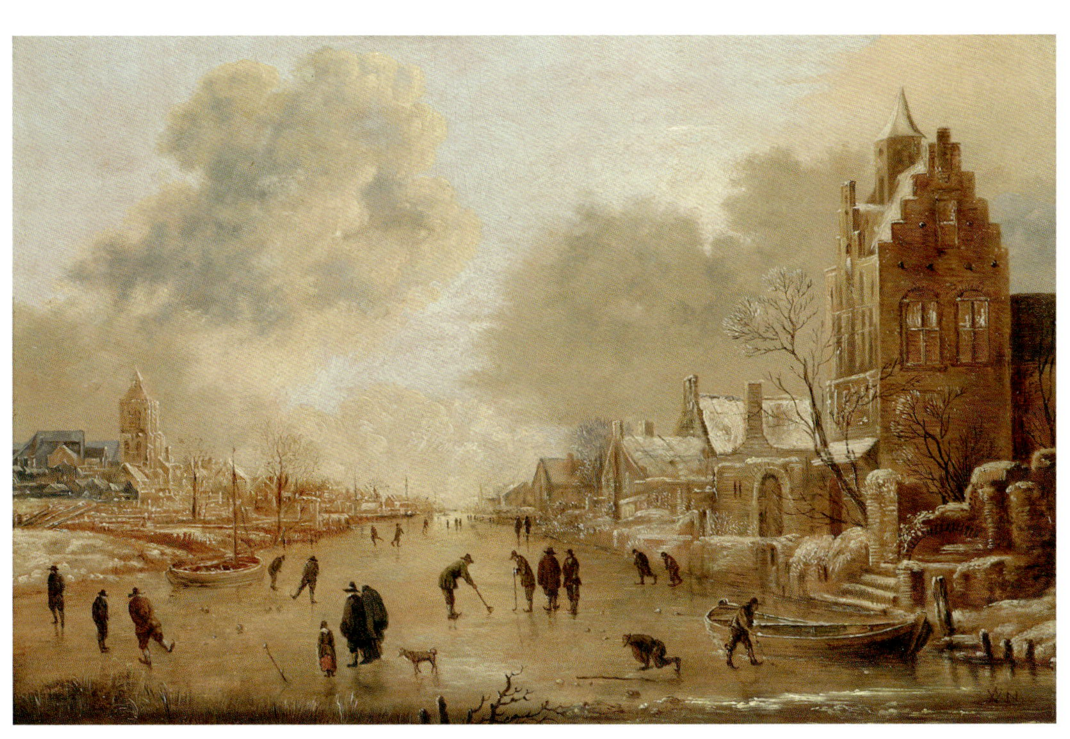

59

PALAMEDES PALAMEDESZ
London 1607–1638 Delft

Cavalry battle on a bridge

Oil on panel, 34.5 × 54.5 cm
Sutton no. 53

Probably born in London and living in his father's home town of Delft by 1627, Palamedesz showed some skill but limited imagination in his short career. He only painted long horizontal or oval battle scenes, cavalry skirmishes and military encampments, of which this is a fine and typical example. It had been thought to be by Palamedesz's brother Anthonie, as their styles and format were very similar. Anthonie's subjects were mostly interior genre scenes, however, whereas Palamedes's were exclusively battles.

This work appears to be completely at odds with the rest of the Samuel collection, but a glance at the picture that hangs beneath it reveals its relevance and the two make a charming and unusual couple. It is the painting that hangs in front of the young boy, who studiously copies it, in the work by Wallerant Vaillant.

This is one of the few works in the Samuel collection that has the type of frame that it would have had in the seventeenth century. Of plain-moulded and polished wood, it was added by Lord Samuel to match the work in its painted representation. Edward Speelman and Lord Samuel agreed that the majority of the collection should be presented uniformly in carved gilt-wood frames, with the exception of this one and the Aelbert Cuyp on the Red Staircase (no. 5). Gilded frames were used in Holland and Flanders in the seventeenth century, as we can see in the interior by Pieter de Hooch (no. 37). However, plainly moulded or simple ripple-carved ebony or rosewood frames, sometimes with a thin gold inner fillet, were the standard. Lord Samuel's taste was for eighteenth-century French and English frames, which were obviously felt to be more suitable to the setting of Wych Cross Place, his country house in Sussex, and complemented his fine English furniture and silver of the same period.

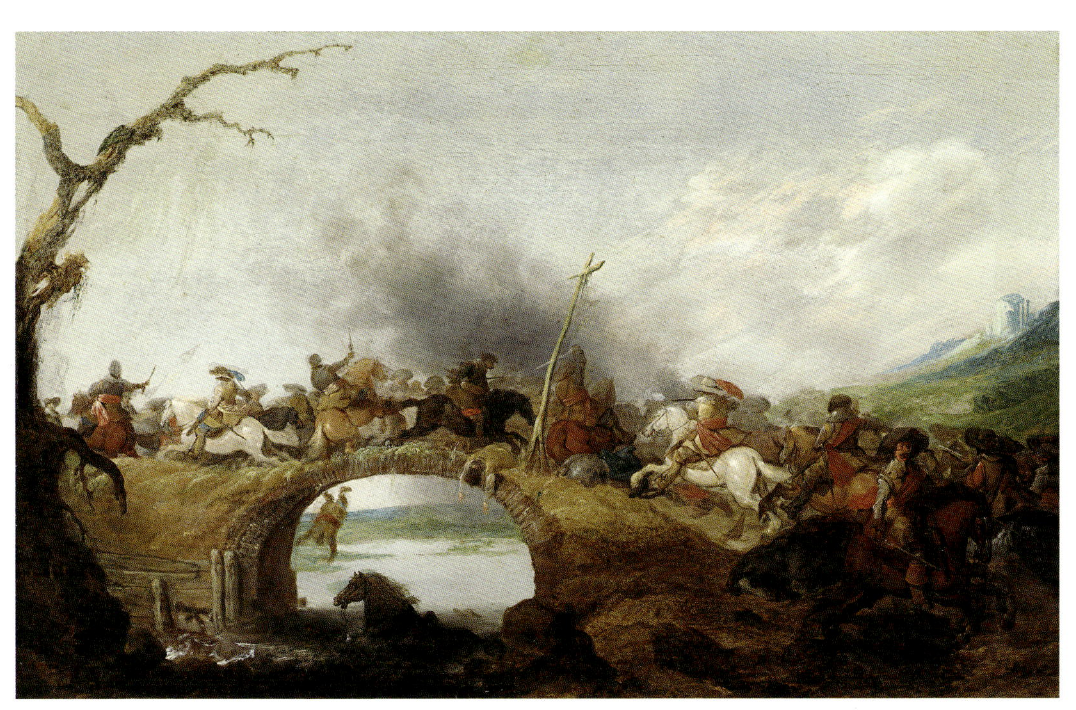

60

WALLERANT VAILLANT
Lille 1623–1677 Amsterdam

A young man copying a painting

Oil on panel, 32.1 × 39.5 cm
Sutton no. 72

Acquired in 1966 as a work by Michael Sweerts, a painter who had also treated the subject of young apprentice artists, this painting shares several qualities of style with his Franco-Dutch contemporary Wallerant Vaillant. Comparisons with two very similar works ascribed to Vaillant, in the Louvre and at Lille, combined with a close analysis of the painterly style, confirm this as an autograph work by Vaillant. The form of the boy's body and hair are fuller and softer than in Sweerts's work, the treatment of the setting less defined and more nuanced.

Originally from Lille, portraitist and genre painter Vaillant was apprenticed in Amsterdam, worked in Germany and France in the 1650s and 1660s and then returned to Amsterdam. He was one of the earliest and finest mezzotinters. This background of mezzotinting – a skill he taught Prince Rupert of the Rhine – was influential in developing his soft, velvety technique of painting, seen in this work, which probably dates from the mid 1650s.

The unusual view shows only the back of the apprentice, who is set to draw a copy of Palamedesz's *Cavalry battle on a bridge*, hanging at a convenient height on a wainscoted wall. A canvas and painter's manikin shows this to be a corner of the master's studio. Despite the soft solidity of the copyist's head and coat, details like the scuffed edges of the portfolio on which the boy is leaning and the worn edges of the black-painted chair rail show a keenly observant artist. Vaillant's accuracy in scale and detail can be confirmed by comparing the painting being copied with the real work. The close proximity of the viewer to the scene is emphasized by the chair-back and the space is admirably defined by the use of strong daylight from the upper left and the diagonal shadow at the lower left. Surprisingly modern in feel, this and other works of young people drawing were to have great influence on the works of French eighteenth-century artists, particularly Chardin. This work is rightly regarded as Vaillant's masterpiece.

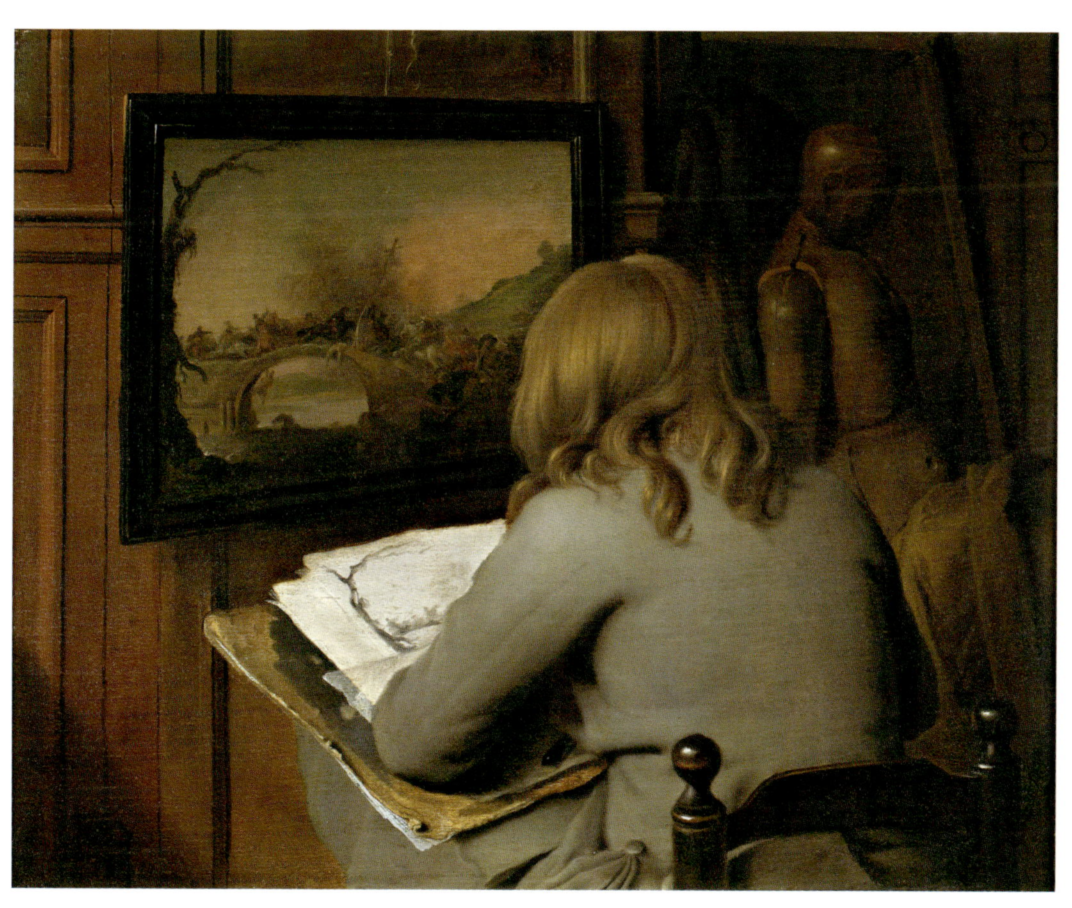

61

GERRIT BERCKHEYDE
Haarlem 1638–1698

The Smedestraat with a view of the Grote Markt and St Bavo's Church, Haarlem

Oil on panel, 52 × 39.5 cm
Sutton no. 6

It is morning in Haarlem – the clock on the tower of St Bavo's Church reads twenty past ten. It is immediately clear that Berckheyde was a painter of architecture rather than a view-painter like his contemporary and rival in the field Jan van Heyden. There are eight architectural paintings in the Samuel collection, indicating a favourite subject. This is the finest portrait of a building, meticulous, atmospheric, accurate and dramatic. As the moment is recorded on the clock, so the figures seem frozen at that moment, stock-still and incidental, adjuncts to the domestic buildings that frame the scene with shadows. The tall, upright format of the panel was required to achieve a full view of the octagonal tower, built in 1519–20, an addition to the largely fifteenth-century church with its distinctive bells, lattice crown and weather-vane. Looking towards the north side of the church, the contrast between the brick, stone and grey slate roofs is emphasized by the raking light, while the wooden tower, sheathed in lead and half in shadow, stands out against the sky.

Berckheyde had, like many Dutch artists, travelled widely in his native country as well as in Germany, working for a time in Heidelberg, making extensive studies of picturesque buildings for use in landscape *capricci*. On his return to Haarlem in the early 1660s he abandoned fantasy for hard reality, showing a marked preference for austere architecture and blank surfaces either fully lit or deeply shawowed. Utilizing the latest theories on perspective, Berckheyde often used multiple vanishing points or placed the points outside the picture plane. Here he has overcome the practical issue that the street is not at right-angles to the church by using two vanishing points, one for the street at a lower level and one for the building itself somewhere outside the picture to the lower right. The curve in the cobbles and the left-hand pavement of the Smedestraat relieves the almost overwhelming strong orthogonals. Nothing in this picture indicates a time of year, but the strong light of morning suggests a chilly day.

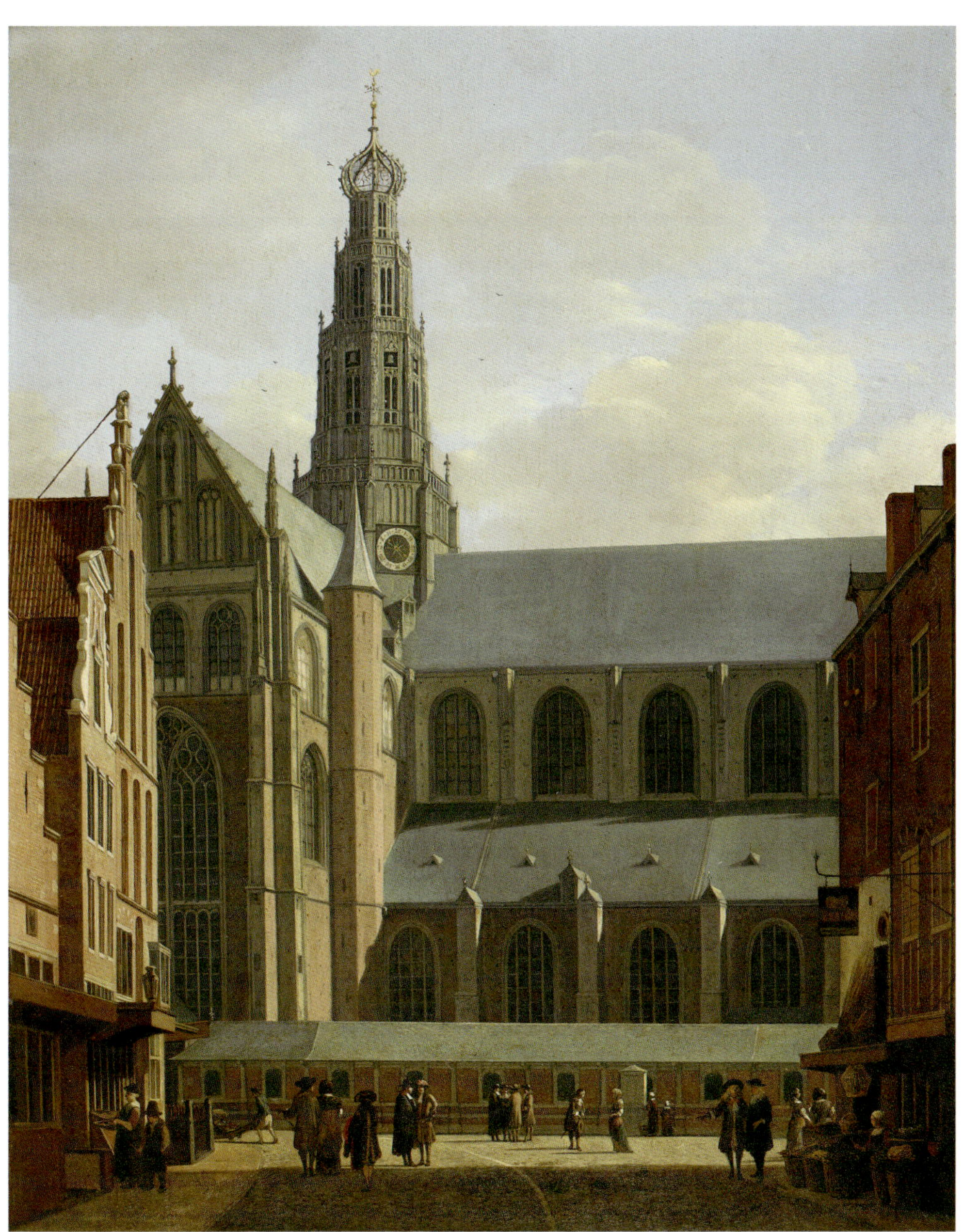

62

EMANUEL DE WITTE
Alkmar 1616/18–1692 Amsterdam

Interior of an imaginary Protestant Gothic church

Oil on canvas, 36.5 × 30.5 cm
Sutton no. 82

Complementing the portrait of a great Dutch Gothic church hanging above
it, this view, though described as imaginary, is in fact based on the thirteenth-
century Oude Kerk in Amsterdam. Dateable therefore to after 1652, when de Witte
moved there from Delft, the distinctive capitals with a wooden barrel vault are
drawn with some accuracy. The dedication of the church to St Nicholas of Bari,
whose relics were saved by South Italian sailors, is reflected in the ship depicted in
the stained-glass roundel of the window. (St Nicolas, patron saint of sailors, was a
suitable dedication in a great seaport like Amsterdam.) The position of the massive
organ on the right is also taken from the Oude Kerk, though in reality it is far
more elaborate and sculptural, while the bases of the piers – painted by de Witte
as black, adding to the sombre tone of the scene – are in fact pale stone. The light
falling from the right, or northern, side would have been impossible. A diamond-
shaped hatchment with the arms of a lady is presumably related to a grave at the
foot of the pier on which it hangs. One of the graves has been opened and a skull
left beside a mound of earth and a gravedigger's wheelbarrow. On the opposite
side of the aisle another memorial records a soldier, whose helm and sword hang
above it.

De Witte, a poor businessman though a prolific and efficient artist, indentured
himself to a number of patrons in Delft and Amsterdam, for whom he produced
church interiors, portraits and genre scenes. His works have a distinctive style and
have always been popular. De Witte was, nevertheless, a difficult and melancholic
character: he was constantly at loggerheads with friends and neighbours, and
his wife was banned from the city for theft. During the bad winter of 1692, after a
dispute with his landlord, he attempted to hang himself but the rope broke and
he fell into a canal and drowned. His body was recovered only eleven weeks later,
after a thaw.

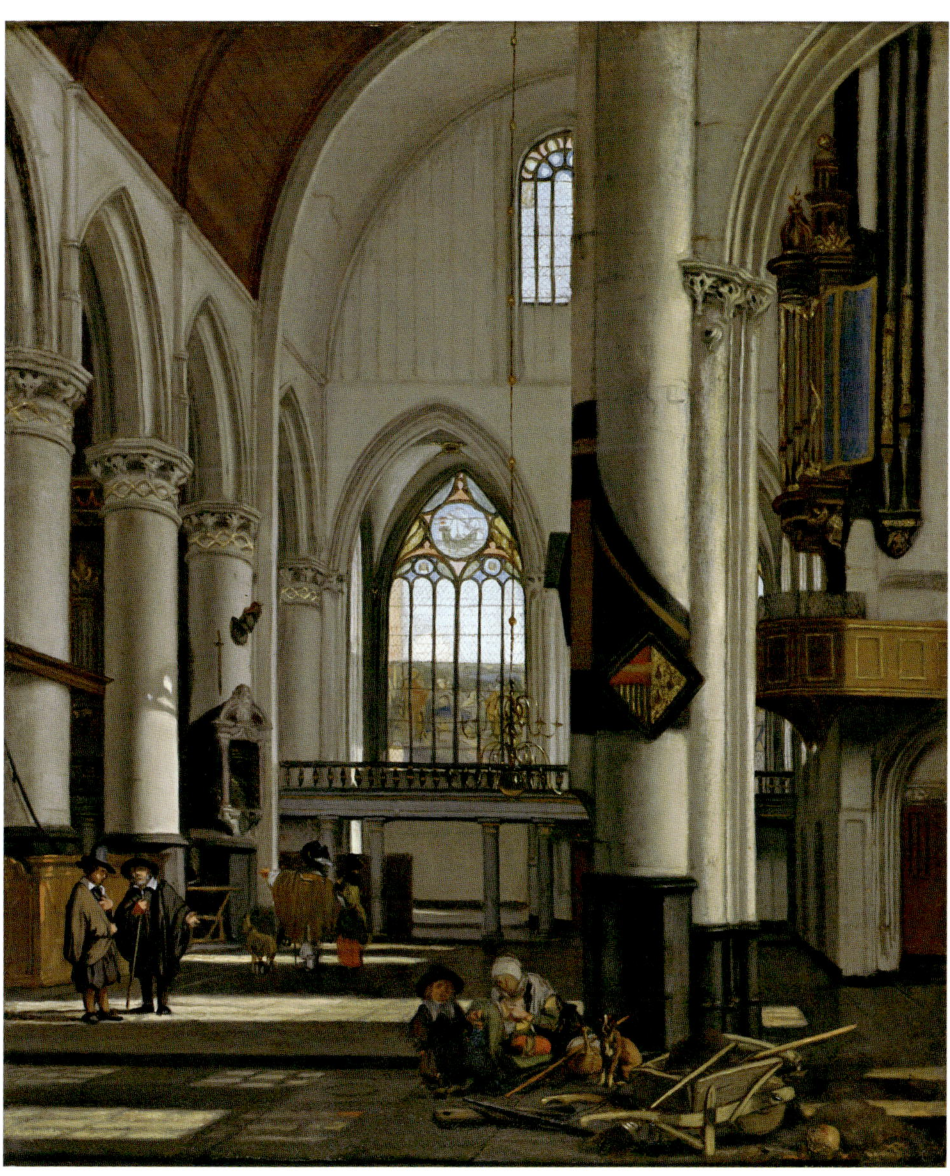

THE SOUTH DRAWING ROOM

Like a mirror image of the North Drawing Room in size and dimensions, here one long wall again provides ample room for a dense hang of the Samuel collection paintings. On the walls flanking the doors smaller, narrow spaces provide for closely related pictures to be hung: on the left the two scenes of Brazil by Frans Post, and on the right two of the finest Dutch architectural works in the collection, by Jan van der Heyden and Gerrit Berckheyde. The arrangement on the long wall is dominated by the monumental panorama by Philips Koninck, a pupil of Rembrandt. It is flanked by a beautiful Meindert Hobbema on the left and a tonal river scene by Jan van Goyen on the right, both significant examples of developments in landscape painting in the Netherlands in the seventeenth century.

The carved white marble fireplace was made by William Daniels in 1822, when these rooms were remodelled, to match the one by John Gilbert of c. 1750 facing it at the other end of the North Drawing Room.

Return to the Salon and turn right into the Salon Vestibule (Passage Room)

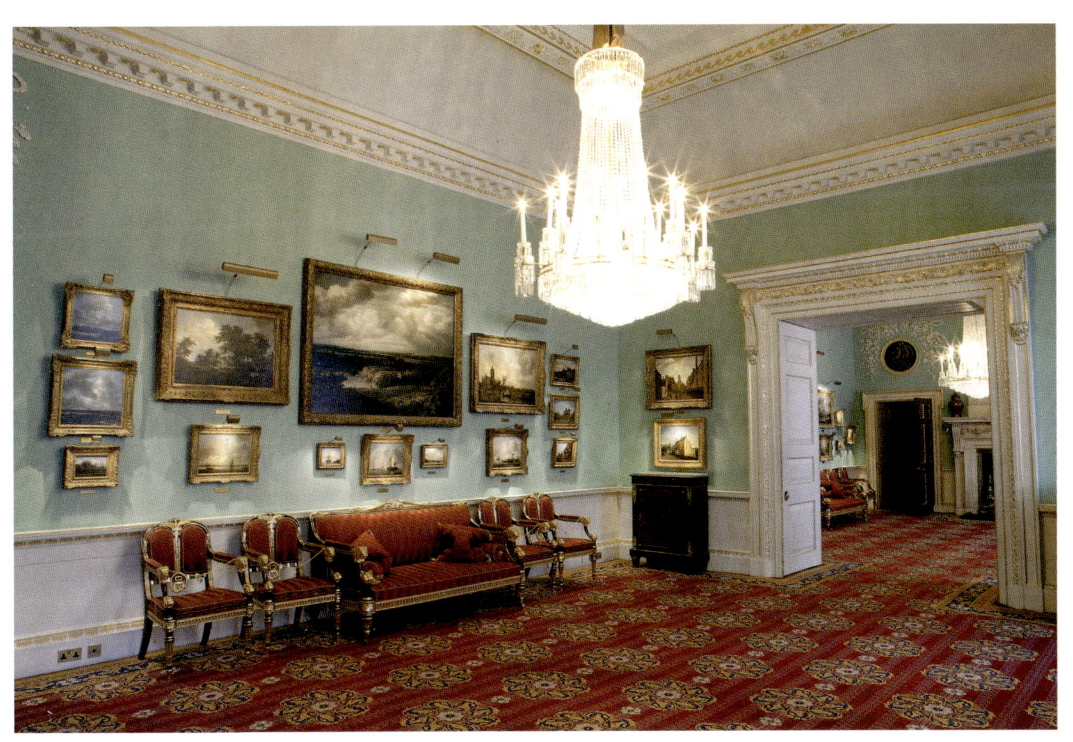

63

FRANS POST
Haarlem 1612–1680

Brazilian landscape with native figures

Oil on panel, 48.3 × 61.5 cm, signed and dated 1666
Sutton no. 55

The construction of this picture – with tall trees framing the view on either side, the dark foreground giving way to a lighter middle ground, and a distant, atmospherically blue horizon – conforms to the principles of design seen in many contemporaneous landscapes in the Samuel collection. The exotic foliage, the figures of slaves and the large anteater and armadillo front left, however, tell us that we are not in Europe. The strong touches of blue on the foliage of the middle distance are unintentional. To create the deeply rich green of the lush tropical vegetation, Post would have mixed ultramarine blue with yellow-lake. Over time the yellow-lake has become fugitive, leaving only the ultramarine.

In 1636 Post accompanied Count Johan-Maurits of Nassau-Seigen to Brazil, where he spent eight years as an official artist. The Count was to be Governor-General of the Dutch West Indies Company for a large coastal area round Recife, formerly held by the Portuguese. Aiming to revive the valuable sugar industry, he built a new settlement called Mauritsstad – designed by the architect Pieter Post, Frans's brother and teacher – on the north-east coast. The venture ultimately ended in failure when the colony was ceded back to Portugal in 1661. Having returned to Holland in 1644, Post spent the rest of his long life painting scenes of South America, usually small in scale and horizontal in format, scenes that were immensely popular, despite being slightly dry, formulaic and repetitive.

The town seen in the distance is probably Ingaraçú, where the Church of São Cosme e Damião was founded by the Portuguese in 1535 alongside the Franciscan monastery of São Antonio. It was captured and looted by the Dutch in 1632, which accounts for the ruinous state of several buildings depicted. The slaves and a single European in the foreground, dressed in a mixture of foreign and native fashions, are seemingly oblivious to the large mammals nearby.

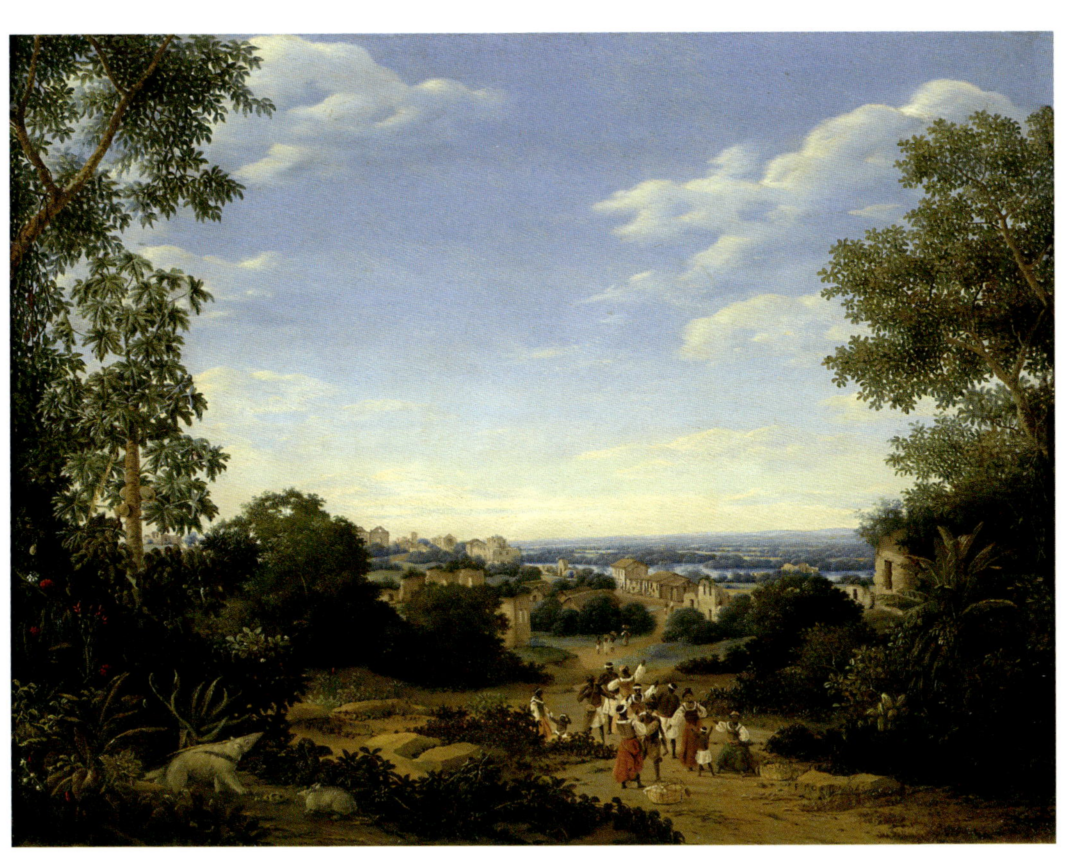

64

FRANS POST
Haarlem 1612–1680

Brazilian village with buildings and native figures

Oil on panel, 49.9 × 69 cm, signed and dated 1643 or 1645
Sutton no. 54

The date is difficult to read. It could either be one of the very rare paintings actually done by Frans Post while in Brazil or it could be among those painted soon after his return to Haarlem. Either way, it is certainly one of the earliest landscapes of South America. All the surviving works that date from Post's stay in Brazil, only seven in number, are from 1637 to 1640: nothing survives from his last four years. This early work still exudes the simplicity, if not naïvety, of the primitive settlements he encountered. This was to dissipate gradually as he matured and improved in style and technique, back amongst the artistic community of Haarlem. He continued to paint views of Brazil for the rest of his life, but the later works lack the frankness and vividness of his first encounters with both landscapes and peoples new to him.

As part of the scientific entourage of the governor, Count Johan-Maurits of Nassau-Seigen, Post was accompanied by fellow-artist Albert van der Eckhout, who was responsible for painting portraits of the indigenous peoples, their dress and material objects, as well as still lifes of exotic fruits and flowers. Post, charged with recording the landscape, besides taking views of recognizable topographical features, also painted what appear to be generic views of everyday rural life, like the present scene.

The European-style plantation house, standing on a ridge with a view of distant plains, has a tiled and hipped roof and a sheltered veranda to catch both view and breeze. Dozens of black slaves congregate in the open space before it, some seated round what appears to be a meal spread out on the ground, while others, to the right, some dressed in European-style costume, dance to the rhythm of drums. While Eckhout portrayed the indigenous people of the colony, Post showed the slave population, originally brought to South America by the Portuguese to work on the sugar plantations.

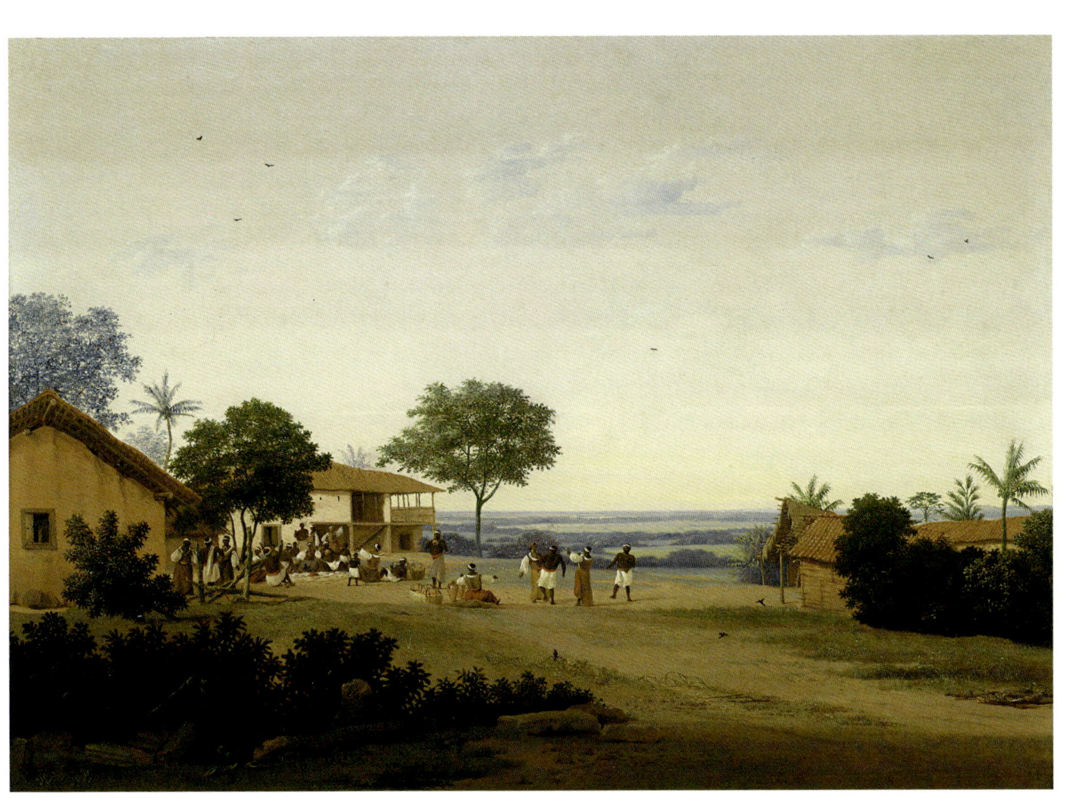

65

JACOB ISAACKSZ VAN RUISDAEL
Haarlem? 1628/29–1682 Haarlem

Landscape with cornfields

Oil on canvas, 35.6 × 33.4 cm, signed
Sutton no. 58

The low viewpoint adopted by Ruisdael did not leave a great deal of space to depict the extensive landscape. Deceptively simple, nevertheless it is packed with a variety of features as a foil to the towering cumulus clouds, grey against the brilliant blue, stretching away into the distance. The road to the right curves round and over the gently undulating ground, skirting the golden wheatfield bathed in sunlight. Forming a *coulisse*, this wedge-shaped diagonal of light thrusts into the heart of the landscape and contrasts with the crisp blue pond in which the strong horizontal of the far wooded bank and red-brick church tower are reflected. This strong horizontal feature, relieved by the church and the white-sailed windmill, is set against a double backdrop of low wooded hills and the distant ridge to the far right, painted atmospheric blue. The monumental landscape of dark and light, near and far, empty and full, has a point of interest and focus in the red jacket of a traveller on the road. The tall tree on the far left and the tip of the church steeple just breaking the horizon add depth.

Though typically both generic and exaggerated, Ruisdael's view is based on reality. The square church tower with a small steeple can be identified as that of the town of Eemnes in the province of Utrecht, where weak dykes often caused flooding and permanent pools, called *waaien*, to form. The wheat crop, which allowed Ruisdael to create a light contrast with the water, green meadows and darker woods, was in fact rarely grown in the Low Countries.

The work was treated harshly in restoration and, when a new canvas was attached to the back, pressure was applied to stick the two canvases together. The paint film pressed into the canvas resulting in the weave becoming visible on the surface and exacerbating surface wear.

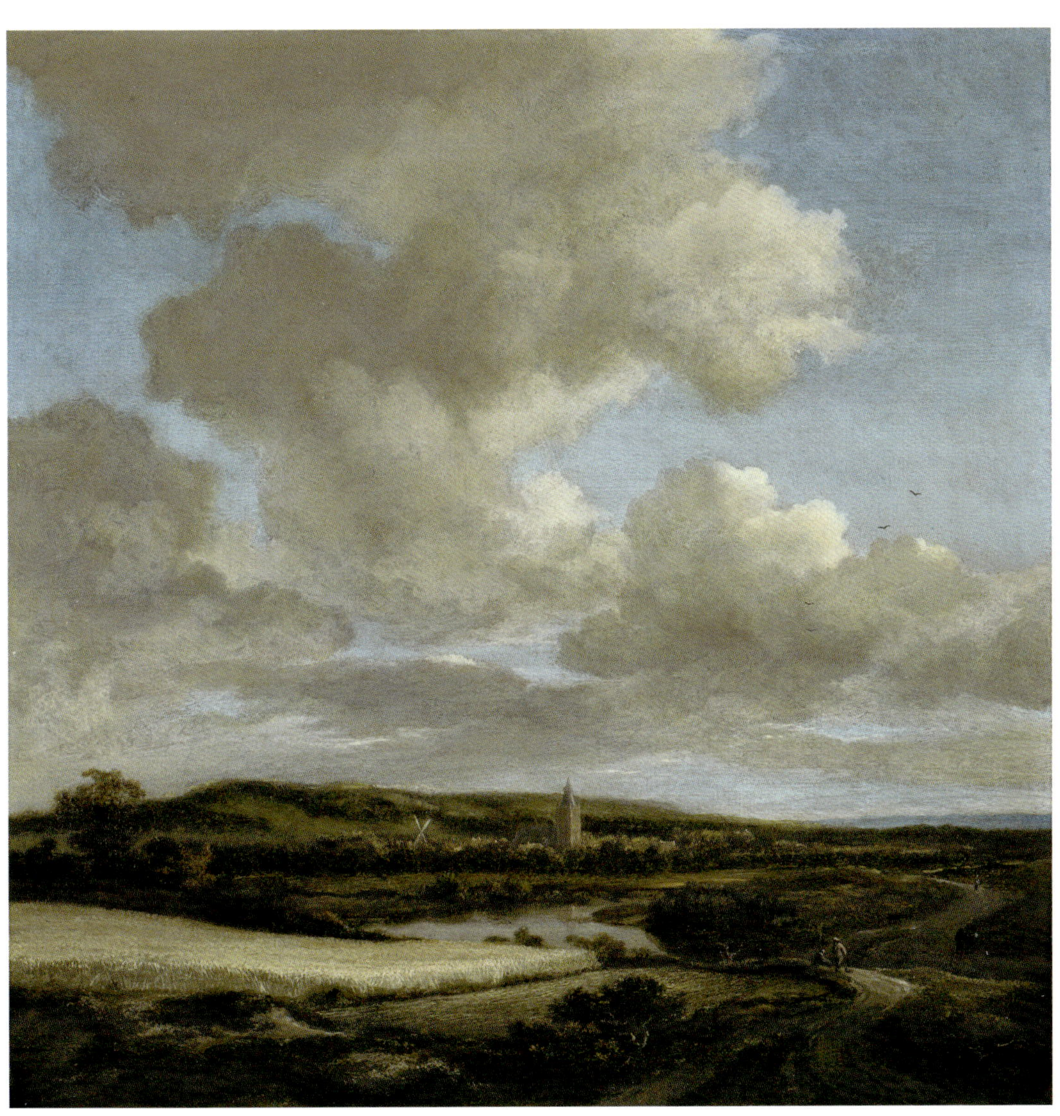

66

JACOB ISAACKSZ VAN RUISDAEL
Haarlem? 1628/29–1682 Haarlem

Panoramic view of Haarlem

Oil on canvas, 43.2 × 41.9 cm, signed
Sutton no. 59

An upright format was one of Ruisdael's chief contributions to the development
of landscape painting in the Low Countries in the second half of the seventeenth
century. His distant views of Haarlem – described as '*Haarlempjes*', or 'little views
of Haarlem' – are seldom dated, but attempts have been made to order them
chronologically on stylistic grounds. This work, a masterpiece of both the genre
and the artist, was probably painted about 1670. On the blue horizon is the Zuider
Zee, so we are seeing Haarlem and the vast St Bavo's Church from the south-west.
The high viewpoint gives a commanding prospect, which has become more a
portrait of the sky than an apparently realistic representation of a great Dutch
city. Ruisdael again exhibits a masterful pictorial organization with a scrupulous
attention to natural phenomena.

The foreground is composed of distinct but subtly coloured diagonals of sandy
heath and woods, with the clouds covering the plain between the foreground and
the distant city with alternating wedges of sunlight and shade. Light falls on the
tops of the near-distance trees, linking the passage of dark to light with immense
sophistication. The deep cerulean blue of the far horizon acts as a stop to the
land itself and as a foil for the bulky church and the spire of the Bakenesserkerk
and the Klokhuis tower to the left and the spire of the Nieuwe Kirk to the right.
We know the elements of St Bavo's from Berckheyde's portrait of it, also in the
Samuel collection (no. 61). Here we see it from afar but in enough detail to make
out the traceried windows. Light falls on the folded sails of windmills and the
red-brick gables of the city's houses, minute in scale but evocative of distance
and atmosphere. But it is the sky, so apparently simple but accurately untamed
– unlike the cultivated landscape below – that is the glory of this work. With the
clouds acting as a moving machine for casting light, Ruisdael captures a single,
splendid moment in time.

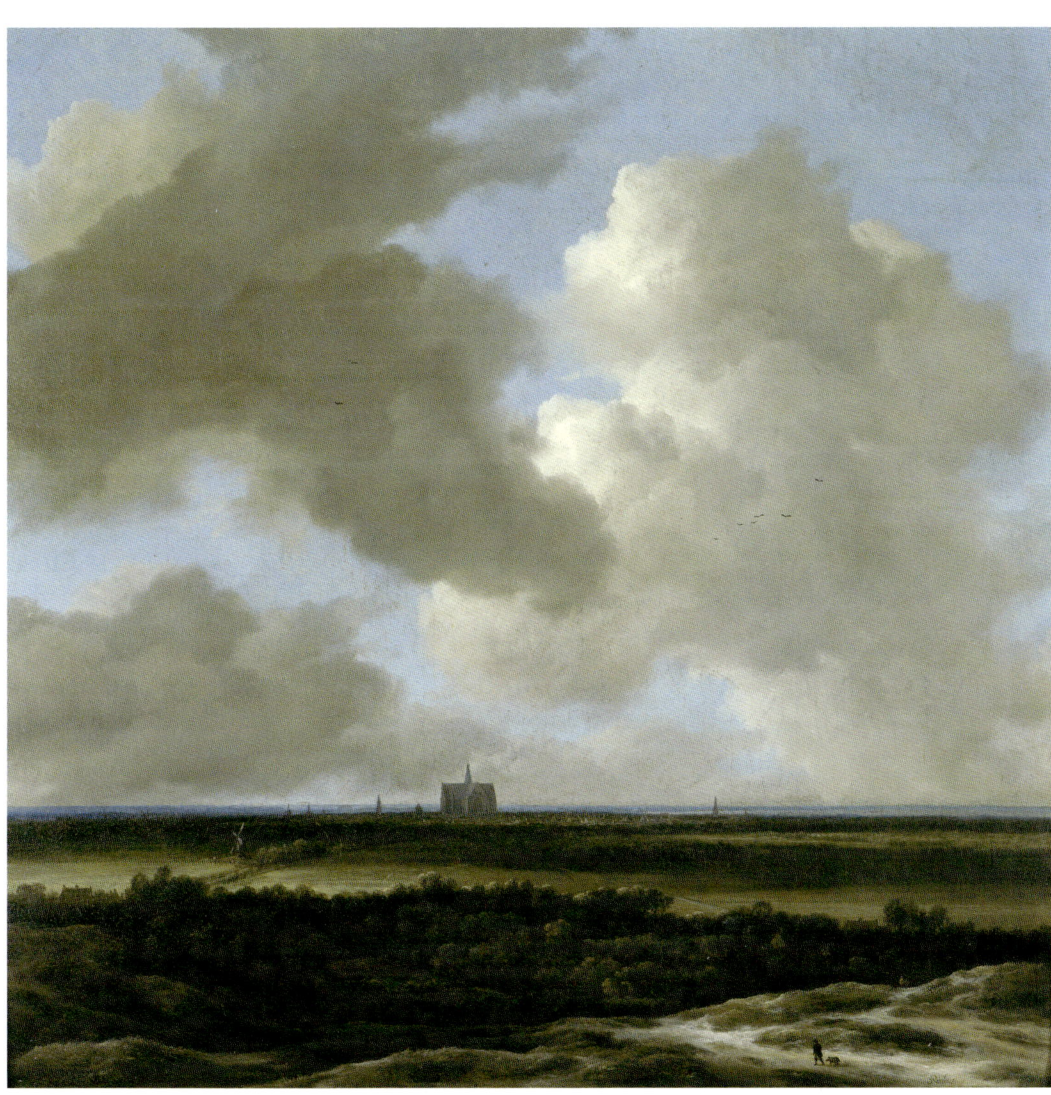

JAN VAN DER HEYDEN
Gorinchem 1637–1712 Amsterdam

A wooded landscape with figures

Oil on panel, 16.2 × 21 cm
Sutton no. 31

Despite its tiny size and apparent simplicity, this landscape is packed with incident and detail. Better known as a painter of cityscapes, van der Heyden extended his range to views of country estates, sometimes with elements of pure landscape. He included trees, despite their intrusion on views of the buildings or streets he was depicting. (Gerrit Berckheyde often excluded them to reveal the buildings completely.) Adriaen van de Velde was often asked to provide 'staffage' for van de Heyden but not in this case, where the figures add to the composition but do not dominate and are by the same hand as the landscape.

On a slight bank that leads into the picture from the right sits a man resting on a staff in conversation with a woman carrying a basket. Further to the left a boy appears to be kneeling to collect mushrooms in his hat. The edge of a wood fills the background and a piece of water to the right is crossed by a wooden bridge. A man carrying faggots on his back and a strolling couple pass by. The skill van de Heyden exhibits in painting the meticulous details of his town scenes – individual bricks and delicate shading of water, stone and wood – is clearly evident in this work, where the grasses of the shady bank, the bark of the tree trunks and the fall of distant light in woods are all rendered with finesse and accuracy.

It has been suggested that the woods near The Hague are the setting for this scene. In 1645 a country house, designed by Pieter Post, elder brother of the artist Frans Post, was built there for the wife of the Stadholder Frederick William of Orange and named 'Huis ten Bosch' (House in the woods). These woods became a fashionable place for riding and recreation and were painted by several artists of the period, including Paulus Potter and Adriaen van de Velde.

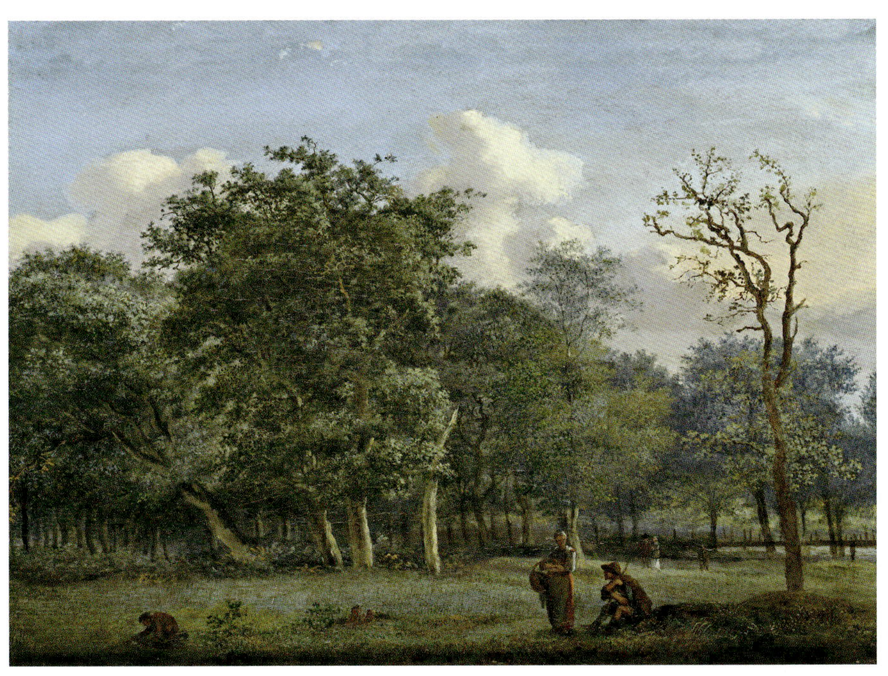

MEINDERT HOBBEMA
Amsterdam 1638–1709

Wooded landscape with the ruins of a house

Oil on panel, 60 × 84.5 cm, signed
Sutton no. 32

With this lush, romantic wooded vista, Dutch landscape painting in the Samuel collection reaches a conclusion. It has developed from simple representation of the canals and polders in summer and winter – Averkamp and van der Neer – to views of travellers and country pursuits or leisure – Brueghel and Cuyp. Gradually the inspiration of nature becomes more important than the figures, and simplicity in design and colouring won through – van Goyen and Jacob van Ruisdael. Now, at the end of the seventeenth century, Hobbema, pupil and friend of Ruisdael, paints landscapes of great depth, strongly coloured, in balanced compositions in a style that is instantly recognizable. Hobbema's influence was long lasting, particularly on the works of British artists like Gainsborough and on French nineteenth-century landscapists of the Barbizon school.

Directional points of interest have multiplied. The angles of recession through the water and the woods towards these points have become more sophisticated. The eye is led left and right, from the reeded banks and the ruined brick house in the foreground, through the darkened middleground of dramatic, writhing trees towards the sun-lit front of the distant cottage, across the little bridge reflected in the still water. To the left the focus point of a red skirt on a woman walking with a man and child leads the eye to a distant blue horizon. On the farthest right a church spire vies for attention above the tree-tops. These contrasting changes of direction, leading backwards and forwards across the picture surface, creates a multitude of vignettes in what appears to be a cohesive and unified composition.

Hobbema's mastery of landscape is reflected in the ease with which he peoples his apparently quiet rustic idylls. There are eight figures in all: a man in red fishes, another strolls away on the far left, a third crosses the foot-bridge and a woman sweeps before the cottage. In the left distance a couple dressed in red are accompanied by a child, whilst on the far right a hatted man sits reading or sketching – the artist?

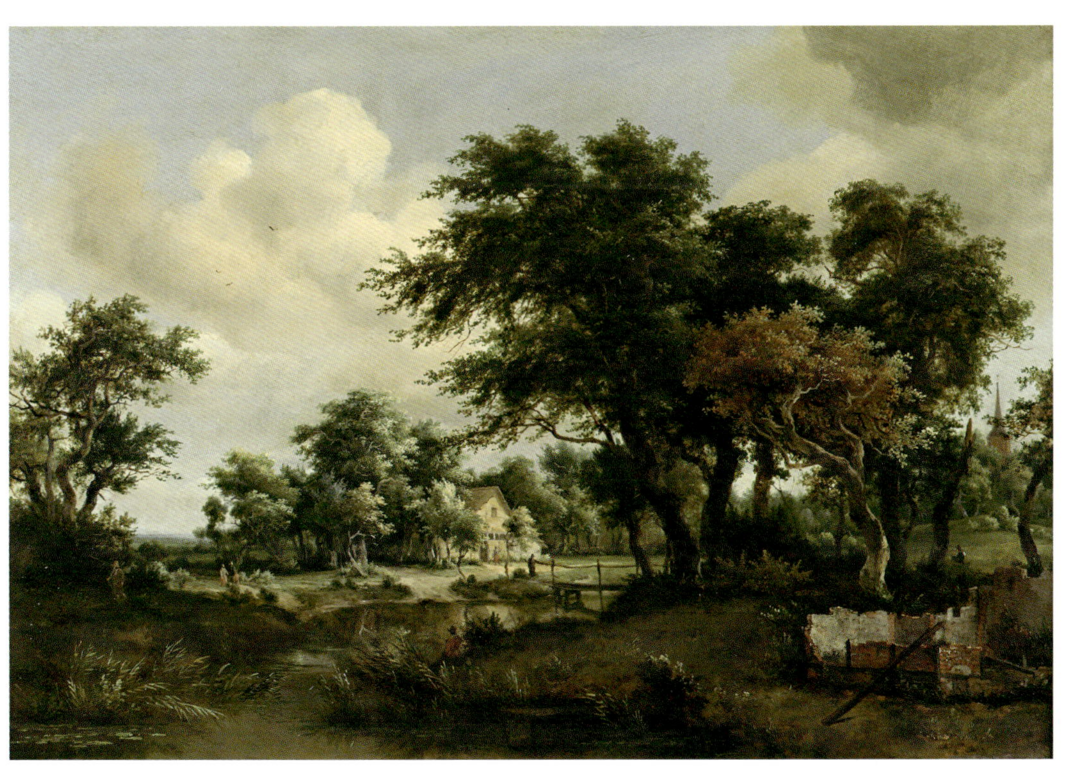

69

JAN VAN GOYEN
Leiden 1596–1656 The Hague

An estuary with boats

Oil on panel, 31.9 × 42.3cm, signed and dated 165(?)
Sutton no. 23

This is a tone poem. With limited colour but rich accents, van Goyen has captured the feeling of an unpromising subject, the muddy estuary of a Dutch river on a cloudy day. A light breeze ruffles the reflecting water and barely fills the sails or lifts the flags of the flat-bottomed *smalschips*, Dutch coastal vessels. The low viewpoint and the large expanse of water in the foreground dramatically limits the area in which depth can be created. The rowing-boat, filled with drably clad figures, moves quietly across the scene towards the prospect of land by the wooden posts of a ruined breakwater on the right. A range of buildings, windmills and navigation posts sit on the spits of land on the horizon, receding in shades of grey and cream. Mirrored by the heavy clouds that break here and there to reveal a blue sky, they contribute to the feeling of calm reflection. Smoke rising from a brilliant stab of flames on the nearest strip of land adds a tiny touch of brightness and focus.

Jan van Goyen was a master of understatement in the depiction of his homeland. His friends and family were artists, like Salomon van Ruysdael and son-in-law Jan Steen, so he was well acquainted with current artistic trends and developments in the mid-century period, when these tonal landscapes were so important. Prolific and by this late stage in his life fluent in technique, van Goyen applied quick brushstrokes with assurance and confidence. He understood the moods of wind and water and, though his subjects are quotidian, his skill was to present the mundane as beautiful, never more so than here.

Dutch artists rarely if ever painted out of doors, directly in front of their subjects, but van Goyen is known to have made hundreds of drawings *in situ* for use in his studio. His skill in mastering the effects of light on muddy water, the reflections of clouds and sky, are all the more remarkable for having been done from observant memory.

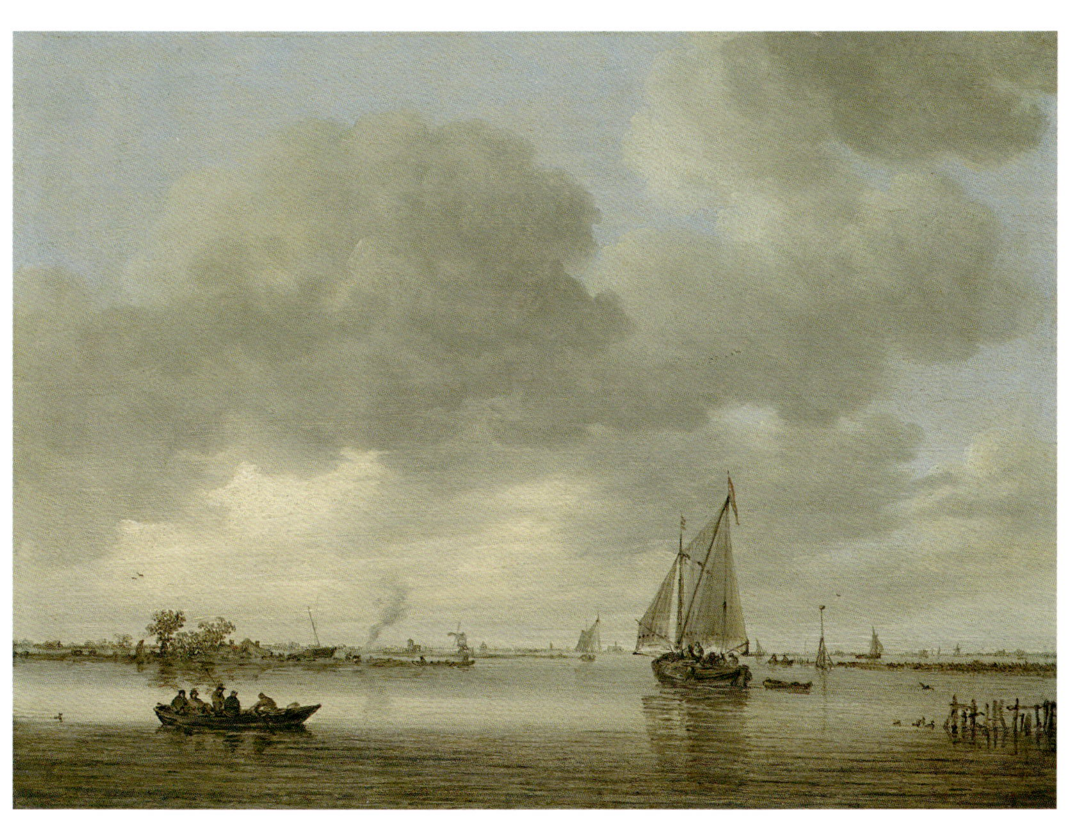

70

PHILIPS KONINCK
Amsterdam 1619–1688

Panoramic landscape

Oil on canvas, 132 × 168.5 cm, signed
Sutton no. 36

The influence of Rembrandt, evident in the broad brushstrokes, sombre golden-brown tonality and grand sweeping composition, is unsurprising considering Koninck is believed to have studied in the master's studio in the early 1650s. Son and brother of Amsterdam artists, Koninck is also known to have painted portraits and low-life genre scenes, but it is large-scale panoramas for which he is most famous, this being a fine example. Like Salomon van Ruysdael and Meindert Hobbema, he repeated compositions making only elemental and meteorological changes. Koninck's repertoire, though fixed, was an endlessly imaginative theme of space, seen from a high viewpoint, of shaded landscapes sent off to a vast, almost limitless horizon.

The foreground, already some distance from the viewer, shows a track running diagonal to the picture plane across a sandy heath, turning sharply towards a neoclassical mansion with a tall cupola lying in a wood below. Tiny figures, incidental to the scene but necessary for scale, are shown on the road and beside the water. Bathed in sunlight that pours through the wind-torn clouds, the piece of water before the house reflects the grey-blue sky. More buildings are revealed in the middle distance. The view recedes to reveal a river, possibly intended to be the Rhine, meandering into a distance of low, sunlit hills, where rain clouds fuse with the horizon. Koninck rarely identified specific locations but used quintessentially Dutch geographical features from the northern part of the western province of Gelderland, called Veluwe, where thick pine forests grow on sandy dunes, some reaching over 300 ft in height.

Broadly painted, with golden tones and skilled use of perspectival atmosphere to achieve the effect of panoramic distance, this work must date early in Koninck's best period, roughly 1654 to 1665. His output fell considerably thereafter. He is known to have had significant business interests, notably the ownership of the inland shipping line between Amsterdam and Rotterdam, that may well have diverted his attention from painting.

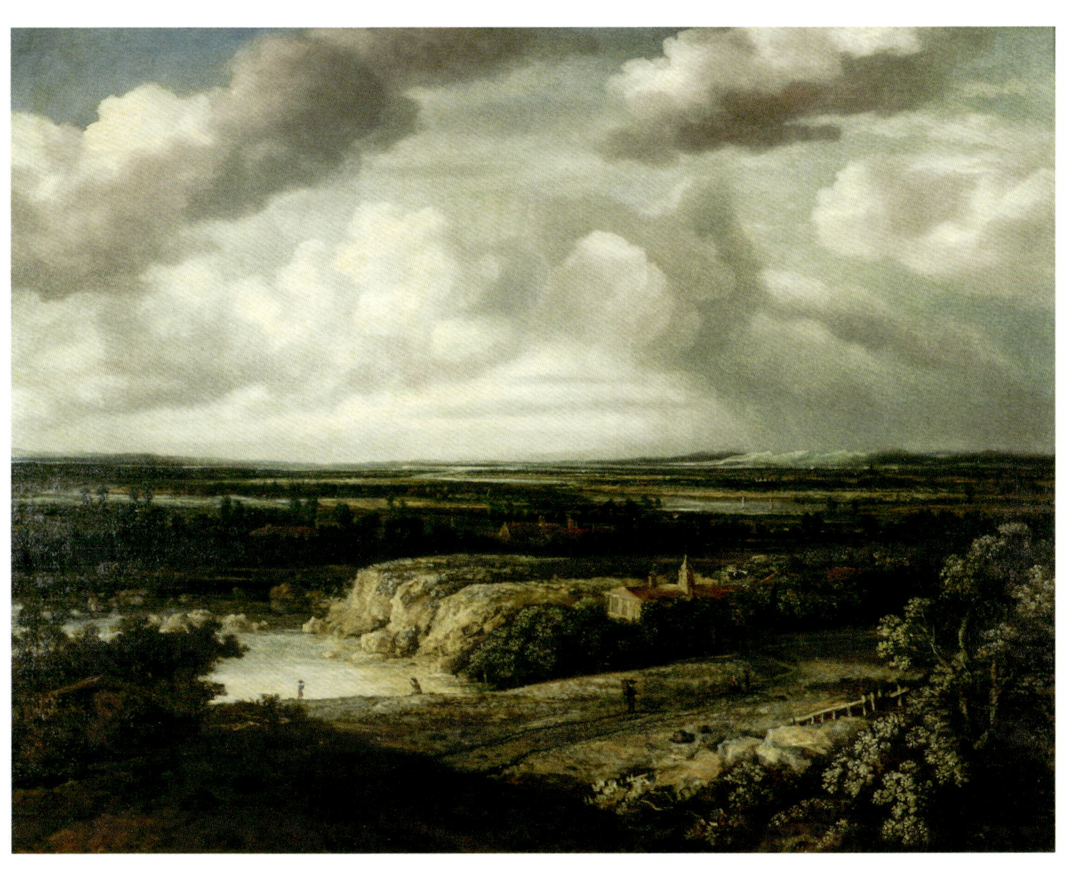

71

Studio of WILLEM VAN DE VELDE THE YOUNGER
Leiden 1633–1707 London

Two smalschips off the end of a pier

Oil on panel, 16.4 × 19.6 cm
Sutton no. 80

The Samuel collection contains several types of Dutch land and seascape painting. There is an excellent group of views of identifiable towns or buildings, almost portrait landscapes; there are the generic landscapes, which suggest to the viewer well-recognized topographical features – canals, dunes, woods, a distant tower or church – and which became increasingly specific by time of year or day as the century progressed; and a third type, like the views of Willem van de Velde, which are instantly recognizable as Dutch, but without any specific feature at all – seasides, ships, figure groups, spits of sand, the feel of a northern sky – identifiable landscape by association.

Here, well-dressed gentlemen awaiting transport on the jetty are respectfully addressed by a man on the right, who has removed his hat. A wherry or in-shore rowing boat draws up to the jetty. Two *smalschips* rest at anchor, the tide being out and the shore therefore visible at the jetty's foot. It is hard to tell whether the artist intended the horizon to be obscured by a hazy atmosphere or if the poor condition of the panel, combined with the studio workmanship, has rendered it barely visible over time.

The painting was bought as a work entirely by Willem van de Velde in the early 1960s, but Michael Robinson in his catalogue raisonné detected that it was an eighteenth-century copy of a 1660s work – competent and no doubt beautiful, but a copy nonetheless. It reflects the problems of connoisseurship faced by scholars, collectors and curators that only direct observation, repeated experiences and continual comparisons can address. It matters a great deal that we are not looking at the work of the master's hand, as that would show his ability, his understanding of the subject, skill in composition and mastery of the techniques of painting. Instead we learn an interesting but salutary lesson on workshop practice and gain valuable insight into the creative process.

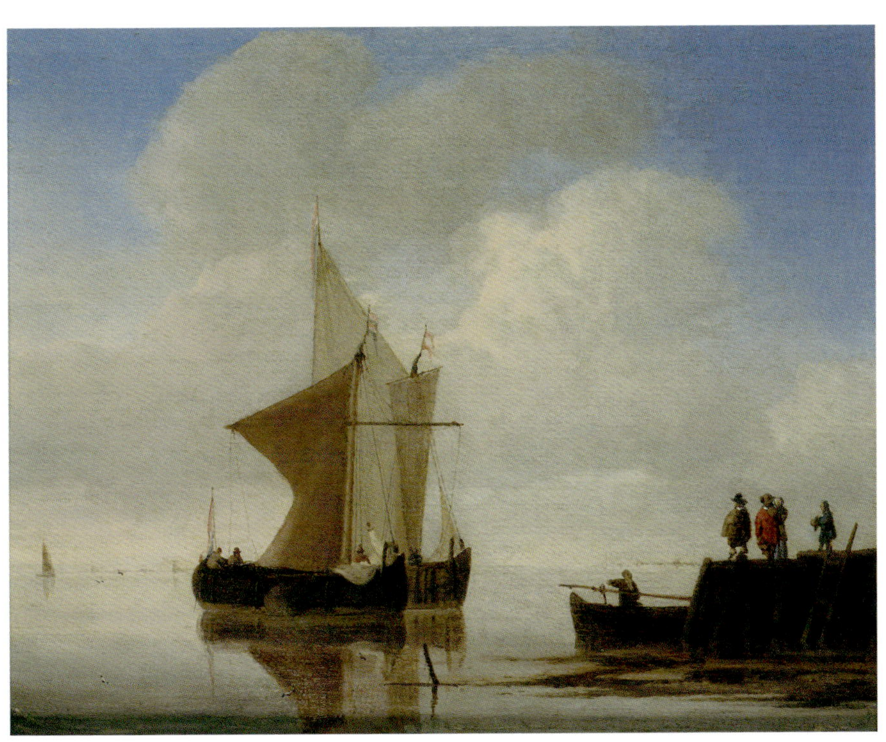

72

WILLEM VAN DE VELDE THE YOUNGER
Leiden 1633–1707 London

A kaag anchored by a sandbank with two other vessels

Oil on canvas, 33 × 39.2 cm, signed
Sutton no. 78

Michael Robinson, in his authoritative two-volume work on the van de Veldes, described this work as "painted probably by the Younger for the Van de Velde studio, c. 1660". This typifies the problems of over-analysis and the difficulty in describing the author of a work without fully explaining what an artist's studio comprised and how labour was divided or supervised. Robinson only very briefly notes that the Younger's son Cornelis was "the most important member" of his father's studio. This is the full extent of any discussion of the van de Velde's studio practice. As Cornelis is recorded as being active from c. 1675, this work cannot be by his hand. Robinson's dislike of the "uninteresting" juxtaposition of sails is a personal aesthetic judgement, but he also queries the form of the distant ship seen broadside in the left distance, regarding it as too long and low for a work of the 1660s. It is on details such as these Robinson relegated this work to 'attributed' status. As the van de Veldes reportedly had a keen eye for detail and would never have committed such apparent solecisms themselves, it strikes the intelligent viewer as strange that they would have had such lax approach to their studio assistants' work.

Despite these apparent problems, this depiction of a cluster of small ships and boats becalmed by a sandbank has the distinctive charm of van de Velde's well-spaced compositions, and the subtle positioning of ships at a distance to one another rings true to life and observation. Depth on a calm sea, with the horizon barely distinguishable, is excellently described. Flags and sails hang limp, the vessel approaching the sandbank only just finding enough wind to move, while the grey cumulus clouds build up, suggesting a change in the weather and forming the perfect foil for the group of cream and brown sails. The subtlety of the colouring, of wood and water, canvases and their reflections, surely denotes the hand of a master?

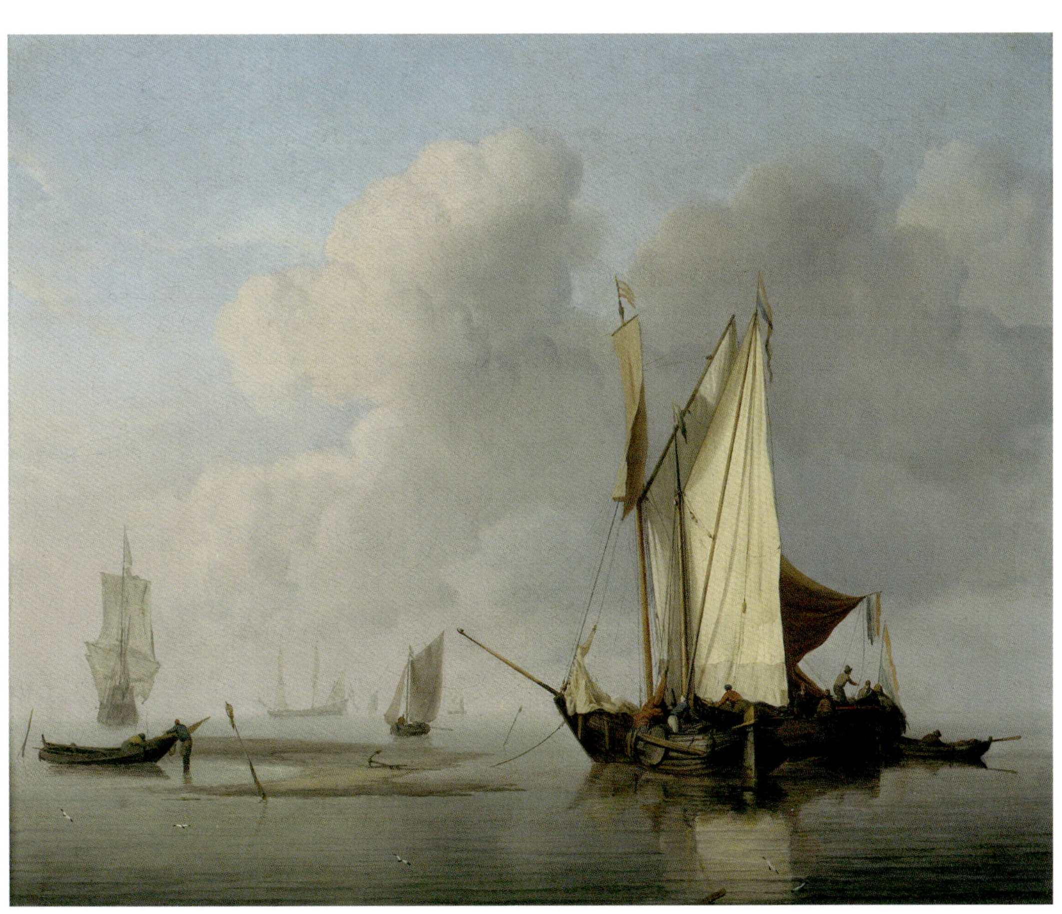

73

WILLEM VAN DE VELDE THE YOUNGER
Leiden 1633–1707 London

A weyschuit coming ashore near Den Helder

Oil on panel, 15.4 × 23.7 cm, signed
Sutton no. 76

Dating from *c.* 1650, when the younger Willem van de Velde was at work in
Amsterdam, the work is set at Den Helder, the northernmost point of the
province of Holland on the strait between the mainland and the island of Texel,
making the entrance to the inland sea leading down to Amsterdam. The small,
coastal, passenger vessel, a *weyschuit*, has drawn in close to shore at low tide and
the travellers are unceremoniously carried ashore. The quantity and size of the
shipping off-shore testifies to the busy traffic through the narrow waterway.
The high sterns of the two larger ships confirm the date to the mid seventeenth
century. Only the faintest breeze stirs the Dutch flag on the ship's boat that is
pulling toward the break in the sea-wall that leads up to a distant building.

Van de Velde was the master of atmospheric seascapes. The low horizon here
gives ample scope to depict the billowing cloud formations, deep grey at top
right, artfully mirroring the solidity of the high sea-wall secured with piles in
the opposite corner. The wall and bank cross the picture as a form of *coulisse*, with
alternating light sand and dark piles reflecting in the water and mirroring the
shadows cast by the darkening clouds above. Out to sea the damp atmosphere of
impending rain is brilliantly conveyed. Though there are at least twenty figures
and fourteen vessels of one sort or another, the impression is of a lonely and
desolate spot.

The condition of this picture is generally very good. However, the finer details,
usually painted in last and with the greatest delicacy and refinement, are the
first to suffer, both from wear with time and poor restoration. The signature at
lower left in the form of angular letters that the artist used at this period has been
subsequently strengthened.

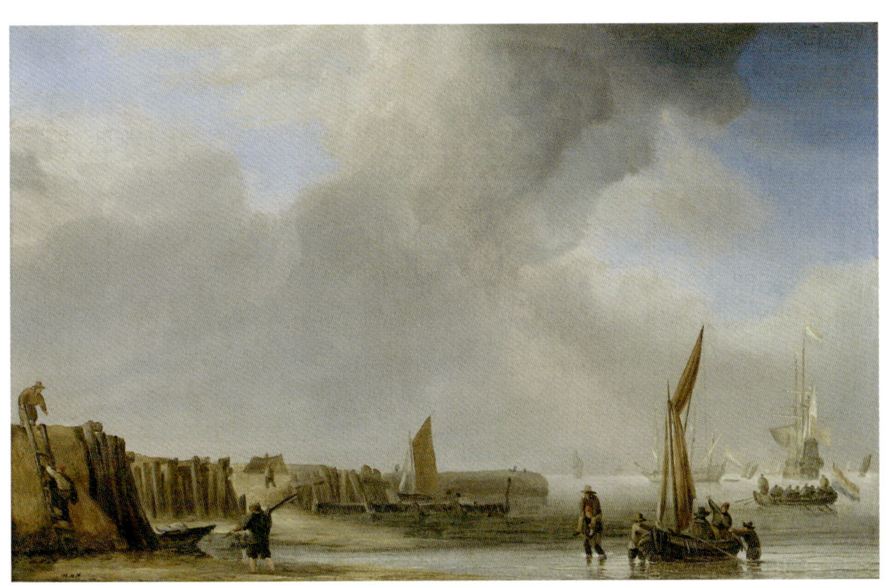

74

JAN VAN GOYEN
Leiden 1596–1656 The Hague

Hofstede Arnstein with Middleburg in the distance

Oil on panel, 64 × 89.5 cm, signed and dated 1646
Sutton no. 22

A recognizable scene is not rare in the oeuvre of van Goyen but for a building to take centre stage is unusual. The tower of the fortified manor house stands at the junction of two canals is the Hofstede Arnstein, which lies a mile or so east of Middleburg on the Walcheren peninsula in Zeeland, between the northern and southern arms of the River Scheldt. The castle, which was demolished in 1871, was built in the late sixteenth century for the family of Adriaen ten Haeff, one of the founders of the Dutch East Indian Company. Nearby, where the River Arne becomes a canal leading into Middleburg, there was also a toll-booth for shipping. The view shows the entrance from the Arne canal into the moat. This area of the Netherlands, in the far south, is protected from the encroachment of the sea by earthen dykes, here strengthened by brick walls around the castle that allow a bridge to cross. In the distance the distinctive tower of the town hall of Middleburg rises over the low-lying polders, with the squat Abdijtoren on the far right.

The work is painted in the fluid, almost sketchy manner of van Goyen's later period but the range of colours is still muted and distinctively tonal. The grey and creamy clouds, broken to reveal some blue sky, and the mellow greens of the trees and grassy sides of the dykes are reflected in the still water. Despite the russets and stronger reds of the brick buildings and the jacket of the fisherman in the foreground, the overall feeling is subdued and sedate. It is unlikely that van Goyen painted this as a commission for the castle's owners, but rather that he found it a picturesque setting with an interesting variety of materials – lead and tiled roofs, bricks and wood – set against the leafy trees and lush green of the polders. The figures must have been painted in last as they have become opaque with time, revealing the details of the landscape underneath.

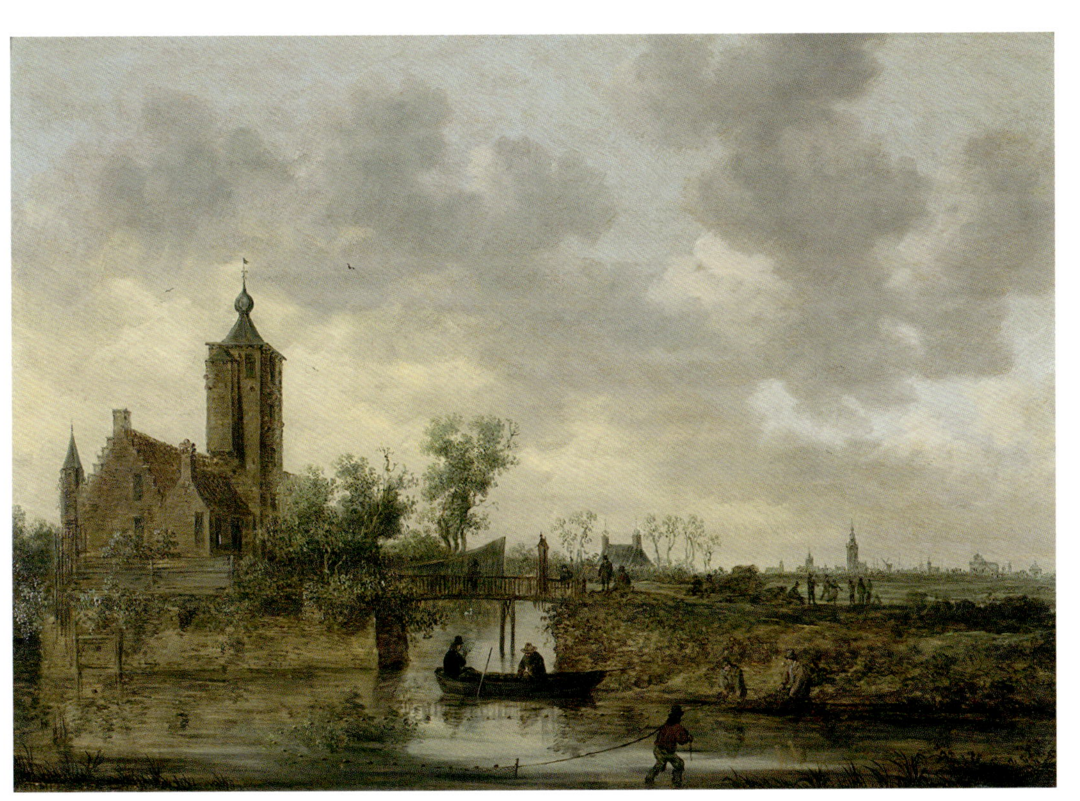

75

WILLEM VAN DE VELDE THE YOUNGER
Leiden 1633–1707 London

A kaag and a smalschip near the shore, with a ship firing a gun

Oil on panel, 35.4 × 44.7 cm, signed
Sutton no. 77

Deriving from landscape artists of the 1620s and 1630s, the techniques of balanced compositions and careful spatial arrangements transferred particularly well at the hands of the van de Veldes to marine views, and the Younger was at his very finest when painting calm waters filled with incidental shipping off the Dutch coast, as here.

The scene is set close to shore, where a group of small, coastal vessels have lowered their sails. They form a tight, pyramidal group, strongly coloured in browns, russets and creams, lit from the left. The strong verticals formed by the group of masts is relieved by elegant diagonals and horizontals made by the sprits of the two larger boats, a *kaag* and a *smalschip*, both light, Dutch coastal cargo vessels of the seventeenth century. There is a great deal of shipping behind them, receding into the distance. In fact, there are so many ships and boats that the horizon is all but completely obscured. A spit of sand entering from the right acts as a *coulisse* to create depth, breaking up the foreground.

The work, small in scale but large in scope, is painted on panel, allowing for a finely finished surface, particularly useful for painting the variety of reflections in the still water – white gun-smoke, dark hulls, the ochre sail of the small boat in the foreground and the piling cumulus clouds with patches of blue sky. A striking contrast is made between the delicate white and greys of the clouds and the stark white of the gun smoke of the large ship, seen almost head-on but slightly to the port bow, which has just fired a salute. Michael Robinson saw a defect in the bowsprit of this ship – it continues at the wrong angle under the furled jib sail – and he detected the hand of an assistant.

The overall effect of sun, sea and sky, populated with industrious sailors and naval ships defending Dutch prosperity, was popular in the Netherlands in the seventeenth century and has continued to be so ever since.

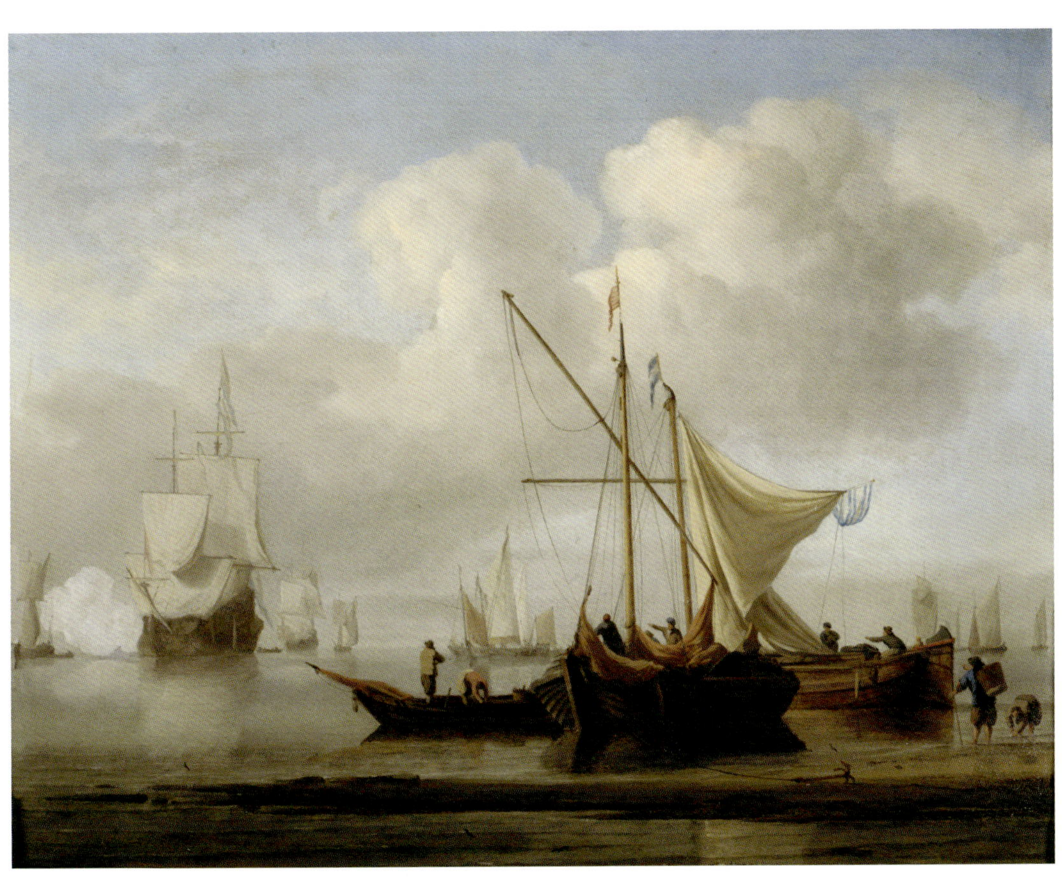

76

Follower of CORNELIS VROOM
c. 1591–1661

Cottage on a canal with a trekschuit

Oil on panel, 28.3 × 38.8 cm
Sutton no. 81

Though fairly undistinguished, this view of a canal is not set in wintertime and therefore helps to fill a small gap in the collection. Vroom, originally a marine artist like his father, gradually transferred his affections to a group of young Haarlem artists who pioneered a new and realistic landscape style. Anticipating the river-shore scenes of Salomon van Ruysdael and influential on the work of Jan van Goyen, Vroom's use of the dramatically lit diagonal *repoussoir* might have been the deciding feature in attributing this work to him when Lord Samuel bought it in 1969.

An anonymous drawing in Berlin, in which a large tree stands on the near bank to the left, has been identified as a preparatory study for this picture. In the painting, the tree has been painted over but is clearly visible, rising to the top of the picture, parallel to the *trekschuit's* mast. The drawing is not by Vroom but may be by one of a group of early seventeenth-century artists working in a similar style that include Esaias van den Velde, Anthonie van de Croos and Pieter Molijn.

An inland network of waterways, rivers and canals was vital to the Dutch economy and everyday life. The easiest and cheapest mode of transport was by small, low boats pulled by men from the bank. Heavily laden with baskets, barrels and passengers, the realistically depicted *trekschuit* casts its reflection in the still waters, passing two fishermen and a pair of goats on the near bank. The quality of the figure painting is poor and the composition, despite the removal of the large tree, is unsophisticated.

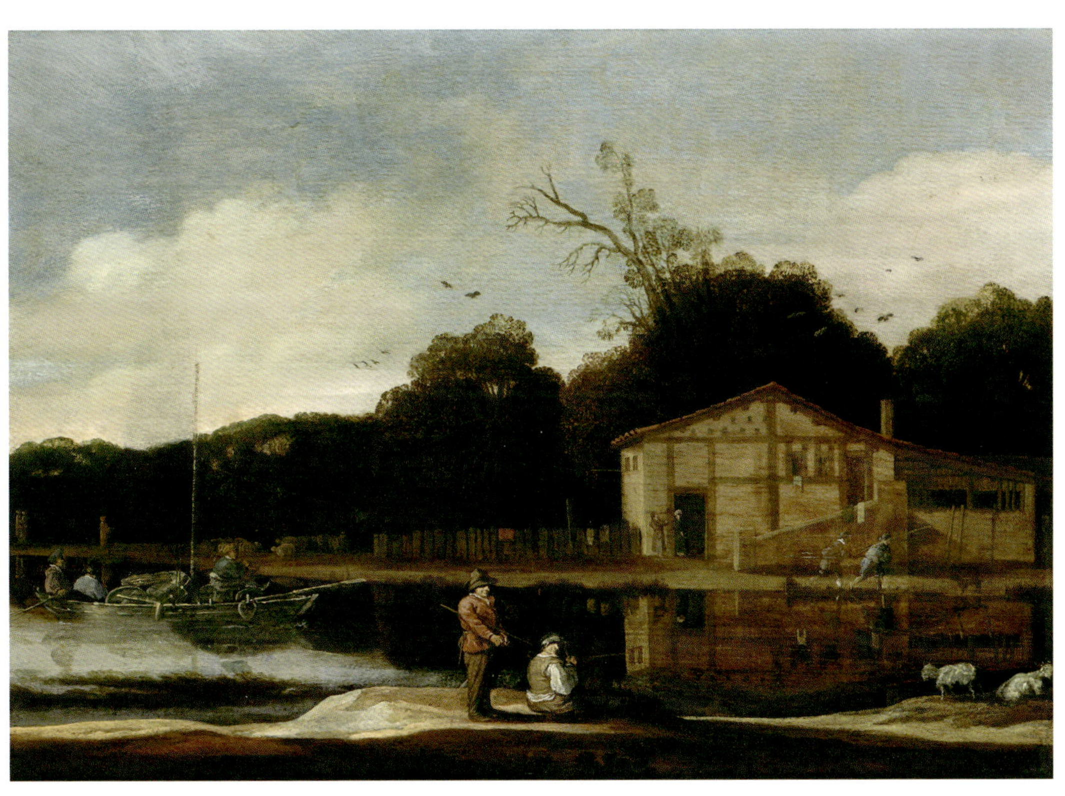

77

JAN VAN DER HEYDEN
Gorinchem 1637–1712 Amsterdam

Cityscape with a church and a square

Oil on metal, 29.5 × 39 cm
Sutton no. 28

Painted on a sheet of white metal, this is one of Jan van der Heyden's finest
works. Based on two dated views he did of the same church, loosely derived
from St Andreas in Düsseldorf, it was probably painted in 1666 or 1667. Van der
Heyden is known to have travelled up the Rhine to Kleves, Düsseldorf and as
far as Cologne in the spring of 1661, making detailed drawings so that he could
reproduce the scenes with imaginative exactitude later in his studio. The Jesuit
– now Dominican – church of St Andreas was built between 1622 and 1629 in the
transitional style from late German Renaissance to early Baroque. The building
is actually faced in plaster with comparatively simple stone detailing, but van
der Heyden has replaced the severe stucco of the original with brick and changed
the plain arched windows surmounted with *oculi* on the aisles with simple
rectangular ones. Dramatically, he has replaced the windows of the towers at
the eastern end with high Gothic lancets. The stucco sculptures of 1650 by two
young Jesuits, Johann Wolf and Johann Hoen, inside the church itself and still
in situ, have been faithfully reproduced but put outside the church. Furthermore,
the tablets, swags and wreaths, also by Wolf and Hoen, are taken directly from
the pulpit inside the church. He has placed a fanciful cupola, based on that of
Amsterdam town hall, on the western end of this embellished building.

The lucrative and distinguished career that van der Heyden had as an
entrepreneur and inventor in Amsterdam curtailed his artistic endeavours,
but this work – mastery of perspective, with its highly imaginative use of real
elements transposed, introduction of streets and buildings that gradually dissolve
towards a hazy vanishing point, all set against a brilliant, cerulean sky – show the
young artist in his prime. Few of his works surpass this one in technical skill or
imagination.

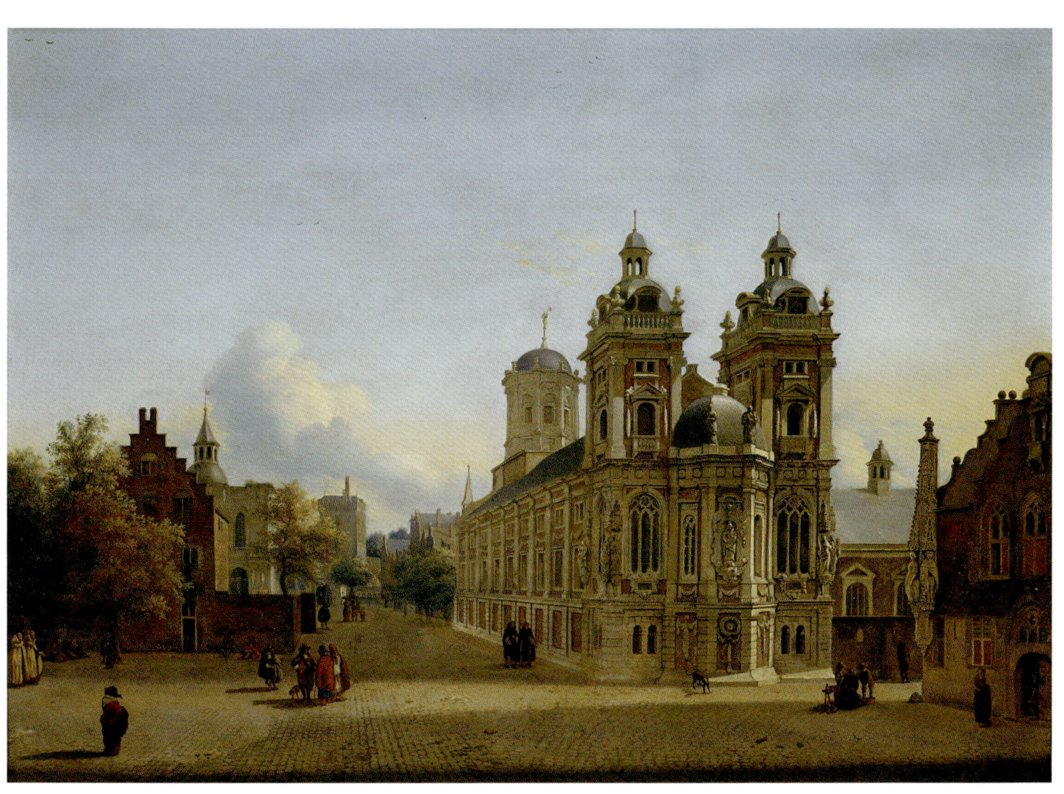

78

JAN VAN DER HEYDEN
Gorinchem 1637–1712 Amsterdam

The Wassertor, Kleves

Oil on panel, 23.7 × 29 cm
Sutton no. 29

After the signing of the Treaty of Münster in 1648, following decades of hostilities, Dutch landscape artists took the opportunity to travel, particularly up the Rhine. Ruisdael and his friend Berchem went as far as Bentheim and Aelbert Cuyp travelled this route as well. Before 1661 van der Heyden went up the river at least as far as Cologne, stopping at a number of port cities along the way. He is known to have made many drawings of buildings and views that he later worked into paintings, like the fantasized view of Düsseldorf in the Samuel collection dating from 1666–67 (no. 77). Here he is at Emmerich, the first Rhine port in German territory after leaving the Netherlands, in the duchy of Kleves. He painted views of the ancient fortifications several times, but he often transposed, adapted and otherwise altered the reality to provide a more pleasing image. This is a view of the thirteenth-century watergate entrance to the town, at the south-east corner of the walls that lead on to the embankment of the Rhine. We know that the view is actually quite accurate, not from any notes that van der Heyden made, but from a drawing made by fellow Dutch artist Roelant Roghman, whose drawings he used in other works. From this drawing we can see that he faithfully followed the view depicted, looking west through the ancient gate, to where on the far side, beyond the standing figures, the river can just be seen. The 'staffage' was painted by his friend Adriaen van de Velde.

The incredible detail of the brickwork, a hallmark of van der Heyden's work, was achieved mechanically – unsurprising considering his talents as an inventor. Pressing etched copper plates that acted as intaglio or cameo impressions into wet paint to create areas of bricks or lines of mortar, he was able to achieve fantastic effects. He made plates of differing angles, sizes and textures, though the exact methods he used are unclear. Despite the fact that this shortcut *prentschilderijen*, or print-painting, was recognized as his particular technique by contemporaries, his work was greatly admired and still is.

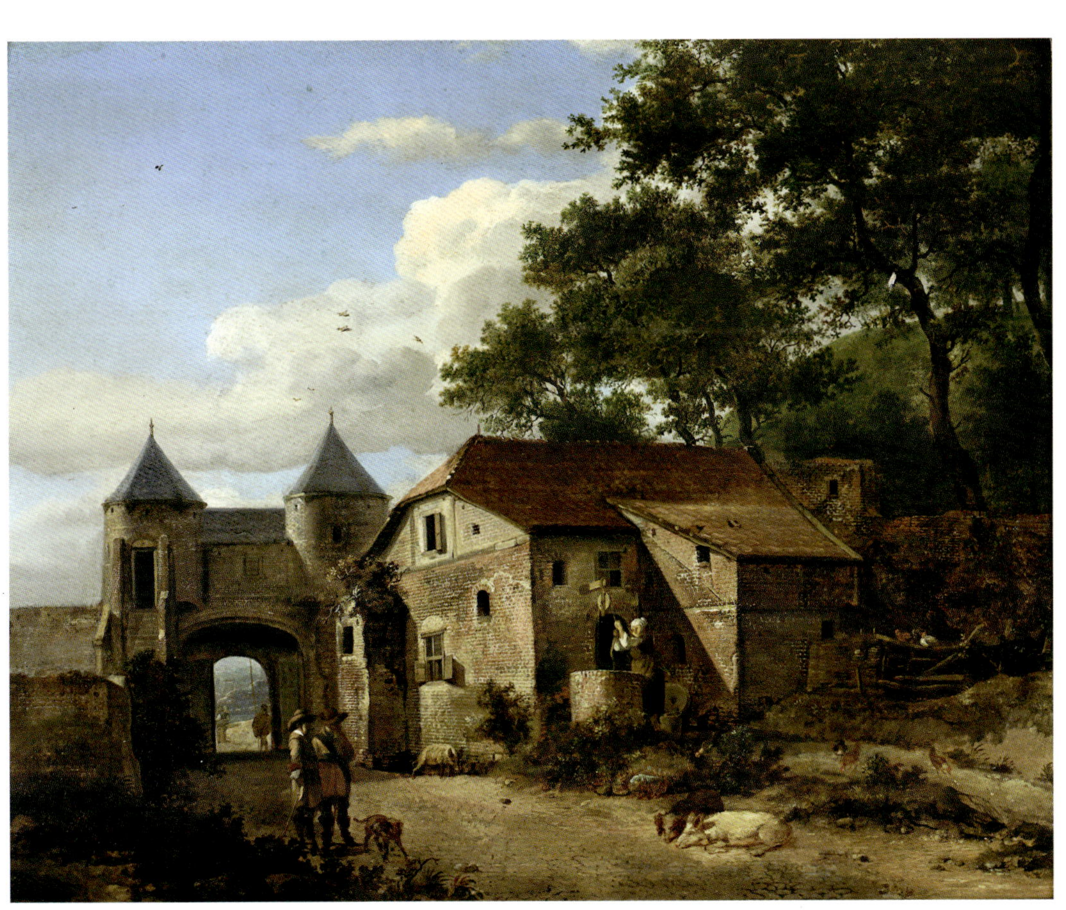

JAN VAN DER HEYDEN
Gorinchem 1637–1712 Amsterdam

View of the Boterbrug with the tower of the Stadhuis, Delft

Oil on panel, 55.5 × 71.2 cm, signed
Sutton no. 26

Lord Samuel, a distinguished property developer, loved Dutch seventeenth-century cityscapes and portraits of buildings. Characteristic of the country and period, the genre became popular in Italy in the following century, in Venice in particular. It had developed strongly by the mid century, specifically in Delft amongst artists like Emanuel de Witte, Pieter de Hooch and Johannes Vermeer. Though based in Amsterdam, van de Heyden travelled widely in the Low Countries and into Germany. This scene of Delft is one of a group of five views by him that date from the 1650s at the very beginning of his career as a painter.

From contemporary prints and extant buildings we know the scene is correct in scale and detail. The early date would account for the accuracy of the small market street depicted, with the Gothic tower of the town hall at the far end. Van der Heyden had yet to develop his skill for improvisation and imaginative alterations seen in later works. The simple linear perspective is also indicative of this period, as he would later use several vanishing points to create highly sophisticated pictorial space. The 'staffage', though animated and accurate, lack depth and are slightly naïve. He sensibly overcame this weakness in later works by asking others, particularly Adriaen van de Velde, to provide the figures. Nevertheless, the textures – of the brickwork, wooden frames for the market stalls and stonework of the tower – show his trademark skills for detail and the overall tones are well balanced.

This picture was treated roughly by critics while in the collection of the Metropolitan Museum in New York, who de-accessioned it in 1972. It was not then fully understood as a fine example of the artist's early technique and his rather dull finish. Recent scholarship, however, recognizes it as an important early work which adds considerably to the fine group of van de Heyden's works at Mansion House.

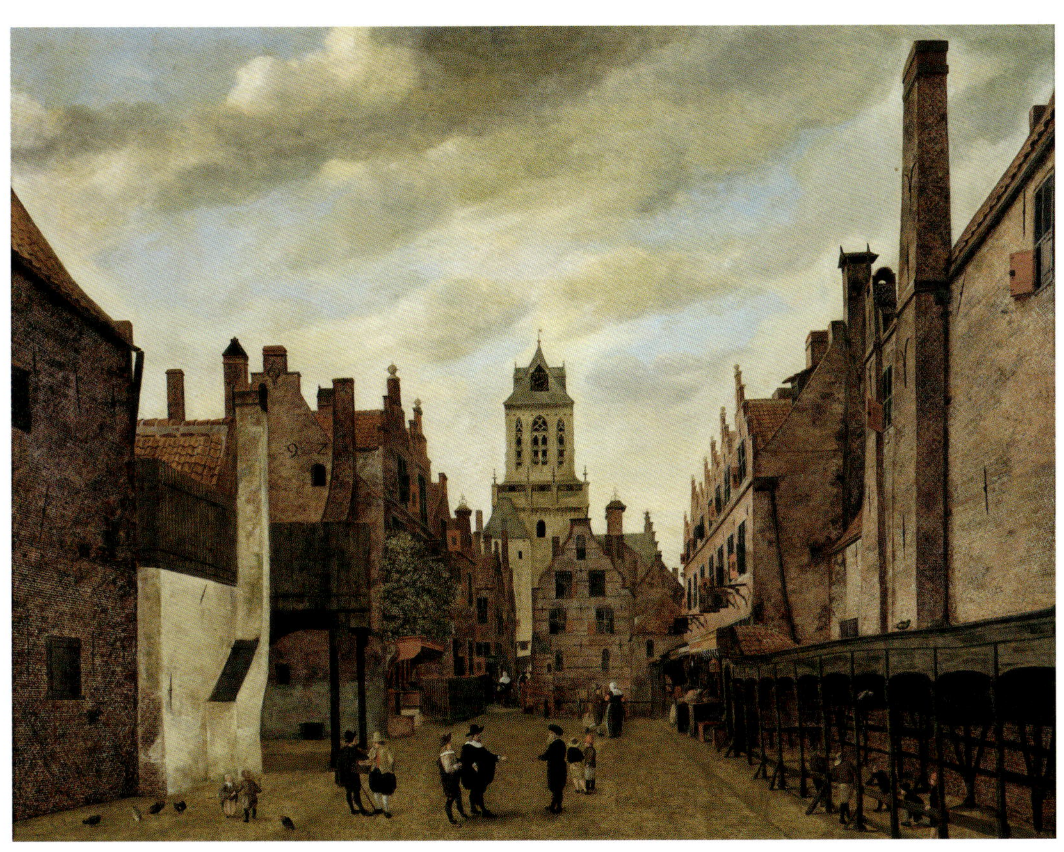

80

GERRIT BERCKHEYDE
Haarlem 1638–1698

The Castle of Heemstede

Oil on panel, 42.8 × 54.7 cm, signed and dated 1662 (or 1669)
Sutton no. 5

The use of two vanishing points – one on the very left-hand edge of the picture
next to the arched gateway, the other outside the picture plane on the right
beyond the stone ball – were carefully considered to provide the best view. The
raking angle at a height slightly greater than eye-line allows a view into the
moat, across to the bridge and two full sides of the castle. Berckheyde drew out
the perspective on the panel in detail before beginning to paint. Meticulously
exact, he was more architectural in his interest than Jan van der Heyden, painting
accurate portraits of buildings and townscapes rather than the often fanciful or
improved views of his contemporary and rival in Amsterdam. His brittle, austere
and sometimes harsh effect is achieved by a combination of painstaking detail
but also the strong and direct sunlight that helps define the spaces as much as the
perspective. The figures in this painting, though slightly stiff and formal, when
viewed with the swans, peacock and hunting dogs, add life and incident to an
otherwise fairly stark depiction.

Heemstede, just south of Haarlem on the River Spaarne, was the magnificent
home of the Grand Pensionary of Holland, Adriaen Pauw. As chief magistrate and
head of the council of Holland, the foremost province of the Netherlands, the
exceptionally wealthy Pauw led diplomatic missions for his country, notably at
the Treaty of Münster in 1648 that ended the war with Spain. He celebrated this
event by building a new bridge across the moat at Heemstede, which he called the
'Pons Pacis' (the bridge of peace), depicted here. Pauw received Queen Henrietta
Maria, wife of the English King Charles I, at the castle in 1644. Pauw died in
1653, at least ten years before Berckheyde painted this view, and the castle was
demolished in *c.* 1810, only the Pons Pacis surviving.

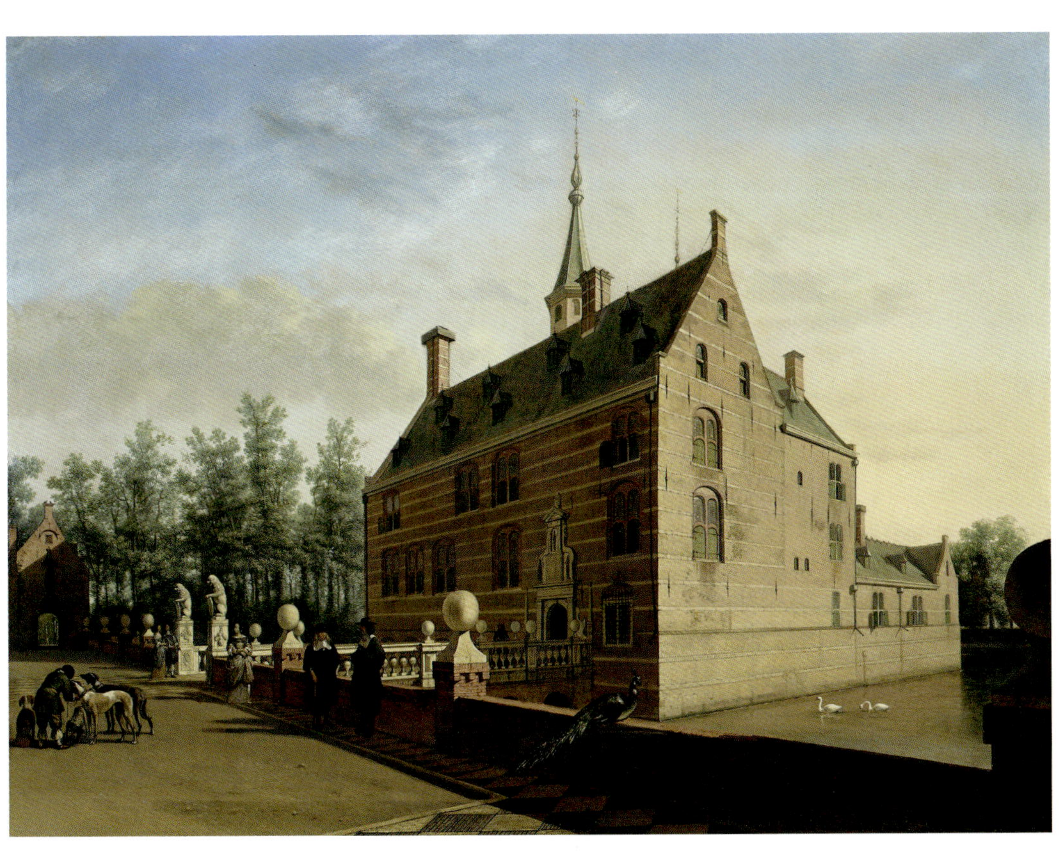

THE SALON VESTIBULE (PASSAGE ROOM)

Leading from the original main door of Mansion House and the Vestibule (now offices) into the central court, this room, lavishly decorated with carved wood and stucco, now acts as an extension to the Salon. The Kentian blank frames on each long wall are embellished with palm fronds with masks, swags and cresting that are matched by the decorated blind *oculi* above the doors. The door on the west side leads to the Lord Mayor's private study (the Venetian Parlour), while that on the east leads to the former Common Parlour or Court Room. The work of John Gilbert, George Fewkes and Humphrey Willmot from the late 1750s, the mouldings – now painted cream to stand out in contrast to the ochre-coloured walls – were originally painted white and set against a stone colour.

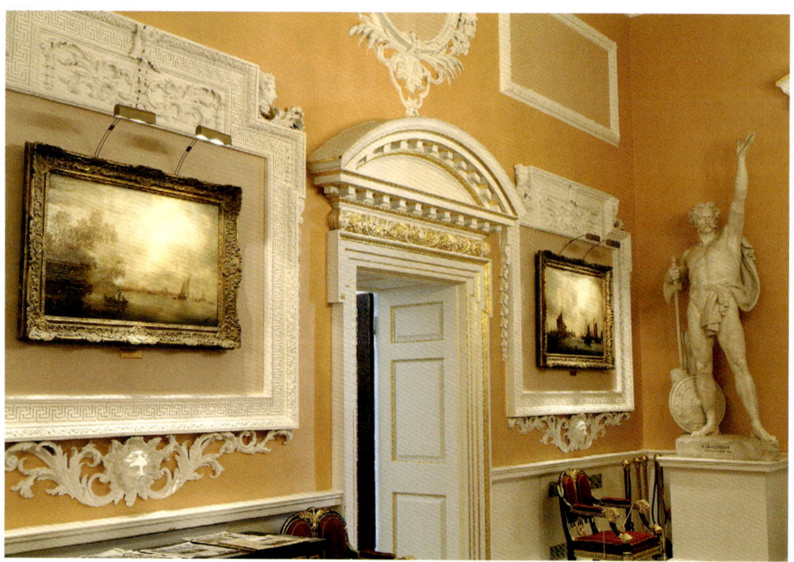

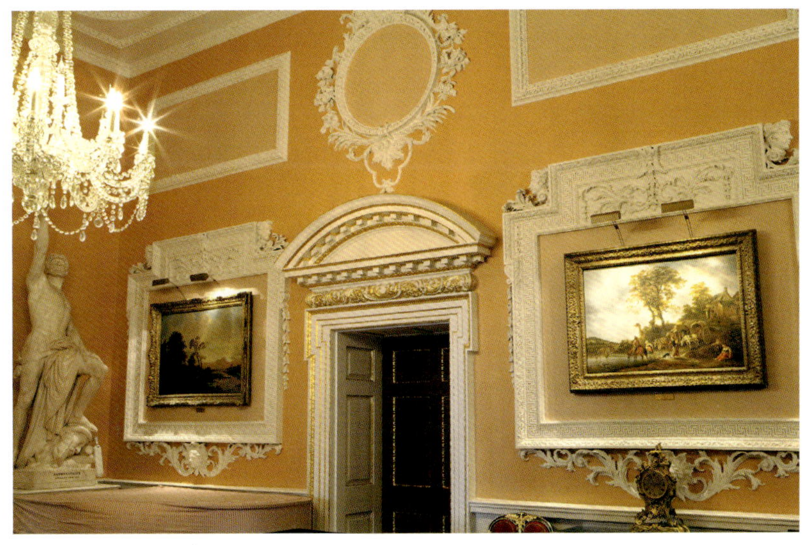

Four large horizontal landscapes and a marine are very suitably hung in the framed panels. They are works by Salomon van Ruysdael, a follower of Jan van de Cappelle, Isaac van Ostade and Aert van de Neer, all of whom are also represented by other works in the Samuel collection.

Exit through the door on the east side to the Red Staircase and the Walbrook Hall

81

SALOMON VAN RUYSDAEL
Naarden 1600/03–1670 Haarlem

View of the River Lek with boats and Liesvelt Castle

Oil on panel, 67.5 × 102.5 cm, signed and dated 1641
Sutton no. 60

Ruysdael was prolific and fortunately in the habit of putting a date on his works, as he has here, along with his signature, across the gunwale of the rowing-boat. We know that he painted at least thirteen other pictures in 1641. Despite the large production and the apparently endless repetition of a simple formula – leafy river banks receding diagonally, cloudy skies, shipping of one sort or another reflected in still waters – he was endlessly imaginative and inventive. Though the majority of these works are not site-specific, Ruysdael certainly included distinctive buildings from a wide range of places across the Netherlands. Unlike his friend and rival Jan van Goyen, who produced many drawings, Salomon van Ruysdael does not appear to have made records for later use, though he must have had some method to allow him to be so precise. Castles and churches were often reproduced in prints or in sketches by other artists. These may have been Ruysdael's sources, but the church tower with corner buttresses and short spire in this work, while cursory and inexact, suggests first-hand observation.

Painted in the tonal style of his middle years, the view is of the south bank of the River Lek, a branch of the Rhine which runs through the polders of south Holland below Utrecht towards Rotterdam. The round tower and adjacent range of buildings constitute the castle of Liesvelt, begun in the thirteenth century but now destroyed. Beyond lie the two churches of the little town of Groot Ammers. The effects of atmosphere complement the sense of depth, particularly where the dark *coulisse* of the heavy foliage on the left gives way to an inlet from which a flat-bottomed passenger ferry emerges, laden with cows and peasants, a charming and recurring theme of Ruysdael's work. The boat in the foreground carries sportsmen aiming, it seems, for the waterfowl on the right. The browns and greys of the cloudy sky, mirror-calm water and receding bank blend together, anchored in the bottom right by the slanting post emerging from the still water.

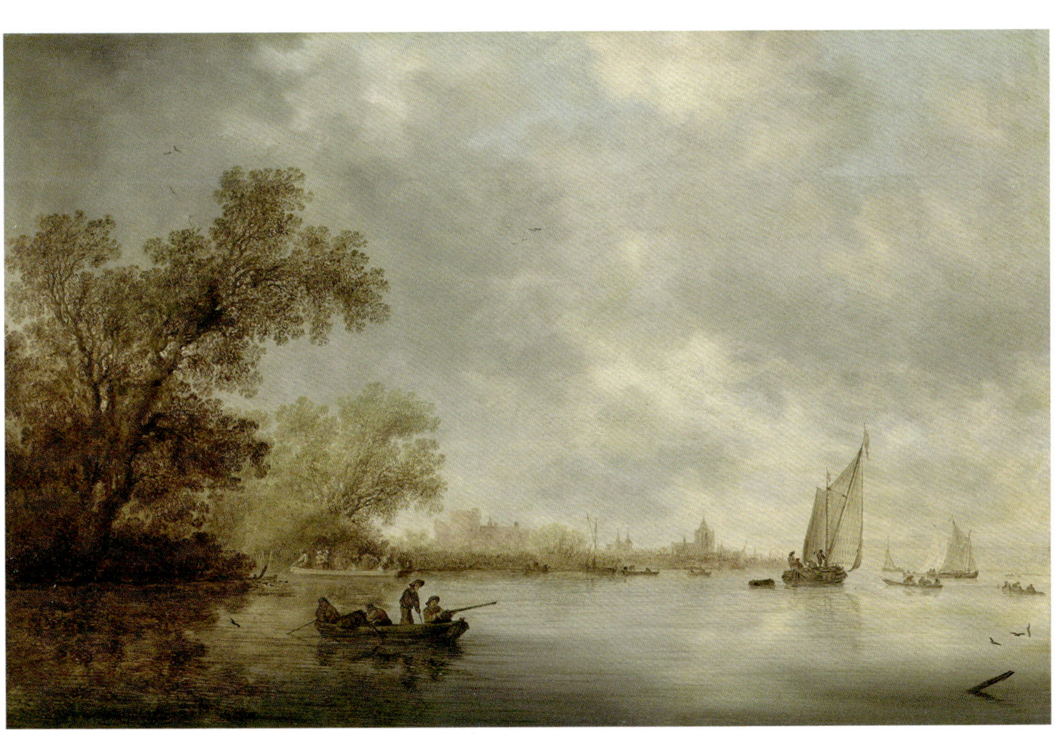

82

Follower of JAN VAN DE CAPPELLE
c. 1626–1679

Ships at anchor in a calm

Oil on panel, 75.1 × 106.7 cm
Sutton no. 13

The towering, leaden clouds reflected at the forefront of this grand scene are
entirely typical of Jan van de Cappelle. So, too, is the elegant composition of serried
ranks of ships and boats, drawn up on either side of a wide river mouth, protected
on the left by a fort flying the Dutch flag. Through this enfilade is a glimpse of a
distant horizon to which the eye is drawn by smaller floating objects in the open
water between – two barrels and a distant wherry. The monotony of brown and
silver-grey, unrelieved by stronger, primary colours, are also entirely characteristic
of the work of van de Cappelle.

Something is missing, however. The paint is much worn in places, which may
impede our reading – particularly evident in the dark areas where detail and
definition is lost and on the glazes in the water that have become fugitive and
transparent over time. Even discounting these factors, though, it is clear this is
not the work of the master. It lacks the refinement and complete understanding
of the variety of tones within a small range of colours that would create believable
depth, in particular in the treatment of the water. Though the copyist (this is
surely a copy of an autograph work) understood the effect of diagonals of light and
dark in the creation of recession and depth, and though he attempts the effects of
reflection for which van de Cappelle was famous, it is not enough. He did not see
that the ripples in the forefront of the picture should be wider apart than those in
the middle distance and invisible in the far distance. Here the intervals are much
the same throughout, lacking the understanding of direct observation.

Sailing out on his own yacht, freed from the cares of earning a living by his rich
inheritance, van de Cappelle, as a skilled autodidact, had mastered the technique
and marshalled the design of marine painting on this grand scale in a thoroughly
distinctive manner – just lacking in this work.

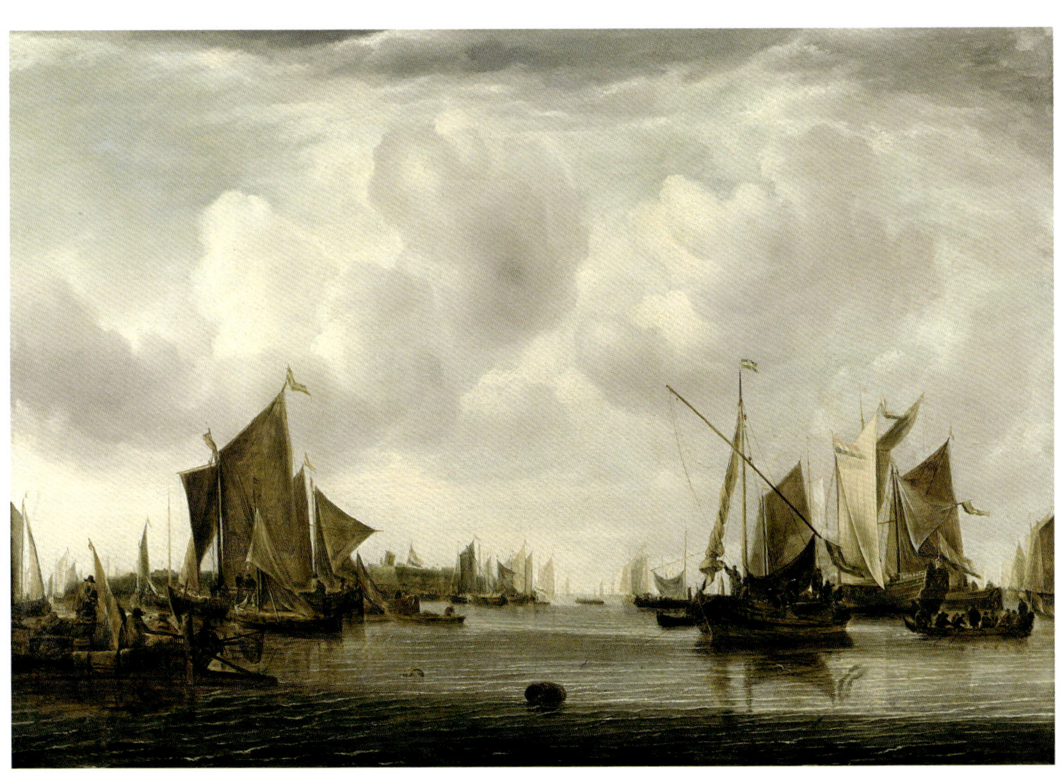

83

AERT VAN DER NEER
Amsterdam 1603/04–1677

Evening landscape

Oil on panel, 84.5 × 122.5 cm, signed
Sutton no. 44

This mellow evening scene shows van der Neer at the height of his powers. The setting sun, hidden behind clouds, casts its pinky-gold light on to the sky, while the deep blue of the gathering evening fills the upper atmosphere and is reflected in the still waters of the canal. The scene is suffused with light and all the various elements are affected in some way. Shadow already falls on the houses of the far bank and the rowing-boats moored to a post are dark against the golden water. Glittering reflections are seen in the distant windows and white highlights on the rumps of the principal horses. Taken from a comparatively low viewpoint, this work is without the usual *repoussoir* across the front of the scene. Instead van de Neer divides the picture plane diagonally, juxtaposing light and dark in the overall composition as well as in the detail (the English landscapist John Constable remarked that *chiaroscuro* is not confined to dark pictures but can also be found in works suffused with light, as it is "the power that creates space").

This work has been criticized for the large scale of the figure groups. They are indeed larger than in other works by the artist in the Samuel collection and also fulfil a more prominent role in setting the scene. A wealthy gentleman on horseback, identifiable by his sword, hound, feathered hat and the fashionable whip he carries upright in his right hand, addresses a respectable black-clad gentlemen on foot, while a maid brings a glass of refreshment to the travellers in the open cart. Arriving or leaving or merely pausing, these travellers are certainly more dominant in the composition than the incidental figures of earlier works and help to date it to the early 1660s.

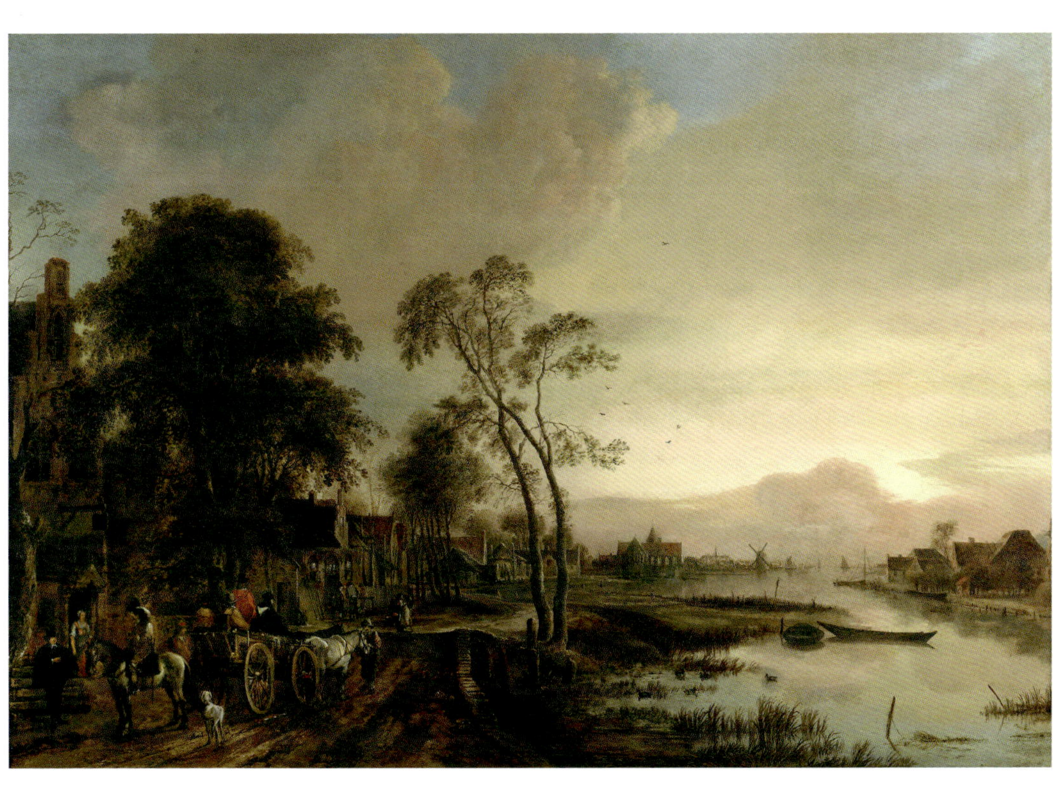

84

ISACK VAN OSTADE
Haarlem 1621–1649

A ford

Oil on panel, 79.6 × 109.5 cm
Sutton no. 52

The theme of inns and travellers was a popular one for Netherlandish artists
in the seventeenth century and the Samuel collection has examples of several,
in very differing styles: Brueghel, Wouwermans and Aert van der Neer all treat
the subject. Here, with a strong diagonal emphasis, the compositional space,
like a stage set, is well conceived to take the figural groups: travellers on foot, on
horseback and in a labouring cart ford a stream in the foreground, while in the
background weary figures sit before an inn. Younger brother and pupil of Adriaen
van Ostade, Isack drew on his brother's established repertoire of peasant scenes,
placing his figures in landscape settings rather than interiors. He also shared the
tonal palette that Adriaen developed, influenced by the landscapists Jan van Goyen
and Salomon van Ruysdael.

The overall mood is sombre, despite the bright relief of reds and whites.
Though the composition is well designed, with the landscape assured and
confidently depicted, the figures struggle somewhat, being slightly awkward
both in themselves and in relation to each other. The woman with a white
headdress and red shirt, for example, walks into the water with her hands at stiff
and uncoordinated angles, while the seated woman on the far right is completely
oblivious to the child beside her. Even the grey horse, tired and straining, lacks
vivid execution, adding to the melancholic effect.

Isack's production was notoriously uneven and this work, by no means a good
example, has been compounded by problems of condition, whereby several of the
figures have lost some definition owing to thin paint layers and abrasion over
time. This is probably a very late work: it is hard to comment as Isack was active
for a mere ten years, dying at the age of twenty-eight.

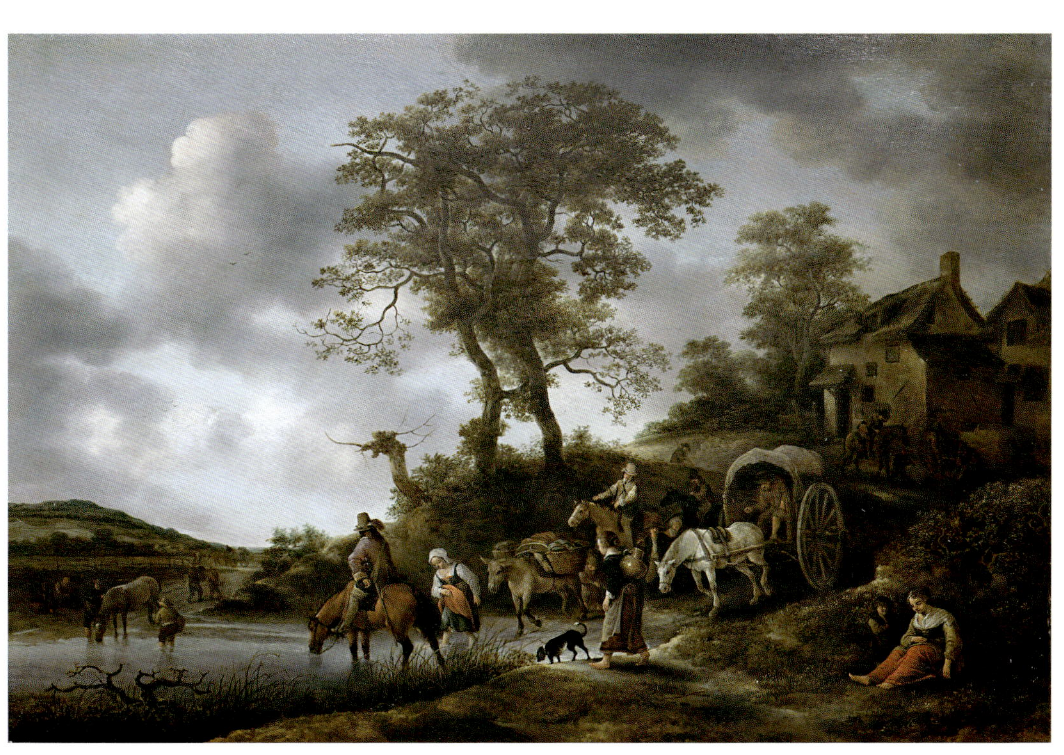

List of Artists

Arent Arentsz, called Cabel nos. 1, 2

Hendrick Averkamp nos. 3, 4

Gerrit Berckheyde nos. 61, 80

Gerard ter Borch no. 43

Jan Brueghel the Elder nos. 27, 28, 30

Jan Brueghel the Elder (copy after) no. 29

Jan van de Cappelle no. 55

Jan van de Cappelle (follower of) no. 82

Pieter Claesz nos. 39, 40

Aelbert Cuyp nos. 5, 52

Gerard Dou no. 19

Jan van Goyen nos. 6, 7, 53, 69, 74

Frans Hals nos. 10, 31

Jan van der Heyden nos. 47, 57, 67, 77, 78, 79

Meindert Hobbema no. 68

Pieter de Hooch no. 37

Willem Kalf no. 42

Jan van Kessel (copy after) no. 34

Philips Koninck no. 70

Nicolaes Maes nos. 33, 35, 38

Gabriel Metsu (copy after) no. 32

Frans van Mieris (copy after) no. 23

Aert van der Neer nos. 9, 54, 83

Aert van der Neer (imitator of) no. 58

Jacob Ochtervelt nos. 41, 44

Adriaen van Ostade nos. 16, 24, 25, 26

Isack van Ostade no. 84

Palamedes Palamedesz no. 59

Frans Post nos. 63, 64

Hubert van Ravesteyn no. 18

Jacob Isaacksz van Ruisdael nos. 49, 65, 66

Salomon van Ruysdael nos. 50, 51, 81

Floris van Schooten no. 45

Pieter Cornelis van Slingelandt no. 22

Jan Steen nos. 17, 36

David Teniers the Younger nos. 11–15

Wallerant Vaillant no. 60

Adriaen van de Velde no. 8

Jan Jansz van de Velde III no. 20

Willem van de Velde the Younger nos. 56, 72, 73, 75

Willem van de Velde the Younger (studio of) no. 71

Esaias van den Velde no. 21

Cornelis Vroom (follower of) no. 76

Emanuel de Witte no. 62

Philips Wouwermans nos. 46, 48